Sex, Spirit and Community

Earth in Spirit,
Spirit in Earth.
May it be so for us,
As it already is.

Sex, Spirit and Community

Mark Josephs-Serra

JON CARPENTER

Our books may be ordered from bookshops or (post free in the UK) from
Jon Carpenter Publishing, Alder House, Market Street, Charlbury,
Oxfordshire OX7 3PH

Credit card orders should be phoned or faxed to 01689 870437
or 01608 811969

Our US distributor is Paul and Company, PO Box 442, Concord, MA 01742
(phone 978 369 3049, fax 978 369 2385)

First published in 2000 by
Jon Carpenter Publishing
Alder House, Market Street, Charlbury, Oxfordshire OX7 3PQ
☎ 01608 811969

© Mark Josephs-Serra

Illustrations © Marcea Colley

ISBN 1 897766 60 2

Printed in England by J. W. Arrowsmith Ltd., Bristol.
Cover printed by Cheney and Sons Ltd, Banbury

Contents

Preface 1

Introduction 9

1

THE PREMODERN ERA • THE FUNDAMENTALIST PHASE

SEXLESS SPIRIT

1. Introduction 23
2. The Body, Sexuality, the World 24
3. Relationships 36
4. Alienation 48

2

THE MODERN ERA • THE PORNOGRAPHIC CULTURE

SPIRITLESS SEX

1. Introduction 61
2. The Question of Certainty 66
3. Split-off Sex 79
4. Completing Adolescence at Forty 94
5. Pseudo-scientific Fundamentalism 101
6. Holism, Community and Religion 113
7. Holism, Community and Politics:
Notes on Holistic Democracy 125

3

A POSSIBLE POSTMODERN ERA • HOLISTIC COMMUNITY

SEX AND SPIRIT

1. Introduction 137

2. Co-creativity and Flexible Form 139

3. An Overview of the Model of the Four Spheres of Community 155

4. The Community Forum 162

5. The Communal Sphere: Initiation 170

6. The Communal Sphere: Partnership 186

7. The Balance Project 192

8. The Blood and Roots of Community 206

Bibliography 213

Contacting Balance 214

Response Form 215

Preface

The Holistic Attitude

More and more people have travelled beyond the otherworldliness of traditional religion and beyond the worldliness of materialism, and now share what might be called a 'holistic attitude'. They respect both spirituality and sexuality. They honour both the journey of consciousness and the cycle of the seasons. They are in awe both of eternity and of change. This attitude has become increasingly influential in the human potential movement, in environmentalism, and in economics and commerce. The question this book addresses (given the disintegration of traditional community) is the possibility of the realistic development of holistic community. It is a book about deep, intimate, meaningful community. It is about growth-work, but it is about growing together. And it is about a politics activated by a sense of shared growth.

We might even say that this book is about the next step in 'the consciousness movement' that has been evolving, large-scale, since the 60's. Through the 70's and 80's that beautiful, adolescent impulse to change the world became reflective and introspective – and rightly so. But, to paraphrase Ventura and Hillman, 'We've had plenty of years of therapy and the world's getting worse'! We need to re-group, and this means community.

In this sense, this book is not about applying an individualistic 'holistic attitude' to a certain subject matter – be it gardening or economics. It is about the next step for the holistic attitude itself. It is about a broadening out. Because how can we develop community while at the most profound, gut-soul level our life-attitude (however holistic) remains secretly, supremely individualistic? And for the most part, it does. For the most part, our growth-work is purely personal. The family is shrinking away. And even our politics is the work of groups of individuals tied only in ideological unity. There is rarely a sense of travelling together – of commitment to each other, to each other's families, and to the local land we live upon together. Why not? Because this would call, and does call, for a new sense of collectivity. Not a new theory of collectivity, but a new experience of collectivity.

While insisting we retain our individuality, holistic community calls for a new humility – a new sense of identity in belonging. It calls for a new sense of self: as both absolutely unique and absolutely the same as everyone else – both apart and part-of. It calls for a new experience of surrender – one of giving all, yet remaining personally present. And although such matters might be far removed from most community development programmes, I believe the feminist slogan that 'the personal is political, the political personal' still holds true, and that deep postmodern community reconstruction must address the interconnectedness of our politics and our ultimate faiths and fears.

Over the last five years I have been dedicated to the practical exploration of holistic community. My experience is that there's fear and resistance (of course), and that many, many people want it – but that within the pressure and rush of modern life people don't have the peace to sit together and sketch and test the means of getting there. There is a deep desire to unite, to support each other, to commit to each other, to surrender to travelling together – to living a deeper, more heart-felt, more integrated community life. And there's a shortage of models and methodology.

The Four Spheres of Community

In this book I offer one possible model, no doubt still in its infancy, which I call The Four Sphere Model Of Community. The model proposes that the project of holistic community involves four interconnected spheres: the existential ('what do we mean by 'holism'?'), the personal (the individual journey into wholeness), the communal (the shared sense of journey, rites of passage, social structures), and the practical (the political and economic sphere of organisation and action). And the implication is that for holistic community to emerge, all four need to be tended.

Much (though not enough) is being said and done in spheres one and two, at the private end of the spectrum – in the realms of new paradigm thinking, and individual healing and empowerment. And much (though not enough) is being said and done in sphere four, at the public end of the spectrum – in the fields of environmentalism and sustainability and alternative economics. Far less is being said or done in sphere three – in the interpersonal sphere, the sphere of community people-structures, the sphere of the collective journey. And unfortunately, it is sphere three that bonds us in community. While we only develop existential and personal holism it remains a beautiful but privatised and socially irrelevant pursuit. And while we only develop environmentalist and political holism, however decentralist and community-empowering, we are only dancing on the surface.

Even if we imagine a local population active at both ends of the spectrum (both personally and politically), unless they share social structures and rites of passage and forms of ceremony and celebration – all of the substance of the communal sphere – they will remain a politically active group of growth-working individualists. Although in such a situation, from time to time, the feeling of togetherness might rise and fall, it is the communal sphere of men's-community and women's-community, of public grieving and celebration, of birth-rites and initiations, of partnership-rites and death-rites, that bonds us in stable, long-term community.

In the last analysis, all four spheres are equally important. Ideology (sphere one) is pivotal, personal commitment (sphere two) is crucial, togetherness (sphere three) is the very essence of community, and unless these first three spheres are reflected in the way we organise our agriculture, building, transport and trade, then we are not propagating a postmodern holistic synthesis, but perpetuating a premodern split between spirituality and the world. But I like to stress the communal sphere. It is the glue. It is in the communal sphere that we regularly go beyond our often tight and tense individualism and touch our commonality. It is in the communal sphere that our hearts get regularly stretched. And if we are to convene community forums, and attempt to weave community, then at least a few stretched hearts can be a definite advantage.

Above all, the model of the four spheres is a practical tool. In any local area there is activity and apathy, history and memory, and a set of sub-groupings with their overt and covert prejudices. The four sphere model can be used to make sense of all of this, navigate it, and offer the possibility of respectful unity in diversity. It can be used to recognise strengths and weaknesses, and to address imbalances when one sphere is highly developed, and another underdeveloped.

The four sphere model carries a context and a vision. In itself it is neutral (it could be used to carry any belief system), but in carrying a holistic outlook, encouraging personal wholeness, and promoting social and political activity that is neither high-and-holy nor hardened and cynical, the four sphere model can provide direction, clarity, enthusiasm and inspiration to travel together in very human, very real, very deep community.

Co-Creativity

Alongside the holistic attitude and the model of the four spheres of community, the methodology of co-creativity is the other central theme of this book. Holism is about not repressing any part of ourselves, nor being controlled by any part – it is about being in relationship with all parts. The four sphere model is designed to help us practically establish holistic community. And co-creativity is a way to do it – it is a way holism can be lived.

At the personal, inner, intrapsychic level co-creativity is about cultivating free-flowing relationships between the crowd of characters that lives within each of us. At the interpersonal, social level it is a way of conducting a community forum, for example. It is a way of including feelings, as well as opinions – so that dialogue isn't fact-obsessed and parched and emotionally suffocating. And it is a way of including all parts of the community. It is the way of relationship. In co-creativity the pragmatic and the spiritual become two equally valid voices of the community body, rather than unconnected, opposed factions.

Finally, at the transpersonal level of our relationship with life itself, co-creativity is an experience of both free will and destiny – both of being guided and of being impelled to sculpt our own future. It is about a dynamic relationship with spirit, or 'the mystery of life', or whatever we might like to call that of which we are part. It is not the philosophy of the obedience of the created to the creator, it is the collaborative expression of the divine and the Divine. Co-creativity is an exquisite feeling of appropriateness – of dignity and simplicity, of vulnerability and responsibility, of aloneness and inseparability.

And again, just as most politics, public dialogue and community development programmes tend not to acknowledge difficult emotions, like fear and shame, they also tend to exclude the sublime. We seem equally ill at ease with the public expression of feelings of love or joy or spiritual sweetness. So it might feel awkward to talk of 'aloneness and inseparability' in the same breath as agricultural reform, or economic depression, or social unrest. We might want to return to comfortable, familiar categories: "Let the priest talk about inseparability, let the politician talk about economics". But that wouldn't be holism. That wouldn't be wholeness. That most certainly would not be the way forward into deep, fully human, co-operative, co-creative community.

Local Community Reconstruction

Over the last thousand years humanity has visited the premodern world of fixity, the fixity of modernism, and the flux of postmodernism. While many Muslim countries, for example, have remained fixed in premodernity, in the dominant culture God has lost his fixed, absolute authority, and relationships and institutions have been opened to question and challenge. And as the bulk of this culture moved into modernity it established a new fixity – the fixity of facts, of pseudo-science, of informationism, of ultimate meaninglessness and sensual indulgence. Then, as even the authority of facts broke down, postmodernity entered, with the final end of fixity, promising the full flux – full freedom amidst complete confusion and disintegration. Today, to various extents, in various parts of the world, all three trends still exist.

What is referred to as 'globalisation' is the ideological, political and economic tendency of the dominant culture to impose its mix of modernism and postmodernism on the rest of the world. There is now increasing resistance to globalisation, to monoculturalism, in principle. And there is also increasing resistance to the disturbingly inhuman and achingly superficial consumerist thrust of this globalisation. However, most of this resistance is premodern (nationalistic or fundamentalistic), or offers no alternative to the values and lifestyle of globalisation. Combating the ethnocidal programmes of governments and multinational corporations is a heroic, heart-rending endeavour. As is combating governmental and corporate environmental brutality. However, slogans such as 'empowering ethnic minorities to determine their own futures' overlook the tragic reality that, increasingly with every generation, we are all internalising the grab-it-while-you-can values of globalisation, and that left to determine our own futures (whether we live in a city centre or a forest) we are increasingly likely to shape a modernist/postmodernist society around ourselves.

Hence the need, alongside direct opposition to the excesses of globalisation, to formulate profound, soul-satiating, cohesive, socio-economic alternatives, such as holistic community. Many people are contributing in many ways. This book is not written in a vacuum. Holism itself is a voice of postmodernity, perhaps its healthiest voice – expressing itself in new approaches to conflict resolution and peace making, new approaches to the wealth, growth and profit, new approaches to nature and agriculture, to transport and trade, to education, to the self, to relationships, and to the mystery we all find ourselves in together. There are innumerable sources of knowledge and expertise we can draw upon to develop holistic community in our local areas. The four sphere model and the mode of co-creativity can be used to manage and apply the knowledge and expertise of pioneers in every field, and to focus it on developing holistic community. And if we can just stay wherever we are, without moving home, and commit to developing our own communities, perhaps we will be automatically shaping a more decentralised culture of the future.

About Myself

This book is rooted in my own experience of the narrowness and arrogance of premodern cultures. It is rooted in my experience of our empty, wonder-filled modern technoculture. It is rooted in my postmodern personal journey into the holistic experience I call 'erotic awareness'. And it is rooted in my longing for community, and in my years of experimentation. My story…

(i)

My foreskin was sliced off when I was eight days old. As a teenager my rage was not only that I had been claimed for Judaism, but that the Judaism I had been claimed for was in ruins – that the altar I had been sacrificed upon was being bulldozed to bits by the lopsided logic of modernity.

I ached for profound and high-sighted community, but all that held our post-holocaust anglo-jewish building together was folksongs, folk-jargon, folk-food, the social habit of synagogue, showbizz rites of passage, our anti-antisemitism, and the memory of horror. I was an outsider among gentiles, and an outsider among Jews. So at seventeen, I ran outside…

(ii)

My hippie days were great. I was a podgy Jewish cleverdick from a soul-dead London suburb, then suddenly, overnight, I was walking barefoot with Pablo and his chillum through the mysterious sand-floored forests of Morocco. He had a wooden bowl strapped to his back, and we lived on salads dripping with olive oil, and flat round village breads. I didn't know why I'd gone – but it was for something huge, something expansive…

I'd been suffocating in central heating and monotonous comfort – suddenly I was sleeping on beaches on Greek isles, riding for free in a transcontinental truck across Turkey, drumming wildly with a blood-mouthed tabla master in Pakistan… My hippie days were great. I took off, I flew… and I got afraid. I got afraid, so I hid inside religion.

(iii)

The rhythm was cold showers at 4am, temple ceremony at 4.30, prayer-beads from 5 to 7, then scripture study, and more ceremony, before breakfast at 8. The day was dedicated to service, punctuated by various rituals, and governed by extensive and intricate regulations. Life as a shaven, robed, vegetarian, drug-free, celibate Hindu was not what that hippie had expected next.

At first it was bliss. I touched spirit. I was home. I was found. Here was community – here was the community of the free! And, undeniably, there was ecstasy in that blind, mindless togetherness. Which is why the doubts and disillusions which came with the years tore me apart. By the time I ran away a decade had passed – and I was in shreds.

(iv)

I wrote like a madman, and smoked and drummed. I hung out in the squats and cafés and street markets of north London. I was back with the bohemians. But now I was a broken, fallen monk. I bought porno magazines. I had girlfriends. We had warm, relieving, pornographic relationships.

But indoors the air felt artificial and stale, and outside it felt filthy and thick – like a smoke-screen between me and life. The buildings and streets seemed hard and everywhere and overwhelming. Everyone seemed disturbed and on edge. Everything felt stuck and ugly and very, very loud…

I was cracking up. I ran. I ran again. Not to spirit, this time, not from spirit, this time – but from the absence of spirit, and from the absence of sacredness on earth. I ran from the modern urban nowhere-land, the porno-land of facades and food with no substance – the world in which reality is just around the corner. I ran into the arms of the earth. I ran to the forest and the river and the vast open embrace of the sky. I ran because I needed holding.

(v)

I had flown, somehow, propelled by drugs and music and recklessness. I had tried donning robes to stay high forever. And for a while I had hovered in spiritual sweetness. Then I had crashed. I had crashed by the grace of my sexuality, my intelligence, and my sincerity. Still – I was in pieces, and I needed healing back together again.

And so I left London for the Devon countryside and coast – and settled in 'new age' Totnes. There I entered the universe of therapy. I learnt to name and speak my feelings. I acquired an emotional vocabulary. Instead of up and out, I now went down and in. I met the crowd that lives inside. I exposed my compensations. I met my fear. I met my pain. And rather than fly away to spirit. I stood in it – at the point where it touches the earth.

Which is where I still stand, ten years on – now with a woman whose passionate journey mirrors mine, and two children, and animals, and a community for my soul. The spirit I came to know through Hindu ritual and meditation lives with me – on earth, in the green wet Devon valleys and hills. The transcendent spirit and the immanent earth are tenderly entering relationship within.

I am no longer so concerned with enlightenment. Anyway, my sense is she will creep up on me only when I look away. I have become more concerned with being truly human than becoming a god. I have become concerned with living together as holy humans.

I have become happy not to know, and to live together not knowing – to suffer together aware of the blessings that fill the air, that descend everywhere, and of the magic and beauty that rise up like dawn mist from the meadows all day every day.

Introduction

"What is this new 'holism'?"
"The union of yesterday's spirituality and today's physicality."
"Can that be experienced?"
"Yes."

Before discussing the social structures or politics of holistic community, I want to look at this little conversation. It hints at a union of the modern and the premodern. It suggests a vast cultural story. And more than that, it holds a promise. A promise at the very core of any attempt to develop holistic community.

And I want to approach it very personally, because I have lived sexless spirituality, I have lived spiritless sex, and from time to time, I have lived the union of sex and spirit. So I will use my life story to illustrate the story of our culture...

I will take up the story where I'm a religious fanatic –
which is, in essence, what almost our entire culture was
until a few hundred years ago.
Somewhere I broke down,
and threw in my robes,
and fell to earth –
which is, in essence, what almost our entire culture did
about a few hundred years ago.
However,
without my vows and prayer beads and holy books
my spirit shrivelled.
As has the spirit of our culture.
But I wasn't going to fake it again.
I stayed down there,
in the emptiness,
and gathered up the bits of myself:
my skin, my sex,
my soul, my heart,
my guts,
my silence, my wings,
my brain –
and I learnt to tend them, to be with them.

Each part of me had a story.
And each story was a part of the story of me.
And my story was a voice, an echo, in a family story
in a cultural story
in a human story
in a story beyond history,
beyond time.

And every word of story, every sound,
told of love and yearning and expansion,
and retreat and shrivelling and distortion,
and the unabatable thrust of life...
And here I am today,
in and out of gratitude, wonder, wholeness and homecoming,
travelling with others like me –
a weaver of social patterns,
offering my designs in exchange
for warmth and wisdom
when certain stories overwhelm me.

Thus three phases of my life parallel three phases of our culture. Within my forty-five years I have lived our traditional religious past, our secular recent present, and a holistic present and possible future...

(i)
As a man of the cloth I regressed
into a childlike dependency.
Renouncing my power, my discrimination, and my heart –
I was owned by sexless spirit.

Parallel:
THE PREMODERN ERA.
Our cultural childhood.
The fundamentalist phase.
Collective consciousness.
SEXLESS SPIRIT.

As a child-in-wholeness I followed other,
and I was no one –
until something slow and tortuous snapped.
My self struck back.

(ii)
I glided over the polished surfaces of the wonder-world.
The earth was on sale in the supermarkets.

The shelves were stacked with empty packages.
I grabbed at them.
I had escaped, but I was lost.
I was floating in a culture without roots.

Parallel:
THE MODERN ERA.
Our cultural adolescence.
The pornographic phase.
Ego, identity, separateness – individual consciousness.
SPIRITLESS SEX.

As an adolescent-in-wholeness I hit out against other.
I followed myself –
I was someone,
but I had no idea who.

(iii)
I flew down inside myself often enough,
and sometimes stayed, lost
in the shadowlands.
And inside me my sexuality left the city.
I found the seasons again,
and my own body rhythms, and my own sensations,
and friends who feel things differently.
Now, as a young adult-in-wholeness, I am carried
as myself.
I surrender,
but I don't give up.
I let go,
but I keep pushing.
I surrender to spirit and I surrender to the earth.
I surrender to the beauty, and I surrender to the beast.
I surrender without losing my centre.
I merge,
but I'm still me.

Parallel:
A POSSIBLE POSTMODERN ERA
Our cultural adulthood.
The holistic phase.
Oneness and difference, individuality and community.
SEX AND SPIRIT.

Thus *the first section of this book* draws upon my fundamentalist phase. It is a crucial element in the dynamic of this book...

Holism implies a valuing of all things – things up and things down, things within, things without. In the past we had a culture of value. But to value spirit and holiness and all things high, we created a devil and devalued all things delicious and dark. There was value, but it was split. And our religion and civil and criminal laws strained to keep that which was split-off from snapping back in our faces.

This book keeps glancing backwards and forwards... 'If we seek value again will we be seduced by the holier-than-thou, by the angelic hymn – or will we be able to place value upon incarnation and intimacy and anger and fear – and also bow before those sacred urges?' 'Yes, yes, yes, the answer's obvious – the holistic direction we need to take is completely clear!' We say this, but we've suffered split-value for centuries, and we carry mistrust in our bones.

All of the discussion in this book pivots and swivels on an old, undefinable feeling – on a cultural memory of purity and spirituality somehow so sweet and right and yet so twisted and wrong. We had a culture with value. We want value back. Not split-value, whole-value. Yes, we're clear. 'But can we trust ourselves?' we ask...

There is a popular fantasy that prophets are perfect and pure, and that their followers then dogmatise and corrupt. However clear we are now, we fear we are also those followers... We don't yet trust ourselves to drink sacredness *en masse* again. And that is good. The collective mind embodies all qualities – and one of them is caution. Here in the present, before we christen the future, we need to name the past.

> *(i)*
> *I am a Jew without a Synagogue,*
> *I am a Christian without a Church,*
> *I am a Hindu without a Temple.*
> *I am a Man of Wholeness*
> *without heritage or community or teacher or book.*

> *(ii)*
> *Fundamentalist religion was the house of value.*
> *For better and worse – it fell apart.*
> *Who'd rebuild in the same mould?*
> *Only the revivalist backlash.*
> *But our globalising technoculture is suicidal.*
> *It is locking out all air.*
> *It is near-blind to the invisible –*
> *it is near-blind to the visible.*
> *It desperately needs a stairwell to silence –*

and to sound.
It has almost forgotten
the value just behind, just inside –
the value beyond a price.

And out of our struggle have come
feminism, gay-rights, the men's movement,
self-help groups, community action,
ecological awareness, alternative management and economics,
healing, growth-work, meditation, counselling and therapy,
health foods and complementary medicine –
a thousand and one voices of holistic value.

We don't want religion back –
but can we re-house value?
Can we build community structures imbued with a holistic valuing –
community structures to hold us,
to hold our days,
to hold our seasons,
to hold our families –
to hold us in mutual acceptance
as we travel alongside each other
on the beautiful, painful journey beyond knowing?

This is a massive and delicate discussion.
Why did religion fall apart in the first place?
Rigidity, dishonesty, fanaticism?
Ignorant, ethnocentric arrogance?
Irrationality, dogmatism?
Misogyny?
Corrupt, disempowering hierarchy?
Repression, denial, escapist transcendence?
We might need a home for holistic value,
but how not to repeat the same mistakes?

(iii)
I was a child of value.
I chose to be outcast.
I chose to walk the path of value in a pathless age.
And I made enormous mistakes.
But I am coming home.
I already have friends –
and sometimes we sit in full respect...
And in that intimacy

we truly know aloneness,
and in that trust
we allow ourselves to be seen...
And we see ourselves –
our insignificance,
and our greatness –
and we tremble...
And we know we can never know –
and we know,
we know,
we know...

(iv)
We desperately need
a holistic cultural architecture,
but can we build conscious, flexible, reviewable structures –
local, manageable structures which don't disempower?
And can we make our altars
not only out of the heavens,
but also out of earth, sky, water and fire?

We need to.
We need soulful social reform.
We need a holistic social infrastructure.
We ache for deep, united community.
We ache for holding,
for shared meaning.
We deeply desire to re-house value –
but we're paralysed, unable to go forwards
because we're terrified of going back.

The second section of this book emerges from another landscape... The backdrop has shifted. I am no longer the arrogant ghost I was, immersed in fundamentalism. I am now out of the clouds – and on the streets. We have landed in modernity.

No longer cradled by the heavenly certainties of the ancient world,
I walk in not-knowing –
dazed in the dazzle of the modern world.
I am on my own.
I am dispirited.
And the temple of sex,
which is the world,

has been desecrated.
On the altar of the earth,
of the womb and the seed and the hand of death –
hangs the picture of an object to fuck.
I enter.
I reach for the chillum again.
I reach for the pile of porno magazines tucked under the altar.
I masturbate.
I have no song of soul,
I have no sacred flesh.
I am split-off from all value.
In the temple of modernity my semen splashes to the floor
  like dirty water.
I become quintessentially modern.

But somehow, somewhere, simultaneously, I stick and cling to my silent journey. I keep the-value-of-something tucked up somewhere inside me – although I no longer have the words to speak it. Like everybody else, I am a teenager on the run from spirit, reconnecting with my uniqueness, but I can't fully surrender to the emptiness of modernity. The-value-of-it-all had been my running-away, but it was also my calling. It had been my addiction, but it was also my devotion. It was my defence system, but it was also my protection.

I write like a maniac. I write for my life. Soon the tension becomes too much. The city becomes a nightmare. My need for healing begins screaming for the countryside. I nearly kill myself. And then destiny picks me up and lays me down in a forest beside a stream, beyond the reach of the void and crazed mass mind – beyond the vibrational influence of modernity. And there, at rest under the stars, I sink into peace. There I unfurl enough to heal.

This section records my road from holiness (via hollowness) to holism. This is the section of my life in which I fell out of heaven, passed through purgatory, embodied, became empassioned, and arrived as all-of-me on earth. This was when I became human. This was my incarnation – not from life to life, but within a life. I began taking birth at about thirty-three – and it took me about ten years.

At first I thought holism meant just being open. I had no concept of integration. I had no psychological imagination. And I had no understanding of the relationship between psyche and spirit – no idea of how I could be both true to myself and true to Truth. Slowly I understood in my mind, then in my heart, then in my hands and feet.

From 17 to 23 I flew madly everywhere. From 23 to 33 I flew decisively up towards a premodern spirit. At 33 I fled spirit, collapsed, and fell to earth. From 33 on I have re-made myself and been re-made.

I have re-made myself and been re-made
in the image of another spirit:
a spirit that gets aroused,
empassioned –
a spirit that mounts the world.
A spirit of silent laughter
and tenderness
and ecstasy and pain.

And I have re-made myself and been re-made
in the image of another earth:
an earth of proud storms,
of minerals and jewels,
of unbearable love and dying and wild celebration –
an earth of sexual oceans overflowing.

And I have re-made myself and been re-made
in the image of their union:
in the tantric everyday –
in the bliss of the bodymind –
in the pain of dying to my lies –
in the cauldron of their bed –
in the erotic inner journey –
in the passion of invisible sex.

This has meant therapy, the study of therapy, relationship work, menswork, support groups, rituals, time in nature, more time in nature, reading on holism, being green, community activism, health foods, holistic medicine, voicework, dance, therapeutic movement, meditation, and esoterics of all sorts. All in all, painfully, naturally, and unintentionally, I aligned myself with the emergent creative belief system of our times...

And that a holistic movement exists – this needs to be stated. That a shared worldview exists (however undogmatic), that a shared sense of path exists (however broad), that a shared ethics exists (however flexible) – all of this needs stating. Especially if the proposition is to re-construct community together. Especially if the ultimate proposition is a community-based holistic civilisation...

At the level of its essence,
a civilisation is a collective energy field.
It is composed of concepts.
The citizens of an energy field feed on it
for existential, personal, communal and practical identity.
They create cultural structures

to embody and transmit their concepts.
When a civilisation disintegrates
the citizens become undernourished.
This is symptomised by confusion, despair,
fear, aggression, compensation.
The culture's structures shatter.
Often there's bloodshed.

But a concept field can only disintegrate
in the presence of other concepts.
Disintegration must be accompanied by emergence.
Modernity is disintegrating.
What is the emergence?
Fundamentalism is regressive –
calling us backwards and upwards to the frustrated tyrannical heavens.
Postmodern porno-techno-fun is the disintegration itself,
the suicidal revenge of the prostituted earth –
calling us further into abstraction and anguish.

Holism is the emergence.
It is integrative.
It redeems both spirit and earth.
It promises a civilisation of creative intercourse.
Today, within the collective energy field,
disintegrating split-down modernism,
regressive split-up fundamentalism
and integrative, creative holism
are co-existent, live, divergent potentials.

It behooves us, therefore,
to name the emergence,
to nourish it and be fed,
to guide it into manifestation,
and to develop cultural structures to contain it.

In this second section I use the story of my own development to suggest the kind of inner journey we need to make, the kind of inner ground we need to be upon – in order to ready ourselves, at a personal level, to participate in holistic community. But before beginning with the local community-development practicalities of Section Three, I end with chapters on holism and science, holism and religion, and holism and politics – in order to offer a larger perspective on the implications of holism, and holistic community, for our civilisation.

Atheistic pseudo-science is the basic creed of modernity. Is then, holism anti-scientific? Or in its call to re-connect with the natural world, is holism anti-technological? And is holistic community exclusive? Does it have fixed boundaries? How does it fit within the existing culture? Can there be holistic community within the existing religious traditions? And what are holistic politics?

Holistic community is not just a comfy, supportive option for people who believe in growth work and who need help with the babysitting! It is not even only about sharing growth paths. People who commit to trying to travel together in holistic community (precisely because it is holistic and must therefore affect their bodies as much as their souls) will automatically start looking at how their food is grown, their houses built, their products and services bought and sold. Again – precisely because it is holistic, it has implications for every aspect of our lives. Decentralisation and community empowerment might mean each community working in its own way, but holistic community has implications for agriculture, industry, trade, education, the law and the arts. Nothing is unconnected. Holism is not religiously apolitical.

The third section of this book is based on articles, essays, diaries and working materials written since setting up Balance about five years ago. Balance is based in the Totnes area of Devon, England, and experiments in developing holistic community.

Community existed in the premodern world. It was misogynistic and self-destructive. It survived on demonisation. And the fundamentalist premodern communities that survive alongside or within modernity remain a threat to themselves and others.

'Eastern' communist community has been another community-of-repression – crushing the long-fought-for dignity of the individual, and denying each person's right to their own thoughts and feelings and gods. And all that denies implodes.

'Western' capitalist community cannot be discussed because it doesn't exist. Such capitalism is separatist and competitive by definition. It is as fanatically individualist as eastern communism was collectivist. Thus it is ethnocidal. It replaces ancestral communal bonds with an every-man-for-himself addiction to consumerism. National community, racial community, religious community, local community, the community of the family – all is collapsed or collapsing under the assault of colonialising capitalism. Whatever community survives does so despite it.

And much does. Whether it is academic community, street gangs, clubs, cliques, community centred around a leisure activity, a school or a cause, cults, surviving premodern religious community, modernising religious community, community by ethnic identification, or the community of the workplace – to different depths and in different ways, pockets of community survive. This last section looks at the development of one such tendency. A hardly formed, hardly articulate tendency. But a tendency that perhaps carries the seeds of a profound philosophical, psychological, social and political alternative – the postmodern tendency of holistic community.

There are many towns around the world where, on a like-attracts-like basis, people with an essentially holistic outlook have been gathering for several decades now – buying property, opening shops and schools, setting up community support networks and growth work options of all sorts, and generally transforming the ethos of the local area. But even in such places, holistic community is mostly unconscious – inasmuch as there is little conscious commitment to staying together, and working together, to develop it. Most people have come from outside the area, don't have childhood roots there, and tend to keep open the option of moving away should, say, an interesting employment opportunity arise elsewhere. There is little commitment to the area – to that land.

Furthermore, because of their ethos, these areas also attract a transient population. People come for healing, and then move on. And whatever structures or support systems emerge seem to do so sporadically, and are hardly ever part of an integrated, overarching vision. Even community forums are rare. Other than to a small circle of friends, there is little commitment to each other.

Totnes is one such town. Although they have their disadvantages, they are ripe for holistic community. But now, as we enter the twenty first century, the expanding health food market, the legitimising of complementary therapies, and our ever-increasing concern with ecological issues all suggest that more and more people are tending towards holistic values. The stuff of this book is not for everyone. But today more people than ever are ready for the material presented in this last section which invites us to come together on the basis of our shared values, and to engage with models and methods that can help us practically (not just theoretically) construct deep, supportive local community.

Section Three explores the four sphere model of community more deeply. It also explores co-creativity more deeply. The aim of this section is to equip the reader with enough confidence to begin developing holistic community in her or his own local area. As a starting point, a centre point, I suggest the community forum – from which all of the spheres can be developed, as each locality sees fit, depending on its own needs and desires.

I do not offer any guidance on developing spheres one and two, since I have said enough about them in the first two sections. And I do not offer any more input on the content of the fourth, political sphere since the basic agenda of green, participative politics is clear, and each locality knows its own specific needs best. However, in discussing community co-creativity, and the importance of the other three spheres, I will be stressing the qualitative reform of our politics.

Furthermore, in placing the fourth sphere as an offshoot of the co-creative community forum there is a re-visioning of community hierarchy. (Without any naiveté as to the persistence and omnipresence of hierarchy) rather than seeing our politicians as our leaders, at the top of the local pyramid, we are placing leadership at the centre, in the hands of the community, with political matters seen as important offshoots, of neither lesser nor greater importance than the matters of the existential, personal or communal spheres.

I will go into further detail about the communal sphere, since (having been the province of organised religion) it is a sphere we tend to shy away from. Besides the community forum, which is communal, I will be looking at how communities can gradually co-create their own meaningful ceremonies and celebrations – whether of the seasons, or birth or death. And I will be looking at perhaps the two most fundamental communal structures – initiation into adulthood, and long-term committed partnership.

All in all, I will be offering you my reflections-so-far. I do not for a moment consider them definitive. As my own experimentation evolves, so do my opinions. My hope is that some readers will be inspired in the community development work they are already doing, others encouraged to embark upon new holistic community development programmes in their local areas, and that both will refine my reflections, combine them with their own, and make the whole project of deep community development more and more popular.

The Premodern Era
The Fundamentalist Phase

Sexless Spirit

Introduction

I left home to find Truth.
I had no idea I was also running away.
I hitchhiked to India with Maria-Cruz.
We were penniless when we left Istanbul.
We sold our clothes on the streets in Afghanistan.
It was beautiful, it was spiritual-romantic –
and we were out of our heads.

By the time I got back to Europe I was walking and praying,
walking and praying...
I had decided I was a follower of Christ –
'but was I,' I cried, 'was I really? Maybe I was deluding myself.'
I prayed for a teacher.
Driven by the sincerity of my quest, my urge to community,
and my fear of sex, conflict, challenge and success –
I was soon a devotee 'at the lotus feet' of a fundamentalist Hindu guru.
I became an easternised monk in a westernised sect –
a modern pilgrim, stuck like a ghost, on an ancient, abandoned path.
It took me a decade to walk out.

What I have since come to understand is that almost all, if not all, premodern cultures follow the same basic pattern: the pattern of the 'revealed' culture. They claim absolute truth was once revealed, and is to be accessed by following the teachings and teachers in the lineage descending from their one revelation. Some premodern cultures might have tended to be more exclusivist (we're the only way), others more elitist (we're the superior way), and within them all there have been individuals and groupings of greater and lesser degrees of devotion/fanaticism – but they all saw themselves as the supreme cultural embodiment of the absolute truth. And they organised themselves in officially-sacred social structures which perpetuated the descent of their revelation – safeguarding its 'purity' and inhibiting 'deviance' – and thus ensuring their survival.

Thus what I experienced was the patriarchal slavery that most of humanity has experienced for most of its recorded history. The only difference being that I experienced it in an anachronistic cultural transplant within the modern western world.

However sincerely, and however unintentionally, I became a part of the fundamentalist backlash to the artificiality and emptiness of the technoculture.

The Body, Sexuality, the World

I took off my shoes and padded slowly into the temple.
A nervousness inside me joked in a whisper:
'it feels like being on the moon'.
It did.
The hall hung suspended in an atmosphere of the otherworld,
thick with sweet incense.
From everywhere and nowhere within this mystic mist came a glow –
perhaps of purity, or of peace.
I felt transported, enchanted.
Then I noticed the moon men...
They were about human size.
They looked like head-sized, skin-coloured balls,
floating at head height, trailing floor-length skirts.
They bobbed along,
obviously in conversation,
oblivious to me –
graceful and wise.
They were radiant.
I was awe-struck.
This was my first visit.
Wherever it was,
it felt beautiful and safe.
It felt like home.

I was invited to dine with them.
We sat in rows on the floor.
They chanted a Sanskrit blessing.
It felt like a spell.
A good spell.
They ate with their fingers,
so did I.
The food was out of this world.
I was over the moon.
I was in heaven.

I studied the scriptures with the moon men –
learnt the mantras and chants,
and copied the codes of behaviour.
I became a neophyte, a monk-in-training.
I had my doubts, but I was easily persuaded over...

Was I my body, or was I the eternal soul inside it?
(Well, the soul, of course.)
And was not the natural activity of the soul the service of spirit?
(Well, yes, what else could it be.)
But how to serve spirit –
could I just call anything 'service'?
How could I know what spirit wanted?
(I didn't.)
That's why I had to follow the guru,
who, by following his own guru, had become one with the scriptures,
which came from spirit.
(Well – yes, that made sense.)

'If you are sincere you will surrender,
and if you surrender you will experience bliss.'
(Well, they seemed to.)

And so I did surrender,
and I did experience bliss.
I was initiated and re-named Gaura Gadadhara Dasa,
and some years later, initiated again –
as a brahman teacher and priest.
And so my first visit lasted ten years...
I found timeless spirit and lost my personality.
I found eternity and lost my life-on-earth.
I too became a moon man –
an inhabitant of the realms of incense, lotus petals, obedience,
self-negation, self-deception, certainty and lies.
I died to myself in order to bask in the glow of the transcendence.
And I too bobbed along,
as cleansed as driftwood,
looking graceful, looking wise,
a living shell,
trotting out sanskrit mantras –
no words of my own –
an innocent, fundamentalist fanatic.

I call them 'fragments'… pages torn from my mind-of-then – a mind captured and captivated by the eternal, and furiously scornful of the temporary. I called this one *The Doll*:

You scoff at the grown-up girl who imagines her doll lives,
who waits on it, bathes and dresses it,
and feeds it and puts it to bed.

But you, every day,
you pamper and preen and fatten a corpse,
every night you lay it to rest on soft cushions,
and from moment to moment
you obey its beck and call.

It is a scoffing poem... 'You scoff at the girl, and I scoff at you. I scoff at you because you are identified with the material body. You are a materialist. I am superior and spiritual. I am saved, you are damned.' And I scoff and mock and condemn the materialist in me. I scorn any pride in my appearance (vanity), any inclination towards bodily comfort (gross indulgence), and all avoidance of physical pain and pursuit of physical pleasure (slavery to the senses). This is the typical premodern, anti-body, anti-worldly stance. It divides us internally and divides humanity.

Worse:
I am tortured,
I am torturing my physicality,
I project this physicality on to you,
I torture you!

Worse:
My physicality must be subdued, it must go,
completely,
it must die –
you represent this physicality, you must die!
This is the final projective logic of the premodern stance.

For the premoderner
the other world is high and dry and good,
this world is juicy and sexy and bad.
The other world is spiritual and value-full,
this world is sexual and value-empty.
And anything that drags us down
into the this-worldly,
in others or in ourselves,
is to be scoffed at, scorned, condemned.

But condemn them as we may,
our limbs and lusts and needs and fears
cry out to us.
We are not moon men or women.
We are not creatures of the heavens.
We are not spirits without flesh or feeling.

We have personalities.
We are people.
We are creatures of skin and emotion and mind –
as well as spirit.
We are good and bad and neither.
We can't split off any part of us.
Well, we can –
but anything split off will seek reinstatement.
It will seek vengeance,
ruthlessly.

As a would-be heaven-bound premoderner –
denying Pan, denying The Green Man –
I went through hell
as these archetypes reclaimed me
and dragged me down to earth.
Pan in my groin,
in my loins,
was piping furiously.
The Green Man
who is the spirit of the forest and the lake,
and whose eyes sparkle in every man,
was screaming in the night.
These noble, wild creatures of the psyche were suffocating
in the rarefied air of the temple.

'Sex bad, spirit good'. Put crudely, this was the basic premodern equation. And this sex/spirit split still hangs today, like stale cloud cover, in the collective psyche. Even though there is a popular fantasy that promiscuity has redeemed sexuality, the modern era has reinforced, not repaired, the sex/spirit split… In turning its eyes from the otherly, it has focused exclusively on the physical. Ultimate-value is no longer situated somewhere else – but nor is it here. For premodernity up was real and value-full (because eternal) and down was all illusion. For modernity down is real (because perceivable) and up is all illusion – but there's still no value down here in the sexual world.

Sex will not be redeemed by promiscuity, but by seeing the ultimate value of our all acts in the world. Only then will sex be hallowed – as it should.

In premodernity the split soul hit back at humanity in witch-hunting and frenzied crusading and obsessive, masochistic spirituality. Today the split erupts in genocide, ecocide, in an all-pervasive, desperate empty sexuality, and in the consequences of valuelessness: alienation, depression, suicide, violence and addiction (to alcohol, TV, ownership, noise, speed, 'doing', and so on). Such is the vengeance of numbness.

A definition…

> *Pornography is not just about sex.*
> *There is a pornographic attitude:*
> *it's about being out for the thrills,*
> *with complete couldn't-give-a-damn.*
> *It numbs the soul.*
> *Modernity inherited a world stripped of meaning –*
> *and fucked it.*
> *This is the definition of a pornographic culture.*

Another fragment from my fundamentalist's scrapbook. This one was called *The Glorious Soul*:

> *The glorious soul, in spiritual destitution,*
> *tramps the allies of birth and death –*
> *ragged and shameless in blood and bones,*
> *scrounging and scavenging dead-end, dog-end thrills.*
> *Sleeping rough in womb after womb,*
> *weathering the seasons of youth and decay,*
> *its memory eroded –*
> *the Child of God is at home in the rubbish,*
> *scrapping for the pick of the bin.*

This fragment is more seductive, but like *The Doll* it shames the body, and rubbishes the world. And although the reference to 'thrills' in both this premodern poem and in my postmodern 'definition' might make them seem very similar – the mood of *The Doll* is 'forget the thrills, there is only pain in this world, it has no value – leave and go back to spirit', whereas the mood behind my definition is 'forget the thrills, go deeper, appreciate, there is value in this world – stay here in openness to spirit'.

And again… this one entitled *Organs And Bones And Me*.

> *I have seen the wax cheek,*
> *the void eye, the unbendable back –*
> *I have seen them, unprotesting, on the pyre.*
> *The lens, the retina, the screen in the brain –*
> *they don't experience seeing*
> *any more than lachrymal glands lament.*
> *The cerebrum, the cerebellum and the medulla oblongata*
> *don't confer, ponder or philosophise*
> *any more than the liver, the pancreas and the intestines*
> *sit down to enjoy a good meal.*
> *I am not collarbones or shoulder-blades or vertebrae or ribs.*

And that meaningless skeletal grin
which will be mine,
won't be me.

And again, and again, and again… I remember it well: the mantra 'you are not your body' echoing through the scriptures we revered, and through the sermons of the spiritual masters we adored…

Our heads were turned towards spirit,
our necks were like iron,
we were identified elsewhere…
'You are not your body'.
The mantra didn't work.
Bodies disagreed.
The great masters ran away with their adoring secretaries,
there was child abuse in the holy schools…
Absurd, traumatic scandals abounded.
I too was traumatised –
by a paradigm which was
endlessly guillotining
the entirety of my being.

The loss of my body, of my embodiment, of my pleasures, of my discomforts, of my aging… The loss of my manhood, of my fertility, of my potency… A decade of loss has taken a decade to redress. The loss of my lust… I have needed to meet with men, to hear similar stories, to hear the archetypal nature of my own.

I haven't been able to just forgive myself, I have needed to be forgiven by others. And I haven't been able to unfold into my wholeness alone, I have needed the company of other men… So much talking, so much honesty, so much tenderness, so much listening, so many evenings together… The prayers, the feasting, the rituals, the wrestling, with different men in different groups – and I'm still travelling…

Tonight I am on a train, on the way to a men's group. This evening's group's on the theme of masturbation. What do I feel? I don't agree 'it's bad', I don't agree 'it's good'. The former is usually the echo of premodern repression, the latter usually the voice of modernist hedonism. I would tend to judge by the quality of the act…

My outlook's this: we need to be aware of the two polarities: solitary fucking, which is, in general, destructive, and solitary sexual-loving, which is, in general, creative. Solitary-fucking-type masturbation objectifies other, and uses him/her – its flavour is of the celluloid magazine. It is emotionally absent, soulless, demeaning and draining. Solitary sexual-loving-type masturbation is relational – it is an intrapsychic affair, between me and me. It is not dependent on other, it is imageless. It is self-honouring, nourishing and balancing – it is celebratory, fulfilling and surcharging.

Solitary fucking takes value from other. Solitary sexual-loving gives value to self. Between these two polarities there are, of course, infinite subtleties. But masturbation which tends towards solitary fucking will repercuss in one's sex with a partner, and in all of one's relationships – both with people and with things – as will masturbation which tends towards solitary sexual-loving.

As I write this, across the aisle a well-bosomed teenager is giggling with another girl who seems to be her French guest. 'Look,' she suddenly, and loudly, exclaims, 'You see that boy's jacket? On the back is written 'wanker', which is very rude.' They laugh excitedly, people look up, the woman opposite me smiles wryly – the atmosphere tingles for a while.

What is 'rude', I wonder? Clearly, for her, it means 'exciting'! But what about for us, the full grown-ups? Why do we not speak openly of self-loving as a private but very pleasurable affair? Why do we hide it? Why is masturbation still such a frightening and taboo subject? Why can't we discuss it freely, and make distinctions between split-off and integrated types of masturbation?

Firstly, we live with murky ancestral shame – with the cultural inheritance of premodern Christianity. We are ancestrally wounded.

Secondly, the porno/techno-culture is prolonging the body/soul split – rather than healing it. The technoculture might insist we celebrate matter, the body, sex – but until it re-enchants the material world, until it returns ultimate-value to matter, the sex it touts will be empty and thus frustrating, and thus ever increasingly distorted. And therefore, to put it bluntly, we don't declare our masturbation because most of it is split-down solitary-fucking – killing of self and other – a murderous, suicidal quick relief. And the whole being we are, somewhere is bowed in shame.

One other thing… Although this solitary fucking/solitary sexual-loving spectrum is important, it is also dangerous. The danger is in self-righteous denial of the solitary fucker, of pretending to be what we think we ought to be, and then of vengeful re-possession – of being taken over and becoming perverts and fakes. The solitary fucker must be named, placed, judged – but also received, understood, embraced.

In both men and women the solitary fucker is the self-hater, and the hater of its lovers – desperately aching-for other. Rather than just condemning the solitary fucker, we need to lead it towards supportive community – in order to enter relationship with all that fears relationship.

And we need to re-dream, and feel our way into, new sexual mythologies – new images and knowledges and laws. And we can give solitary sexual-loving a go! For me it has been powerful and beautiful in the forest – pulsing in resonance with the trees…

Here is a holistic sexual mythology. I call it *Erotic All The Time Everywhere*:

When time not only stops,
but is gone,
when you know you are
nowhere,
when the simplest
act is laden with symbolism,
when everyone is a character
in an impossibly complex epic,
when objects are magical
and life is alive –
could that be
the eroticism
we're so lustily chasing?

Have we been tricked?
Could it be a question of split terms,
of philosophy and theology that control
the way we explain ourselves to ourselves,
that control the way we understand what we feel – and cripple us?

The experience of a childlike magnificence.
So natural.
Effortless unveiling.
Stillness
holding all...

That state called 'centred', 'present', 'aware' –
so full,
so overpouring,
so voluptuous.
Could we also call it erotic,
natural-erotic –
body-spirit,
spirit-body
sacred-erotic?
Can spirit reach the flesh?
Can sex pull us up
out of the body?
Can solitary sexual-loving be an oblation,
a prayer?

'Om bhur, bhuva, sva, tat savitur varenyam bhargo dimahi.' –
'with the water of the Ganges I worship the Ganges.'

The air moves against my flesh,
smells, colours and textures seduce me.
The myth I walk in
is an odyssey of wholeness.
What is spirit?
The energy beyond me?
What is sex?
The energy within me?
Where am I?
Where do I end?
At times like this I am turned inside out.

If I was always whole
I would walk in eroticism
all the time everywhere.

If we were always whole
sexual love with each other
would be holy communion.

And the sex-honouring community would be
the holy congregation.

My aim in writing this last piece is to suggest an alternative, holistic philosophy of sex. As I have said, promiscuity has not redeemed sexuality. Split-off sex is just frantic fucking. The holistic myth redeems sex by re-valuing it.

This is not to say that spirituality is sexuality, and sexuality spirituality. They are not one. Sex is sex, and spirit is spirit. Sex is the song of the earth, spirit is the song of heaven. They can be separated. They can be divorced from each other. But they need each other. Without the presence of spirit, sexuality becomes pornographic. Without the presence of sex, spirituality becomes inhuman. They can be separated – but in life-before-death they belong together. And there is an experience of their unity. There is a day-to-day holistic experience. It is neither split-up nor split-down. It is not genitally focused, but it is simultaneously sexual and spiritual. It is the erotic experience of the eternal within the everyday. The sexual act is its sacrament.

But if we don't experience it in the everyday, how do we expect to experience it suddenly on entering the boudoir? We can rub genitals forever, but we will never taste the erotic bliss we seek until we can feel the sacredness of all our physical acts, from eating to sleeping to walking through the air. First we need to open our hearts to the numinous sensuality of the everyday. Then, perhaps, we'll find it in bed.

This is a myth – an existential context. It is not a final truth claim. But I believe it is a critical myth for our culture. The holistic experience redeems the physical dimension, the realm of matter (denigrated by premodernity and desecrated by modernity) by acknowledging its immersion in spirit.

And the redemption of sex is also the redemption of spirit. Spirit becomes real again. We get to give God guts. And we need to get to grips with spirit, with the intangible. We need to touch its reality. We need it as present and as exciting as sex.

As I see it, this holistic experience of sacred eroticism lives at the core of holistic community. It is its essence. It is its beauty. Just as Christian community invites us to heaven, and Buddhist community invites us to nirvana, holistic community invites us to be aroused together to the sacred erotic journey.

And ultimately, I believe, unless people are tempted to the fruit of the holistic promise, there will be little impetus to develop holistic community... Holism means samsara is nirvana, and that God is with us as intimately on earth as he is in heaven (without denying the distinctions). But because its apotheosis is in the here-and-now, it does away with the traditional sex/spirit split that has tyrannised the world, east and west, throughout the patriarchal millennia. The rejection of the world, and thus of the body, and thus of relationship, and thus of our humanity – which inevitably leads to appalling inhumanity – is the side-effect of lopsided traditional religious promises. They offered understanding, compassion – we felt seen in our suffering. And they offered redemption – they offered an end to that suffering. Which was obviously tempting. But it was a false promise. Because suffering cannot be avoided. It cannot be transcended, only embraced. Thus the holistic myth of erotic awareness invites us towards sensual alertness and full-body appreciation for the unfathomably sacred world around us all day everyday – in all of its beauty and all of its pain. It is not constant genital arousal. It is an eroticism of the soul. It promises the absence of fear, complete trust and relaxation, and direct perception of spirit – here, in our bodies, with each other, and the birds, insects, animals, plants and trees.

And this myth is very important in terms of the four sphere model of community, which begins with the conceptual level (the collective energy field). We need clear concepts if we are to construct community with clarity. We cannot just assume we know each other's visions. It is also central to the second sphere, the sphere of personal path, because although the holistic experience might be immediately available, as usual, paradoxically, it is also a lifetime's work. To trust and open and relax into the place of erotic awareness requires enormous sophistication. To truly relax into an open heart we need to be able to parent ourselves – to be able to tend our brokenness. To truly relax into spirit we need to know our eternal core. To truly relax into our sexuality we need to be masters and mistresses of our boundaries. And heart, spirit, sexuality – all three need to be open to experience sacred-erotic awareness, spirit-in-the-flesh. And they do all open, sometimes, and they usually close again. It's hard to be in so much pleasure. And what does all of this mean?

That, although it might take a thousand different routes, there is an essential holistic path.

And how we conceive and live our personal paths will obviously shape the way we develop the third sphere, the communal sphere of shared path. And finally, our attitude to the practicalities of life, to the fourth sphere of community, will also be totally informed by the core-note of holistic awareness. After all, it's mainly in our everyday working, doing, creating lives that we have the opportunity to practise opening up, being physically present, being in-relationship, and enjoying our sacred-erotic emergence.

Finally, to clarify the myth of holism, I'd like to make a distinction between holism and 'green spirituality'. We need to heal the split , to welcome in wholeness, yes. The holistic movement appreciates this. But its blind spot, as Ken Wilber has so brilliantly explained, is green spirituality.

It's like this:

- for premodernity heaven was real and value-full, and earthly existence was just the vestibule of eternity.
- for modernity life on earth is real, but valueless, and heavenly existence is just a fairy tale.
- for green spirituality the earth is real and value-full, and heaven is a myth of the past.

In green spirituality's denial of the otherly is a continuation of fanatical modern empiricism. It might be called a philosophy of fundamentalist immanence: even though it does accord great value to where we are – only the here exists. The pattern looks like this:

Premodernity:	Hate Earth	Love Spirit
Modernity:	Hate Earth	Hate Spirit
Green Spirituality:	Love Earth	Hate Spirit

Green spirituality is an attempt to return value to the world. And in that it is admirable. But in rejecting the possibility of the otherly, the transcendent – it is hardly holistic. To return value to the world, to our daily lives and to our nighttimes, we do not need to reject the possibility of that-which-is-beyond.

In suggesting that sexuality and spirituality belong together, therefore, I am not preaching green. I am not trying to suggest that there is no beyond, no totally non-material dimension. I am not preaching immanence, nor anti-transcendence. And in stressing the one-dimensional nature of green spirituality I am not preaching some new doctrine of holistic dualism. By definition, there can be but one whole – but there's more within it than will ever meet the eye!

To try to walk in wholeness is to love the earth, and to love spirit – and to sometimes struggle with them both! It is to be open to value – without any pre-decided denial.

'God is dead, long live the Goddess!' This is just a reactive position. But it is subtly, unconsciously widespread in supposedly holistic circles. Maybe it's an unavoidable phase – which could postpone holistic community for centuries. But then again, maybe it's a necessary phase. Maybe we need to pass through a predominantly matriarchal age – to become balanced enough to enter a holistic age. The aim of this book is to encourage the holistic movement to develop holistic community – now. But collective energy fields, although they can undoubtedly be influenced, have an impetus and a wisdom of their own. Time will tell.

(i)
For me, for us,
sexual loving
is a temple,
a place of surrender,
a place of self-forgetting and self-discovering
and flesh and sweat and bliss.

And once inside,
Elisabeth and I,
we climb upon the altar,
and move impossibly slowly,
like snakes,
until our wetness begins to crackle –
and the blazing tongue,
the downward flame,
consents
to ignite the earth.

(ii)
And when I'm up in the luscious hills,
in the green rain,
among the trees,
I chant and drum with sticks on logs
and chant and drum with sticks on logs
and chant and drum with sticks on logs
until the whole forest is singing,
and the rain starts lifting
me higher and higher,
and the whole forest's flying –
like kindling tossed upwards
by some mad, ecstatic angel
into the sizzling fire-throat of god.

Relationships

I'd like to open this subject with another fragment from my fundamentalist's scrapbook…

Ron and Julie are in their autumn years
yet their affection is adolescently fresh.
Julie's shelter is Ron's armoured arms,
his bravery, his benevolence, his know-how,
and his handiness with a hammer and nails.
Ron's shelter is Julie's charm,
her chastity, her maternity, her patisserie,
and her worship of his uniqueness.

Infinitesimal, relative actors
oblivious to infinite, absolute truth –
no circumstance, they believe,
could be crippling enough to curb their private jokes,
their pet names, or their innermost intimate silliness.

Ay! Which yearning soul does not search fulfilment
in another unfulfilled soul?
Or hanker for an ever-waxing honeymoon
with a never-waning mate?

Countless melancholic melodies
of nostalgia for a phantom love
jerk countless tears from haunted hearts
unable to accept the axiom:
two theatres never make one truth.
But Ron and Julie are ever-valentines.
They have eloped beyond all logic.
For them two relative infinitesimals
make one infinite absolute.

More monk's poetry. This one extends the laughter of that tight-lipped, self-denying, split-up fundamentalist to those dizzy, maya-tossed individuals who, rather than sensibly aim their hearts at eternity, are foolish enough to actually love each other. It mocks their cute, sentimental co-dependency, and argues the insufficiency of personal love: 'Some simple-minded souls might put on a show of satisfaction, but factually, because we are tiny spiritual beings whose fulfilment is in relationship with The Limitless Source, it is ludicrous to seek fulfilment in each other…' It was either-or – one loved either God, or a human.

Thus the premodern individual was bereft of the world, bereft of his or her body, and bereft of deepest intimacy. Couples lived together at a distance, supporting each other in developing the detachment needed to achieve salvation. Marriage was a best-avoided, usually-unavoidable way through life – whose whole reason-for-being would begin after death. Life on earth was cold. But Heaven would be warm. Kissing? Cuddling? Making love at the fireside while the children were asleep? Feeling heard and seen and held? Sharing one's heart with another? All of such weak, selfish, indulgent, ignorant, escapist urges were to be quashed. But enlightenment would be cosy – forever.

Thus not only did the split-up premodern paradigm prohibit physical pleasure, it forbade emotional pleasure. Only sublimation was legitimate. The premodern individual was allowed no needs on any level. Stoic and resolute – she was to give herself to Truth, casting off all personal want.

The mentality was collective and renounced. Its shadow was the held breath and puffed chest of the fanatic, harshness, cruelty, guilt and shame – and as with all that is split-off, it has hit back: it has flipped in the face of humanity in the form of a modernity that has ripped up collectivity (community), and sunk itself in an unabashed competition for pleasure.

> When I began to doubt Hinduism,
> and my divine will weakened,
> and I began to become human –
> I softened to my needs.
> I went to see my superiors,
> who proposed an arranged marriage.
> I accepted their proposal,
> and somewhere in the women's quarters soon after,
> a celibate sister named Bhaja Radhe
> accepted a similar proposal.
> Thus we married the tradition,
> not each other,
> and were wed to the classical premodern framework
> in which, as marriage progresses, it is hoped
> that couples will become more and more
> detached from each other.
>
> Unfortunately, being children of modernity,
> and only recent converts to the antiquity,
> our early conditioning awoke within us.
> We couldn't resist our affection
> or sexual attraction.
>
> The traditional Hindu law is that sexual intercourse is only for procreation,

and that couples should only mate once a month –
and even that
only after extensive purificatory ritual.
This became impossible.
We broke the rules.
We didn't do the full rituals.
We had sex more often than we ought.
We enjoyed – and we tortured ourselves for it.
We suffered such anguish, such remorse, such confusion...
We felt such hypocrites.
We felt we looked so pure and talked so purely,
but that inside we were
dirty and degraded.
We had neither intellectual understanding,
nor spiritual, nor psychological insight.
We couldn't cope.

I resented the relationship and became more fanatical –
a common pattern, I later found out.
But the religious doubts were mounting up,
even straightforward fanaticism had become problematic.
And our unspeakable shame
was taking us further and further into isolation.

Finally, we escaped the whole split-up mindset,
and found ourselves adrift
in split-down twentieth-century London.
My sister let us live in her empty bedsit.
We shared this flat for a year.

But premodernity hung about the two of us like fog.
We didn't know what it was,
and couldn't shake it off.

We couldn't heal in each other's presence –
and Bhaja Radhe and I divorced.

This story will always make my heart ache. We were so lost, we struggled so much – and despite it all, we loved each other… And this story also makes me angry at the lack of deep guidance I received, and at the lack of deep guidance in our culture.

And although this is a personal and specific tale – of a premodern relationship, in a particularly strict, artificially premodern environment, between two essentially modern individuals – it is also typical of premodernity. The overflow of 'weakness', and the self-inflicted torture, have long been the stuff of the confessions of the good and great.

Today the split-up model of marriage has fallen apart. Over the last few centuries the whole premodern cosmic edifice has collapsed – and from the rubble the modern Romantic Model, blurry eyed and lusty, has stepped forth. It is the Hollywood Model. It is idealised hedonism. It is the over-the-horizon, happily-ever-after model. And it is this superficial romantic marriage which my monk's poem – from its austere, sublime premodern tower – so arrogantly scorns.

The no-fun social norm gave way to the all-fun social norm. Child-like collectivity meant no room for one-to-one support. Today's adolescent individualism leaves us murmuring 'you are my everything'. All-distance has given way to all-closeness. The modern model is a fun-fun-fun symbiosis. But, as anyone who has been in a modern relationship for more than a few years knows, the ever-waxing honeymoon does wane – insecurities and strategies come to light, there is disillusion, and then resentment, withdrawal, anger and conflict. At which point we either split up and go back to the movies, or settle into an arrangement of ruts, avoidances, appearances and stupefied contentment (the Ron and Julie option parodied in the poem).

And of course, it's not as clear-cut as this. I'm generalising about a million and one couples I've never met – and there is a third, holistic possibility. But these are the bare bones of the cultural situation. The collective energy field whose externals were no sex before marriage, no co-habitation, and no divorce, has disintegrated – and the self-assertive and naive, teenage collective energy field of modernity is now reflected in an immature approach to relationships and an increasingly unstable and grief-stricken social situation.

The energy field was once anti-earth, anti-woman, anti-sex, anti-pleasure – and manifested crisp, clean, cruel, frigid, lying spiritual relationships. Now the mass mind is anti-heaven, anti-authoritarian, to-each-their-own and have-a-good-time - and manifests in cheap, quick, directionless, messy, abusive, unsustainable relationships.

As this situation becomes ever more obvious, and ever more fraught, and as the collective holistic energy field expands, the possibility of another relationship model is emerging: a psychologically literate long-term journey of awareness and awakening.

I met Elisabeth three years after I had separated from Bhaja Radhe. By then I had broken down enough, and been put back together again enough, to be open to the holistic possibility. Elisabeth had passed through a long Buddhist phase which had been as disciplined and rigorous as my Hinduism. And like me, she had acquired the language of therapy. We had both done some groundwork for entering a holistic relationship. And over the years, as we've let ourselves become human, we've grown the eyes of gods…

(i)
It felt like
spiritual incest.
We were twins.
She was me
in female.
We fitted
with a pre-arranged perfection.
We were inseparable.
She was Woman –
archetypal, glorious.
I was nobility itself.
Bliss span up and down our spines.
We were immediately together forever.
I loved her,
I worshipped her.
I was adored.
Life was alight.
There was only beauty.
There was only magic.
There was only meaning.

Every cliché of
a dream come true, of
feeling made for each other, of
feeling as if we'd always known
each other –
every cliché,
every corny love song,
all of it –
yes! Yes! Yes!

(ii)
And now I can look back and say –
of course, in order to grow,
we needed to un-merge,
to become two again,
to become ourselves again.

Now I can look back
at when we just had to
start saying
we were feeling suffocated

by each other,
we were feeling rejecting
of each other,
and, worst of all, that sometimes
we weren't loving each other.

I can look back and know
we needed to individuate
in order to be together as ourselves.
Yes.
But it was a long painful fall
from grace.
It was a tortuous descent
down the holy mountain.
Every psychic muscle got torn apart,
every last holding-on torn away –
again and again and again and again.

(iii)
And now I see Elisabeth
isn't Woman –
she is Elisabeth-Woman.
I do not love her goddess-like perfection –
I love her divine humanity.

Nor am I any longer Tarzan and Jesus
merged as Ideal Man.
I am loved as Man
manifesting as Mark,
(which feels much more comfortable than before!)

And within our loving
we accept and reject each other
quite regularly now,
it seems.
How unthinkable
that would've once been!

There's something strange about watching yourselves fall
and somehow,
even if it's only slightly –
looking down with compassion.
Somehow as we let ourselves become human
we grow the eyes of gods.

Now
the bliss in the spine isn't spinning anymore –
it's humming.
And we're no longer dancing on air –
we're dancing on sacred ground.

On one level the journey of relationship has three stages. On another, it seems we visit and re-visit these stages. It's as if relationships have their premodern, merged childhood of mutual loving acceptance; their modern, self-reclaiming conflictive adolescence; and, potentially, their postmodern holistic adulthood. And perhaps, if we can stay just-a-little-bit-conscious through the relationship's teens (and every time we re-visit those teens), trying to avoid disrespect, trying to avoid bruising the relationship, we can emerge into a place of union and independence, of oneness-and-difference, and a wholesome love large enough to hold all of our pain, our rage, our hate, our shame.

After a year or so we established weekly 'circles', as we call them – mornings set aside to tend and nurture the vision of the relationship, and to give space to the psychological issues which are always struggling to express themselves within the busyness of the everyday.

Vowed, as we have always been, to no conscious deceit – these 'circles' were spaces in which we voiced our loves, our fears, our weaknesses, our vulnerabilities, our depressions, our angers, our hates. Sometimes they were the garden of eden, sometimes they were the end of the world.

And sometimes we didn't meet weekly – there was too much anger, or resentment, or confusion. As with every great adventure – sometimes we went through hell. But throughout we were carried by a sense of our relationship as a shared soul-journey, as a path of love offering us the opportunity to unfold to our wholeness.

While preparing to marry we'd put our vision of our relationship into words and music. And we chanted those words to each other at our wedding. Then each time we began our circles, sitting with sacred objects from our wedding in front of us, we chanted them again – to reconnect with the holding-vision of our union. These are the words of our chant:

A journey
of balance
on the edge of life –
into wholeness,
into eternity,
into love.
To heal our wounded personalities,
to open to all parts of ourselves.

To stand as man and woman,
letting our hearts burst open
to the immensity of life.
Treading with courage and gentleness
on the edge
where the known and the unknown meet.
There
celebrating
the joy and the pain
of living with another
and becoming
undivided wholes.

In our local area, around Totnes in Devon, there is an 'alternative' sub-culture with a wide range of non-materialistic beliefs. There's lots of ascensionism – echoing premodernity, but lacking its surrender and austerity, and there's lots of green spirituality which, as we have already discussed, is a kind of 'descensionism'. But a more mature holism is also very much present, and in these groupings there are many couples struggling to be together holistically – with hardly any role models of what that might mean.

Over the last few years Elisabeth and I, alongside our experiments in private, have been convening partnership groups for these couples to come together and support each other in exploring this uncharted terrain. Premodern relationships were split-up. Modern relationships are split-down. No culture has ever attempted to model relationships which are neither split-up nor split-down. Few, if any, of us have experienced our parents or guardians living holistic marriages. And although there are some excellent books about – it's just not in our blood.

We are searching for a new model of long-term commitment. Because, it seems to me, for deep healing to happen there needs to be trust – not least of all, that we are not going to be left when the going gets tough. And it will get tough, and it will take a long time. Some couples separate saying, 'We completed working on the issue we needed to look at together.' Well, sometimes that might be true, and sometimes it might be an avoidance, but in neither case is it the kind of holistic soul-journey-union that could come to replace premodern marriage and modern romance. We are looking for something that is not entered into, or exited out of, quite so quickly. We are looking, I believe, for bonding that is total and eternal. Eternal not because it will last forever (we don't know what that means, anyway), but eternal because it is at the level of the soul. And total because it is a large enough concept of the journey-union to accommodate and embrace everything we are.

Every union is unique. But as each new couple struggles to articulate its own purpose, and to construct its own means of re-visiting that purpose and nurturing it, I can hear their vows echo each other. In different tones and intensities there is a not-so-different statement of intent...

> *We are knit in commitment*
> *to truth first,*
> *and then to each other –*
> *and only therefore*
> *to each other in truth.*
> *We honour the sacred-erotic spirit*
> *in each of us.*
> *Without this honouring –*
> *who will be there*
> *to hold the pain?*
> *But we especially honour our immaturities –*
> *the under-formed, the unformed, the deformed*
> *in each of us.*
> *These speak of the soul's secret purposes –*
> *of its call*
> *to incarnation, to completion.*
> *And we honour the easiness,*
> *the lightness, the laughter, the fun.*
> *We honour the love-making,*
> *the familiarity,*
> *and the caring.*
> *We honour the routine, the responsibilities.*
>
> *In all things together*
> *we walk the mystery and the promise*
> *of personal love,*
> *as perhaps the most complete,*
> *painful*
> *and exquisite*
> *path of truth*
> *through this dimension we call*
> *planet earth.*

To know the importance of having a vision, and revisiting that vision, is fortunate. Having a sense of the emerging holistic model of relationships, and having a sense of the phases through which relationships pass, is also fortunate. Then comes the experience, the painful, growing experience, of learning new ways of walking...

After the honeymoon,
as couples slide back to earth,
and things get sticky,
and they start getting stuck in their 'stuff' –
those ever-recurring, overlapping, interlocking patterns –
new ways of walking will be called for.

They will have to learn to walk hand in hand
with the pain
as well as the joy.
They will have to learn to walk with respect for other
even though it seems other's the source of their pain.
And they will have to learn to walk with respect for self
even though it seems other has seen them
at their worst.
They will have to learn to trip and rise gracefully
thousands of times.
And they will have to learn to tend bruises
and not to let fester.
And they will have to learn to watch themselves walking
as if from above...

And when they're walking above,
watching themselves walking below –
and they're loving themselves –
then they'll understand
the sublime sense of journey-home of the premoderns
(without the shame),
and then they'll understand
the archetypal yearnings of our Hollywood age
(from deep in the belly of all the glamour and the glitz).

And
(just as the good book said they should),
their hearts will be fixed on eternity –
and
(just as the big screen told them it would),
their honeymoon will know no end.

This last piece might sound like a have-your-cake-and-eat-it proposition - and it is! Inasmuch as premodern relationships were heaven-bound marriages, and modern relationships are (albeit value-lacking) earth-romances – holistic partnership is the marriage of heaven and earth. There is both journey and heart.

Thus, in his aptly titled book, *Journey Of The Heart*, John Welwood writes: '(holistic partnership) is a pact between beings, rather than between personalities. In effect, my partner and I say to each other "whatever problems our personalities have together, we will not let them get between us. If our egos are at war, we will not let that ruin our deeper connection – we will always come back and meet on this deeper level. We will help each other wake up and become all that we can be. We will keep opening to each other and to life itself in and through this relationship". Without such an alliance between our beings, our egos will likely conspire to perpetuate old habitual patterns…' (p.101)

Holistic partnership, as I see it, can't just be about untangling our behaviour. It can't only be something we work at. It is also loving and sexual and foolish and fun. But for the love and fun not to get tangled, messy and dirty, we need to hold a vision of the relationship's ultimate direction and purpose. Holistically, although every couple might express it differently, this is a vision of a shared journey of opening to our sacred-erotic wholeness.

And there are vows (particularly, I believe, the vow of honesty), that uphold the vision. We stick to them for the sake of the vision – even when every bone cries out not to. This keeps the union-vision clean. It keeps the atmosphere of the relationship open. And in fact, it is only in openness that we can really 'make love'.

If there is no larger vision – even if there's plenty of good intention to 'heal our wounds together' or 'grow together' – the tendency will be to get stuck in the bog of our 'stuff'. And the relationship will become heavy going… heavy, getting heavier… until the same modern options are there: to split up and get into another 'growth relationship', or to succumb to a dull dead end.

This heavy-going-growth-work tendency is another symptom of the green spirituality syndrome. But to be only-earth, to be only-emotions, only-psychological, and to rebel against the guiding spirit (having known it only as god in heaven, father of an abusive patriarchy) and to thus reject vision-in-relationship – is a sure recipe for ending up in the therapeutic bog.

The flexible model of postmodern holistic partnership I see emerging is more than a therapeutic alliance – it necessitates a transpersonal, or trans-personality, trans-patterns, trans-'stuff' dimension. It is as full of ultimate value as premodern marriage, but it completes it by including the value of earth, home, possessions – and of all that we feel about each other, and say to each other, and do to each other. Although holistic partnership, at this point, is in its infancy, and socially almost unperceivable, it presents us with the possibility of redeeming the social structure of marriage – of it becoming a journey, once again. But not a blinkered, squinting journey into the light – rather an expanding, holistic journey into the unknown.

And it's tough. It's tough to keep going amid the racing hubbub of techno-life – with kids and pets and the million and one comings and goings. It's tough because there's hardly any extended family, because we're often cut off even from our neighbours, and because the ethos is every-house-must-have-it-all and every-house-must-go-it-alone. And it's tough being continually bombarded with valuelessness.

We can read books, or occasionally attend a couples' workshop – but it just isn't enough. As couples we need to offer each other regular, ongoing, intimate support. It's all very well to say 'we need to include the transpersonal' – but as a couple, have we actually articulated our overarching vision? And have we found our ways of sustaining that vision? And can we stay with our vision as it evolves? And can we stay with our vision when we're deep in our 'stuff'?

We need to invent and re-invent our own relationship structures, and the community structures to hold our relationships. We have very, very few holistic married ancestors or elders or community guides. We find ourselves with a little self-respect, a smattering of psychology, and a hunger for value. Little of substance. Within such a demanding, distracting culture, we need deep, strong support. The partnership groups we've been setting up might be one good idea. We shall see. To us, they feel enormously, vitally important. At the moment, in society at large, they're a spit in the ocean.

Holistic partnership is not an easy option, but I see no positive other. At the moment relatively few couples are ready. That could change radically in just a few generations. The family – and at its core, the adult relationship – is generally, universally, the central and most crucial communal structure within a community. If we are to develop holistic community, therefore, we need to practise holistic partnership. I discuss all of this further in The Four Levels Of Partnership, in Section Three.

I want to end this chapter on relationships with a note on the commitment ceremony, on the actual act of wedding. I don't see the form of the ceremony as problematic in itself. Many couples are creating new ways to ritualise their wedding. I have attended many beautiful-looking non-traditional rituals. What does trouble me is the question of credibility.

The cynical and sad question that comes up, for me, as I watch couples wed is 'yes, now your eyes are full of tears of joy, you have such high hopes of each other, of your togetherness... how long will it last?'

I look upon these often young couples, and I know they don't have the understanding or the skills to live a postmodern holistic marriage – that the romantic modern marriage is by definition doomed, and that they don't have the tight beliefs or the discipline to live a premodern marriage.

How then will they fare? I wish them well. My heart goes out to them. And I feel the suffering to come. An old diary entry reads: 'I looked around the crowd. Many of us were in a second or third 'marriage'. There were several single parents. There were couples who were struggling. J. was there – who's splitting up with B. at the moment. I wondered what was going on in everyone's heart. What credibility does such a ceremony have nowadays?'

Later, in the same diary entry, I speculate into the future: 'give me a community with a recognised two or three years' "engagement" phase, a phase in which the relationship purpose is defined and tested – with love, but also with brave honesty and openness. Give me substantial engagements which have been witnessed within the community – not just publicly, but also in intimate couples' support groups – and *then*, despite all the pain and confusion and casualties – *then* a marriage would have credibility.

'*Then*, when the other couples from their group came forward in the ritual, and spoke before spirit, and said "we vouch for this couple, we have seen them in love and we have seen them in hate – and we stand as witnesses to their commitment to each other" – *then* I could believe in a marriage. Then I could believe in marriage'.

Alienation

Here is another fragment from my own personal premodern era, a piece I called *Other People's Thoughts*. Written right at the end of that era, just before my de-robing – it is a passionate letter to my sleeping self…

> *Other people define the divinity,*
> *draw up the doctrine,*
> *sanctify the heritage,*
> *and anoint the infallible priests.*
> *And you, you huddle up and sleep brainlessly*
> *in their cradle of absolutes –*
> *incontrovertibly cosy*
> *on the One Perfect Path.*
>
> *Don't be fooled by those monstrous, pompous*
> *citadels of impregnable truth*
> *with their bugles and drums, their ritual regalia,*
> *their awesome towers, their agile sophism,*
> *their hushed ceremonies, their quick tongues,*
> *their strength in numbers, their roots in time…*
>
> *Don't hand over your mind, coward,*
> *don't squeeze your brain*
> *through the venerable contortions*
> *recommended to acquire*
> *quite the standard vision on things.*
> *Don't succumb to the pressure, weakling,*

don't succumb to the promise.
Don't get carried away, foolhardy,
don't sell your soul –
it's madness
to only think
other people's thoughts.

As a premodern man I had no body. As a premodern man my heart was not my own. But I was also alienated from my own thoughts, my own opinions, my own judgments, my own decisions. I was constantly betraying my body, my feelings, my intuitions, my intellect and my will.

Today I wouldn't say I was 'mad' – anymore than a child is mad to imbibe the outlook of its parents. I was given over – and I had given myself away. I had chosen to sleep 'brainlessly', no one else was to blame. That was the way of premodernity. Everyone was a child. The collective energy field, the societal superego, was both mum and dad – and there we all suckled. If we wanted to argue that we were all mad then, (and if we wished to be consistent) then we'd have to accept that we're still all mad – after all, it's not by coincidence that as a culture we now almost unanimously believe in be-your-own-person and live-and-let-live. It's just that the energy field has shifted, grown up slightly, been filled with a more adolescent imperative – and got us all running about preening ourselves, and proving ourselves, and frantically individuating.

Or, then again, if we look at our collective journey into maturity and wholeness as a journey into sanity – then maybe we are a little less crazy now… But alienation in the revealed world of premodernity was very different from the alienation-from-value of modernity…

(i)
I wasn't there.
I was a walking-deadman –
because suicide of the personality was my cult.
I was hollowed, possessed –
occasionally by something spiritual,
constantly by the spirits of ancient fairy-tale monastic towers.
My mind danced with their sophism,
their quick tongues danced in my mouth.

We were all the same.
We all wanted to be the same.
We all wanted to be no one.
We all wanted to be one.

Through empty eyes we saw it clearly:

you had to get out of the way,
so that when you weren't there,
spirit could act through you.
Unfortunately, because there was nobody there,
there was nothing for spirit to act through,
and all that came out,
from mouth after mouth,
over and over again,
was the same old split-up patter.

(ii)
At best, from time to time we touched eternity –
we had union with the world beyond worlds.
The moderner has no such grace.

The moderner is an information maniac,
cut, like we were, from sacredness-in-matter –
alienated from the elements,
from the seasons,
from moon and sun cycles,
from wildness and creativity and imagination,
from all feeling that cannot be wrapped or boxed or canned...

But hollowed and stuffed with info.,
over-packed with endless important facts –
the moderner is also alienated
from universal purpose,
from personal unfoldment,
from relationship with eternal value.

Theodore Roszak has written eloquently of 'the artificial environment'. And the autistic alienation of modernity within a synthetic, sterilised culture-space has been protested since the Romantics. Today most of us have premodern, modern and various postmodern tendencies within us. We are not exclusively modern just because we are alive in modernity. And we don't have to take any criticism of modernity personally. Nevertheless, to understand the holistic proposition, I feel we need to name that which is quintessentially modern, that which is alienated from both spirit and matter: modernity might not appear to be alienated from the physical, but it is matter-minded and phys-ical not out of an embrace and valuing of the natural world, but in pursuit of anaesthesia.

But in my poem I cry out to myself, and to all who remain hypnotised by traditional truth-claims, to snap out of the alienation of premodernity. My mind was not my own. I spoke as if I knew – but I didn't. I lied obliviously in the name of a theoretical eternal truth. Other people's voices, ancient foreign voices, spoke through me. I wasn't me. My true self walked behind me like a ghost.

I am not about to go on to suggest we oppose all of our ancient traditions. The suggestion that is often made today is that we listen to our bodies, hearts and minds, and to our souls' knowing – and that, from the traditional, we accept all that we feel holds value, and reject all that we feel is split, defensive and elitist. In general terms, I would agree with this, but I would stress that we need to do this together, in community. Academics have contrasted premodern ultimate-authority (which descends from on high), and 'new age' ultimate-authority (which rests within the individual). Here we will be looking at authority being held in co-creative community. However, this pick-'n'-mix approach to tradition is a postmodern way of approaching the premodern – and how much ancient tradition such an approach will finally leave in tact is a discussion in itself (see Holism, Community and Religion in Section Two).

But just as we need to name the information-littered void of modernity, we cannot gloss over or romanticise the fanatic, split-up, fundamentalist, premodern mentality. This is important today because premodern fundamentalism, modern mechanism, postmodern deconsructionism and postmodern holism are co-existing – and within the subtle realms of the collective energy fields, vying for control. And alienated-up fundamentalism has become an option with a following. And regression into the childlike security and sublimity of the premodern is an understandable choice whilst modernity decays and holism is hardly known.

And the premodern payoff is not only mental and social security, it is also the light-filled bliss of surrender to the divine. The part of us that longs to let go, to become one again, to offer itself, to give itself up, to give in – this part is valued by the premoderns. Whereas people who sang or danced or meditated in cosmic bliss would soon find themselves ostracised in modern culture, I can still remember a freedom of spiritual expression which today I would feel inhibited to display – even in most circles schooled in holistic inclusivity.

> *I can't deny it:*
> *I felt secure –*
> *I knew the rules,*
> *I belonged.*
> *I was on The Path.*
> *I felt the bliss.*
> *I paid and received,*
> *and the price was myself.*
> *That was the premodern deal.*
> *And it was a con.*

Because all humanity that's been murdered
seeks its resurrection,
and calls to us
from graves all along the spine –
until, when it's begged long enough,
and been rebuffed long enough,
it becomes ruthless and obsessive,
and sets out,
for its sake and ours,
to survive.

And so, inevitably,
pitilessly,
my safe reality was dismantled.
And the bliss that was based on denial
shattered like the end of a world.

If I had to find one image for premodernity I would choose clouds. If I had to find one image for modernity I would choose a shopping mall. For green spirituality I would choose a garden. And for holism I would choose an image of depicting relationship...

(i)
The premodern image is of a ladder of clouds of light.
Countless souls climb and float heavenwards.
They are ghosts,
they are angels.
Their physical bodies, meanwhile,
somewhere far, far below.
guzzle, grunt, burp, fart, fuck and fight.
The gross noises these bodies make are a hateful racket
clashing infuriatingly
with the soft, lovely melody wafting down from above.

(ii)
The modern image is of a shopping mall
of marble and chrome and glass.
The marble is cut to perfection,
it fits perfectly,
it shines the perfect shine.
The reason there are no entrances or exits is because
there is nowhere other than this.
It is impossible to know if the shops are open or shut.
It is impossible to tell if there are millions of shoppers or none.

When it seems that there are shoppers,
they push their noses up against the marble, chrome and glass.
It is impossible to tell if they are trying to get out or in.

(iii)
To be alienated is to not belong.
To belong somewhere is to feel value there.
In the premodern world we were alienated from here
because value was elsewhere.
(We weren't alienated from heaven.)
In the modern world we are present,
but still alienated
because there is no value here.
(Nor is there somewhere a heaven to belong to.)
For the deep psyche
that which has value is real,
that which has no value is illusion.

For premodernity there was a reality, however ethereal –
and in its reflection even illusion glinted with a relative truth.
For modernity there is no reality –
only surreality –
only shifting surfaces –
only streets with names which could change
leading into streets leading into streets –
and a sense of running on the spot.

(iv)
The green spiritual image is of an earthly heaven –
of pathways lined with rows of knowledge trees,
fat with apples.
Here, in this heavenless eden,
people eat without shame,
and end at death, like all creatures –
humble in their mortality.
Here the Goddess cradles all.
It is She, The Mother, who smiles the smiles of birth and death.
By Her grace the generations of woman are sown and reaped.
Her children are without ambition,
their dwellings are simple,
they do not question, they dream no further.
Inside the apples on the knowledge trees
there is only flesh and seed.

Just as the bright, blinding invisible spirit of premodernity
was cut off from the wet, dark earth –
green spirituality is alienated
from that which is beyond the elements,
from that which is timeless and placeless.
It is blind to the vision on high.
It flows on
regardless of the unchanging.
Green spirituality is split-down, but value-full.
It thus inhabits a partial reality –
with the rest, the beyond,
out of bounds.

(v)
The holistic image is of relationship –
of the ghosts in the clouds
and the shoppers in the mall
and the bodies in the garden,
all meeting.

Of the ghosts receiving personhood from the shoppers
and getting bodies from the greens.

Of opening,
in the shopping mall wall,
a window to a light blue sky,
and a door with a path to a river.

Of the greens receiving,
from the shoppers,
the gift of doubt –
and from the ghosts,
the gift of sight.

The holistic image is of relationship.
It is of blessed sexuality –
of loving angels watching with delight
as our naked bodies express their 'yes'
to each other,
and earth, and life, and the unknown.

The holistic image is of relationship –
of physical prayer:
of digging the ground as meditation,
planting seed as oblation,

harvesting as sacred ceremony,
and eating as spiritual joy.

The holistic image is of near death experiences,
and reincarnation,
and leaving and returning to bodies –
of mystic visitation,
and enlightenment.
It is the love affair of matter and spirit.
It is the eternal passion of earth and heaven.
It is the creative intercourse
of the worlds.

Holism is in relationship with everything.
It can travel anywhere –
and everywhere it goes it feels value.
And because, for holism, there is everywhere value,
everything is real.

Returning to the theme of alienation, I'd like to include one more fragment from the final pages of the diary of my premodern mind. I called this piece *Words From Nobody*. It draws me into reflections on the social and political dangers of alienation, whether premodern or modern – and on the need to develop deep communities as places where we can work at the relationship between our hearts and our economics, between our souls and our political policies…

In the pulpit and in the pews
there is a personalityless person –
persuaded of its insufficiency,
it has surrendered itself,
and follows selflessly,
mindlessly.
No longer perceiving people,
it accepts and rejects feelinglessly,
philosophically.
No longer itself,
it thinks unconsciously and speaks unthinkingly –
it is an avid opinionless preacher.

That preacher was, of course, me. Again I am struck by the image of the zombie, the walking deadman. And I find it chilling. I find who I became chilling. And I see zombies amassed. I see processions and parades of empty-beings. Preachers, like me, all me – and I see tribal wars and jihads and conquistadors.

Premoderners, earnestly striving for righteousness, were seething with shadow. On top of this, being absent-to-themselves, premodern good-people could be filled with absolutely any pseudo-holy rhetoric. And being will-less, they could then be marched off in any direction. Which is what happened.

And alienated moderners are no less open to manipulation. Being cut off from value, they have no reality of their own. Uprooted, adrift in a surreal make-believe world, out of touch with their humanity, and hyper-logical – they can be logically persuaded to the most inhuman acts. The communist massacres are good examples.

The Nazi massacres of the mid-twentieth century might be analysed as a mix of premodern and modern alienations. The mood was typical of premodern fundamentalism, the mode was typical of modern empiricism.

But whether modern or premodern, alienation is a dangerous condition. When we become alienated we become capably cruel. Whether holy or profane, in alienation we are cold-skinned and untrustworthy. We are split, in conflict and at war in ourselves. We must, we can't help but, project out. We must, will and do create splits, conflicts and wars around us. This is the familiar and unfailing mirror of the inner and the outer. This is why holism is not only a philosophy, not only a psychology, not only a social strategy, but also a political imperative.

Looking, today, at photos of myself as I was, (as I wasn't), I remember the payoff of alienation: my eyes are blank, but oh-so-peaceful. And I re-feel my love of my fellow monks and nuns... Love? But haven't I written that I was feelingless, distanced from my own heart? Well yes, well no...

While 'other' was aligned with the revelation, while other abided by the vows, while other was nothing but a receiver and transmitter of our truth – then I was allowed to love that other. Should this other become non-aligned, wander from the path, quit the pack, no longer collude in our outlook – my love became a patronising compassion. I would then behold that person with an arrogant pity. From high, high above I would offer my benign, pure hand.

My heart switched on and off – not according to any like or dislike of my own, but according to other's degree of adherence to the lineage. In order to belong to the salvation-bound in-culture, I was switched off to all outsiders, to anyone elsewhere-bound. My parents were heartbroken. My brother hated me for it. I was serenely indifferent to the protestations of outsiders. Family bonds meant nothing to me – better the in-love of a community of value than value-empty blood.

This is how the premodern heart operates, and is operated. This is why, in their righteousness, premodern men and women, past and present, have committed atrocities and felt no contradiction. Their feelings were (and are) not their feelings. Their feelings were (and are) totally culturally conditioned by an alienated culture.

The only difference in manipulating and mobilising alienated moderners is that the heart-switch is labelled efficient/inefficient, rather than good/bad. Different alienation, different switch – same result. Yesterday's crusade, today's genocide. They too are not themselves. Their feelings are also totally culturally conditioned by an alienated culture.

But, to a large extent, is not all feeling culturally conditioned? Yes. Which is why we must develop an integrating culture. And not spread alienating conditioning, but rather encourage our children to be all of themselves – to be in touch with their bodies, to be close to their hearts, to hear their dreams, to know their fears, to notice each other… This is a kind of anti-conditioning conditioning. It is a conditioning that will encourage   de-conditioning, self-hood and authenticity. If, to whatever extent, we are creatures of cultural conditioning – then let there be a cultural atmosphere of integration not alien-ation, of taking-responsibility not denying, of co-existence not annihilation.

Has there been any advance, then – any real maturing? Or is the moderner as much of a non-person as the premoderner? In premodernity we struggled to be identical. Modernity often seems like an absurd parade, in which everyone is identically impelled to strut and exclaim their differentness.

We have shifted from the otherly-limbo into the porno-limbo. But are we any less cut off – from self, from other? Has there been any real decrease in our capacity to be cruel *en masse*?

I don't know if we can answer this question in terms of 'more' and 'less'. It isn't so straightforward. Our overall psycho-socio growth from a collective childhood into a collective adolescence doesn't mean that we have therefore, automatically, become less alienated, or less dangerous. In a sense – just as adolescents uproot – we are more alienated than ever. In a sense – just as children are naturally, unconsciously rooted – we were less alienated in the premodern world. The relevant clichés might be 'it's all part of growing up', and 'it's just a phase they're going through'. We hope.

Perhaps, if modernity had a voice, it might tell a tale like this:

'Once upon a time, I guess, we all lived happily in heaven. And spirit was always right (we thought). Anyway, after a while, we got fed up with always having to do what we were told. Which, to be honest, included some pretty dodgy stuff. We began doubting spirit, and also, we wanted to start thinking for ourselves. And so we did. We left. And we found a place of our own on earth – which is where we are now…

The latest thing is that we've been having a bit of a party, and the earth (who wasn't even there when we were growing up, and who we don't even know) has started getting really angry. Some people say that we were close to the earth even before we lived with spirit, but that's not much help right now. The fact is that we don't know the earth, and we've lost touch with spirit, and we don't know where we're going, and we don't know what to do. Yeah, and sometimes we do have a laugh – but I just don't know what's the point of it all.'

The question becomes the development of adulthood, of an integrated, non-alienated, adult postmodernity – a culture which encourages us not to follow value, nor to deny it, but to explore it.

Whether this is attainable within a century, a millennium, or ever… I don't know. My local area, around Totnes, has been called a 'new age' centre. And many locals believe this new age is a forgone conclusion – a predestined happy ending. Most people in the mainstream would say that's nonsense Personally, I believe collective adulthood is a realistic possibility – but that it will not happen without our private participation, and public collaboration.

We might consider where we are 'in cultural time'. A sketch of the recent history of our cultural consciousness might read something like this: having rejected the value-full otherworld, we entered a value-empty this-world – which was existentially excruciating. All we had left was ourselves – but we analysed. And psychoanalysis led to psychotherapy and to the path of whole-ness – and to entering the twenty-first century with an entirely new emotional-spiritual vocabulary. The beginnings of the psychological society, perhaps. Because there is, alongside whatever other trends might be evolving in other directions, an undoubted mass movement out of our nihilistic descent – into new schemes of values. But this time value has not descended, it seems, by revelation, but ascended from the depths of our psyches…

But to go beyond the individual torment and despair, and the terrifying mass-consequences, of both split-up-premodern and split-down-modern alienation we need communities of relational adults. Once we are committed to the holistic path, we are ever learning to honour all parts of ourselves, to honour others, and to honour spirit and nature. This is the holistic path: the path of relationship. And this honouring, this entering into respectful rela-tionship is, almost by definition, the antidote to addiction and alienation. Whether premodern or modern, alienation means being out-of-relationship, and we need to call upon the spiritual and psychotherapeutic skills which can restore our ability to be in-relationship.

The Modern Era
The Pornographic Culture

Spiritless Sex

Introduction

One night,
on my own,
after a decade as a would-be-obedient renunciate,
I smoked a huge grass-stuffed joint.

The premodern labyrinth door flew open.
I was ready.
Out I floated.

I had a few hundred pounds
(which I gave to a stranger who was sleeping on the streets),
and a passport
(which I burnt).
I was joyous.
I was sure I would wander
barefoot
on pilgrimage
to nowhere
forever.
I was to be
free.

A few days later I was arrested –
curled frozen
in a shop entrance
at 5 am.

Bhaja Radhe got me out.
And we lived together in my sister's vacant flat,
which she'd said we could have for a year.
But it felt impossible:
all that we were both being cleansed of,
the other had ingrained in their skin –
we were both addicted to the torture we'd escaped,
and both incapacitated by the harshness and emptiness
of our bright new world.

When the year was up,
we separated.

There was a squat in North London with a free room.
I cleaned it,
and hung silks on the walls,
and made it mine.
And I wrote.
I wrote from midday to dawn.
I wrote my beliefs.
I wrote my bible.
I wrote and justified and affirmed my decision,
my departure, my escape, my de-robing –
my utterly abrupt change of universe...
A year before, in just a few days,
I had travelled from 15th century Calcutta to 20th century London.
I was still in shock.
I was still in breakdown.
I wrote.

Then one bizarre bohemian night I took magic mushrooms at a party –
the same guide-drug that had taken me into fantastical worlds
in my hippie days,
when I'd been filling baskets in the orange groves of Crete.
But I was no longer hippie and high,
I was disturbed and down –
and the mushrooms dragged me into a dark purgatory:

I'd been writing over and over about honesty and courage and the unknown.
Walking fast through the night,
past factory walls and closed warehouses,
the never-ending traffic grinding my mind –
I came to feel that my most-real, deepest, underlying, driving force
was the fear of death,
and that my only noble option
was to throw myself under a car.

Then I heard:
'you've taken mushrooms,
you're in no fit state to decide such an act,
you need to get out of London, you need trees and grass and quiet'...

I stumbled on,
half-in-nightmare, half-awake –
past an underground station closed with corrugated iron –
and must have spoken words
to a taxi driver who must have understood.

I clambered up the bare wooden staircase at the squat
and collapsed on the mattress in my room,
and Rebecca, my girlfriend, held me from behind
while I curled like a foetus
and urinated for half an hour.
Thank you, Rebecca, forever, for that.

Then I slept.

I slept and awoke
and swore I was going.

A month later I'd left London and settled near Totnes.

The Devonshire brooks and hills,
the woods and birdsong,
the cattle and horses and foxes and badgers,
the Dartmoor tors and wind and mist –
they soothed my whole being. I wept gratitude and relief.

The questing, 'alternative', small-town atmosphere of Totnes was just the setting I needed. 'Flakey Totnes' some people call it, putting it down – implying that it is a shore where the spineless and spaced-out flotsam and jetsam of our culture gets washed up. And maybe it is. I was washed up there. But on that shore I found healing. I found Totnes was full of the open, confused, searching, kind people I needed. There was support there. I wrote on. The writing became less heady. I re-wrote. I re-wrote again. Over the years that manuscript had two main titles: 'I-Don't-Know-Ism' and 'The Open Attitude'. And the 'fragments' of this section are extracted from it.

This section is not intended as a portrait or appraisal of modernity – I have already sketched modernity: the tight materialistic fundamentalism, the technoculture, the synthetic environment, the grab-it-while-you-can, the porno-culture, the desperation…

It documents my own emotional, sexual and ideological interface with split-down modern crassness – freshly distressed after prolonged immersion in split-up premodern escapism. It is about my dialogue with the value-stripped bare bones of modernity, while clinging precariously to invisible, all-pervading value – but having lost any worldview to explain it or express it.

This was the time of my re-evaluation of the beliefs and moralities of modernity – its open-mindedness, its honouring of the individual, its sense of equality and tolerance. I face the modern world I'd fled, see its integrity, integrate its procedures with my own sense of inexpressible value – and emerge into a holistic perspective. I emerge into the holistic trend that was already there. I come, in my own way, to join the many others who'd already seen how the best intentions of premodernity plus the best intentions of modernity equal holism.

In terms of 'best intentions', our premodern phase of split-up fundamentalism was also the era of the affirmation of the supra-human value of existence, the age of innocence, humility, surrender and community. And our split-down pornographic age is also a time of rigorous unsentimentality, of coming face-to-face with doubt and mortality, an age of great honesty and risk and self-affirmation. Add these two together, not theoretically, but personally, dynamically – add the ancient declaration of value to the rigorous and risky honesty of modernity – not artificially, just day to day, and gradually one breaks through into the sacred-erotic holistic experience.

By not denying the Unchanging, by allowing one's sensitivity to that Presence to just be (whether it's measurable, or even conceivable, or not), and investigating *within* its vast orbit (rather than discarding it in the name of empirical neutrality), a holistic experience begins to crystallise in which value is neither above nor below, but everywhere... We come to feel how we are children of spirit, sparks of the divine, not only spiritually, but also mentally, emotionally and physically – how we are children of spirit and sex. We come to feel the inseparability of all levels of ourselves. We come to know that we are both unchanging and forever in flux. Here is holism – the combination of our best intentions. The route, perhaps, to the best of all possible postmodernities. We need to talk about it, and we need to practice it. And we need to come to it one by one, in ourselves.

In the third section of this book we will be looking at how we might develop supportive holistic communities. But we cannot assume shared understandings. By 'holism' some people mean green spirituality, for others it means anything vaguely 'alternative', for most it is allusive. So I will conclude my parallel story of the rise of holism in me, and within the dominant culture, through its less and more mature forms. Then towards the end of this second section I will broaden out slightly – into the fields of science, religion and politics – in order to do the final groundwork for entering Section Three.

My intention throughout these first two sections is to clarify and strengthen the united understandings that need to be firmly rooted at the core of any attempt to develop holistic postmodern community. Not that everyone needs to agree on everything. Not that there is a fixed and final holistic position. Here we are all pioneers. As the Spanish poet has said, 'the path forms itself by our walking it'. But we do need a shared vocabulary. And we might not need detailed architectural plans, but we do need some agreed broad lines.

Put more esoterically: my intention is to strengthen the collective holistic energy field. Without a strong, clear collective energy field, our efforts to develop holistic communities, however well intended, will be premature and impositional. I have already touched on the image of social structures manifesting out of a civilisation's collective energy field...

If we teach our children to honour
animals and the land,
and to honour their personalities
(both their qualities they like and their qualities they don't)...

Teaching by example,
always by example...

If we teach our children to honour
the fact that we are all
always
knowingly or unknowingly
walking the unknown –
so that they can find humility
and dependence on each other –
(the very heart-weave of community)...

Teaching by example,
always by example...

If we teach our children to honour
the essence of their beings,
and of being –
everything will come.
Everything will come.

Everything always comes.

Social structures don't sprout in a vacuum. Without the energy field the structures can't grow – it's not yet their time. We need to nourish the holistic energy field – so that we can feed off it and be inspired to develop stable, new social structures. Then it becomes cyclic: the energy field feeds the structures, which reinforce the energy field, which then manifests even stronger social structures, and so on... We feed it. It feeds us.

And it's already happening. It's happening alongside other trends, other vibrations-of-intention, other evolutionary possibilities...

The Question of Certainty

Again: the story of this book is both mine and ours – both autobiography and cultural history…

> *When the sky came crashing down,*
> *and the face of our culture no longer had a God to look up to –*
> *when we realised we'd killed Him*
> *and His creation –*
> *when the mind of our culture took control*
> *and set about manufacturing eden –*
> *when there was no good or right or true anymore –*
> *when all value was produced by us –*
> *that was when the cultural soul became frantic*
> *and desperately brave.*
> *It slipped out of the cultural body and wandered like a shadow,*
> *sickened, stricken…*
> *'Where is home? Did I ever have a home?*
> *From where this loss? From where this need?'*
> *It wandered with a demented intensity*
> *of honesty –*
> *possessed by its quest…*
> *'From where this memory of belonging?*
> *What is home? Does home exist?'*
> *There is nothing more fearful than doubt.*
> *But a ghost is fearless,*
> *because a ghost is already dead.*

The character in these next two 'fragments' is that cultural soul. He is also me. Whether by leap or push, or by inevitability – to suddenly lose one's cosmos is devastating. His torment, his desperate earnestness – this is the horror of identity crisis. This is when the mirror is blank…

1

(a)
A distressed man was stopping people on the street in Belsize Park.
I stopped to hear what he was asking them.
It was as if he was lost….

(b)
'Excuse me, Sir, where are we?'
'This is Belsize Park.'
'Where is Belsize Park?'

'It's a part of Hampstead.'
'Yes, but where is Hampstead?'
'Are you joking? It's a borough of London.'
'Yes but, Sir, where is London?'
'Young man, are you trying to make a fool of me?
London's in England. Look, I haven't got time...'
'Sir, where is England?'
(readying to go) 'England, young man, is in Europe;
Europe's on the planet earth;
and the planet earth is in the solar system...'
'And?'
'That's as far as I know.'
'You don't know where the solar system is?'
'No.'
'You don't know where we are?'
'I suppose not.'
'OK, I'll ask someone else then.'

(c)
'Excuse me, Madam, where's the solar system?'
'What was that, my child?'
'Excuse me, Madam, where's the solar system?'
'The solar system? Well it's below heaven and above hell...
so let's make sure we're on the way up!'
'But, Madam, where are heaven and hell?'
'That, my child, that only God knows.
(going) God bless you!'

(d)
'Excuse me, where are heaven and hell?'
'Wow, what a question!
I thought you were going to ask for money!
Heaven and hell, man?
They're part of the whole, that's what I think –
everything's part of the whole.'
'But where's the whole?'
'It's everywhere, man, everywhere!'
'But where's everywhere?'
'Wow, what a question!
Everywhere's everywhere man! Everywhere!'
'It must be somewhere.'
'Well I don't know where everywhere is!
It's everywhere!'

'OK, I'll ask someone else then.'

(e)
As I left, he was shuffling up to the next person,
and I could hear him muttering to himself:
'Yes, but...'
Yes, but...'

2
(a)
Yesterday I passed the distressed man in Belsize Park again.
I caught these two snippets...

(b)
'Excuse me, but – what are you?'
'My name is...'
'No, no, I don't want to know your name...
What are you?'
'Well, I was born in...'
'No, no, I'm not asking your place of birth...
What are you?'
'Well, I'm a human being.'
'What's that?'
'A human being is made of flesh and bones.'
'What are they?'
'They're made up of atoms.'
'What are they?'
'Matter.'
'What's matter?'
'I don't know.'
'You don't know what you are?'
'Well, I guess not...'
'OK, I'll ask someone else.'

(c)
'Excuse me. What are you?'
'What am I? The 'me'? The real 'me'?
The real 'me' is a soul.'
'What's that?'
'It's spirit.'
'What's spirit?'
'It's life itself.'
'What's that?'
'What is life?'

'That I don't know.'
'You don't know what you are?'
'Umm...'
'OK, I'll ask someone else.'
And so it went on...

As a premodern man I had known who I was, where I was, why I was, whence and whereto, and how to get there. I had known the names of the different heavens, and the categories of hell. I had known the specific pieties and sins that got you where. I had had the absolute, eternal and utterly certain overview of the snakes and ladders board of life...

I had advised and admonished
with ease and precision.
From the pages of the scriptures shone the timeless, enlightened truth.
A timeless succession of enlightened gurus had passed this truth
through the generations to me.
I too spoke the timeless, enlightened truth.
I,
and no less my comrades-in-truth,
lived in a universe in which
every action, every word, every thought,
was a throw of the dice with a predetermined outcome.
All was known.
Our cosmos was sacred,
our cosmos was worthy of reverence,
but above all –
it was certain.

For a decade I'd always known the way. Now my existential compass had shattered. I just didn't know anymore. Thus I tumbled into modernity, at the end of the 1980s. Where had I arrived?

The scientific optimism of the turn of the twentieth century was long gone. All plans for a mechanical paradise had been scrapped. Modern medicine wasn't going to defeat disease. War wasn't going to end by logic or rational debate. And the high ideals of 'liberté, fraternité and égalité' had largely deteriorated into the equal and fraternal freedom to shop. Modernity had also lost its cosmos. Here I was, then, not knowing – in a culture that didn't know. A wreck among the ruins.

Many of my peers de-robed and broke their vows, and felt utterly fallen. They felt they had 'fallen back into the ocean of birth and death'. These casualties, although they had physically left the ashram, were still psychically alive inside the premodern Hindu cosmos. They were still psychologically and spiritually stranded in the ancient Vedic world. They had been absolutely certainly found and saved and good and right, and now, by the same standard, they were absolutely certainly lost and damned and bad and wrong. I, however, had escaped the whole mental time-warp, I had travelled out beyond the edges of the whole ancient Hindu frame of reference – I thought.

In my heart I knew my leaving had been an act of honesty, humility and courage, but intellectually I struggled. I had my doubts… 'After all, was I my body, really? Not really. Had I, then, just been seduced by 'maya'? Had I left out of strength or weakness?' A part of me, whether I liked it or not, was still mind-locked in the ethics of medieval India. I felt my leaving was right – but could I be certain? Back at the temple they had a whole holy epistemology, a whole science of certainty. What was mine? A part of me had to prove them wrong to prove myself right. I was still stuck in their terms…

I re-read my notebooks. Endless letters to premodernity that I had nowhere to send. One reads 'Can you deny you're in a mental box? Can you deny you believe the planet's more or less round? Can you deny you'd have believed it flat, had you been born just a few centuries ago? Can you deny the relativity of your outlook? Can you affirm your absolute objectivity? Can you deny you'd most likely be in a Muslim mental box, had you been born in a Muslim family? Or do you think it's just coincidence, that Hindus give birth to Hindus, and Jews give birth to Jews? Can you deny your thinking is conditioned? Can you deny you're locked in a mental box?' With the whip of postmodern relativism I lashed out at the arrogance of premodern certitude. In my heart I felt I knew they didn't know. And in my heart I knew I didn't either. But from my head I tried to prove their certainty uncertain, and my uncertainty certain. This just got me in knots.

Here, for example is a fragment I called *The Certainty Of Certainty (CC) versus The Certainty Of Uncertainty (UC)*…

> *CC: You condemn the intelligence*
> *as a source of absolute knowledge,*
> *and yet you employ your intelligence to do so –*
> *you could also be wrong.*
> *You disclaim the possibility of certainty,*
> *and yet you're so sure.*
> *CU: You're right, I can't be certain we can't be certain.*
> *But this is a confirmation, not a contradiction.*
> *It is further proof of the impossibility of certainty.*
> *CC: No – if we can't know, if we can't be certain,*
> *if we can't state with certainty that we can't be certain –*
> *then the possibility exists*
> *that we can be.*
> *CU: No, maybe we can be certain, maybe we can't –*

we can't know.
CC: No, maybe we can be certain, maybe we can't – so we can,
and you can't say we can't.
CU: No, maybe we can be certain, maybe we can't – we can't know.
CC: No, maybe we can be certain, maybe we can't –
so we can –
and you...
Ad infinitum.

I needed to prove premodernity wrong because I felt that would make me right, and that in my rightness I would be safe. I needed security. I needed ideological security. I needed to know where I now stood in the universe. Writing was a process of philosophical and psychic grounding.

And it was a process of de-alienation – of re-connecting with myself. Through the long nights I spent alone with my thoughts and feelings I began to get reacquainted with myself. But as I examined my posture of certainty-of-uncertainty more closely, it became slightly suspect... I called this next fragment *The Motivation Of Certainty Of Uncertainty – A Conversation Between The Certainty Of Uncertainty (CU), The Certainty Of Certainty (CC), And A Referee!*

CU: What's your motivation, you fanatic?
CC: And what's yours?
CU: Why are you trying to prove certainty?
CC: Why are you trying to prove uncertainty?
Ref.: Are you not both in 'the proving game'?
CU: All right, but let's be blunt about it –
he's not certain he's certain,
whereas I'm certain I'm uncertain.
He can't be certain of what he claims,
because his certainties are unascertainable.
But I can be certain of my certainty:
subjectivity precludes objectivity –
therefore we're certainly uncertain.
CC: On what basis is he certain he's uncertain? How...
CU: I...
Ref.: No, let him speak.
CC: Anyway, it doesn't matter:
whatever basis he employs to establish his certainty,
I claim the right to use it to establish mine!
CU: I have no basis.
It's because no basis exists
that we can be certain we can't be certain.
Ref.: Your certainty must be based on something.

CC: His certainty is based on logic, that's all.
And even if he can defeat me logically – so what!
Logic is uncertain, so its conclusions are too.
CU: All right, I admit it –
I despise your lies, your pride!
Yes, I've had to take a radical stand –
I've had to go from 'I don't know' to 'we can't know'.
If I'd admitted it's possible to know –
on whatever basis –
you'd have leapt up on that base
and started shouting your deceitful rhetoric again!
I've been pushed by your arrogance.
Ref.: So your motivation is to disprove untruth,
not to prove truth –
and you feel it justified to be untrue to do so...
CU: But my lie is liberating, his is oppressive...
CC: Your lie is depressive...
Ref.: Gentlemen, please.

And here I am only including some of the shorter and lighter pieces. I have heaps of longer, heavier pieces challenging the premodern doctrine of absolute-truth-by-revelation. I argue, for example, that acceptance always involves choice, even if it is of a revelation (especially nowadays when there are so many varieties on the market). And, I press on, choice is always human – made with fallible human faculties, and therefore fallible. Again and again I try to knock premodernity off its pedestal of absolute, infallible, revealed truth. But in the end, as the piece above confesses, to say 'you don't know the absolute truth' presumes the speaker does – or at the very least, that she or he has some higher criterion by which to judge. And I didn't. I just knew I'd been a split-off, fanatical liar, and that now I was being true-to-myself. I was angry with myself, I was angry with my past, I was angry with premodernism, with fundamentalism, with split-up scriptures, with manipulative hierarchies, with gurus and with God. But that was no excuse to become a fundamentalist of uncertainty.

But writing and re-writing, proving and doubting, asking my heart and asking my soul – perhaps this is what kept me on the path towards holism. Because the cultural soul, for the most part, in its own reaction to revelation, did become a fanatic – a fanatic of pseudo-science, a split-down preacher of scientism – the doctrine of the non-existence of the immeasurable. The bulk of the cultural soul did sacrifice honesty for security. It broke out of heaven, and then locked itself up down on earth. This has been the great cultural flip of the last few centuries, from one extreme to the other: from twisted religion to distorted science – from the full split-up to the full split-down in a split second of historical time.

And an easy flip to understand. To have no understanding of life or death, no translation, no explanation, to have nowhere to situate one's existence, to be adrift in this great, unspeakable reality – is terrifying.

We will discuss the relationship between scientism and holism later in this section, but personally, I could formulate no neat, protective doctrine – even though I knew what I believed. It all seemed to come down to an attitude – to maintaining an attitude of openness. And to close openness in a set of tenets was obviously contradictory. If anything, this openness became my security. It became my dogma – a kind of anti-dogma dogma.

I felt this attitude was quintessentially religious and scientific. I felt openness-of-heart was the Judeo-Christian message of service and love, openness-of-spirit was the Hindu-Buddhist message of presence and awareness, and openness-of-mind was the modern Materialist message of unsentimental empirical enquiry.

In this openness the essential appreciation-of-sacredness of premodernity and the essential excitement-of-discovery of modernity seemed to meet. I imagined premodernity as the felt, 'yin' universe, and modernity as the thought-out, mapped-out, 'yang' firmament. And the 'yin' and the 'yang' seemed to flow into each other in this attitude of openness – which felt like the all-embracing, undefinable river of the Tao.

And I still feel this openness is at the core of holism. What has changed is that, as I have tried to live it, my openness has gathered a context around itself. Not to be split-up, to be open to matter, not to be split-down, to be open to spirit – this is wonderful. But what does one do with that to which one opens? How does one hold one's experience? It's all very well to open, for example, to one's rage – but what does one do with it once it's opened up? How does one integrate it? How does one introduce the different parts of oneself to each other? And what about the parts that wish to remain closed? Is there a place for openness to closure? And which option to be open to? And when? And how far to go?

Questions such as these, I believe, are being maturely posed and responded to within transpersonal psychotherapy. But at this point I was barely psychologically literate. I was still on my way from saintliness, via openness, to holism. As yet I had hardly any context, hardly any concept of wholeness. I was perhaps immature, but in the simplicity of my openness, I was bravely walking the no-man's-land of not-knowing. Thus this next fragment: *Certainty Plus Uncertainty Equals Openness…*

> *There is an attitude that is not a belief in certainty,*
> *nor a belief in uncertainty –*
> *but a belief in both.*
> *Because*

there's certainty in uncertainty,
and uncertainty in certainty.
Uncertainty seems unavoidable,
and yet, to conclude anything –
even skepticism –
to believe anything –
even agnosticism –
is always to accept the certainty of one's methodology.
And so certainty seems equally unavoidable.
Thus: I'm sure I'm not sure.
This certainty-and-uncertainty,
in practice,
we might call –
openness.
It is not a selective openness,
not a conditional openness –
but an openness that lets in ridicule and pain,
that is ready to dis-cover self.
Such openness is sure of itself –
sure enough to be unsure,
sure enough to reconsider itself.
Such openness is certain of itself –
certain it is the way in.

On the beam above the door are inscribed the words
'open-heart, open-mind',
and in the slab of stone on the threshold are carved
'honesty and courage'.
Such openness is so certain
it allows all uncertainty to pass.

This then, was the philosophy of the adolescence of my being – a reckless, scattered, uncontained kind of holism. Later, as I matured, I settled comfortably into a more rounded, crafted, soulful holism. But meanwhile, I walked the artificially lit streets of modernity on the edge of openness. I believed in honesty. Openness was honesty-in-action. Honesty was truth-in-action – and what but truth could lead to truth.

And I could feel the truth, in my fingertips and in my stomach, calling to me all the time – in the surreal jagged cacophony of the city, in the wind in the trees and bushes and grass, and above all, whenever I was close to my body or heart. Somehow, because of and despite my sincere, naive, precarious philosophy – I was arriving. And teachers like Carl Jung, Fritz Perls and Roberto Assagioli were preparing the ground for honest, lost people like me.

While the mainstream of the cultural soul took shelter in modernity's vast, empty indoors, a small current of the cultural soul had stayed out in the open air – flowing on ahead.

These mentors would come to parent my journey. At that time, like all teenagers who come to see the fallibility of their parents, I was struggling with disillusion, with uncertainty, with self-image, and above all, with rage. In a fragment I called Intolerance Of Intolerance, for example, I constructed a dialogue in which I was trying to reconcile my openness with all of my 'negative' anger. I asked 'Is it intolerant to be intolerant of the intolerant?' 'Yes' was the response. 'Is it intolerant to be intolerant of intolerance?' I asked. 'Well, yes – to be intolerant is to be intolerant.' 'But surely it isn't intolerant to reject intolerance – if we accept the intolerant.' 'To reject is to reject.' And so it went on. There was no way out.

> But I did hate.
> I hated them all –
> the strutting dead –
> all of those conceited fake-holy zombies –
> who'd promised me knowledge and light,
> and sucked me dry and spat me out.
> I hated them
> and I hated their whole cosmic show.
> They had the planets and stars,
> and the elements and seasons,
> all in chains.
> They had everything visible and invisible in chains.
> And above all,
> they'd had me in chains.
> And above all,
> I'd volunteered to be chained.
> And above all –
> I was angry!

The holistic ground into which I was about to be welcomed would invite me to open to my anger, to hear it, to honour it. And I did. And beneath it I found feelings of grief and worthlessness – these too I was invited to hear and honour. And gradually I have come to know many parts of myself, to befriend them and introduce them to each other... Even the concept of 'parts of me' has been a gift from holistic therapy that has allowed my attitude of openness to find its maturity. As has been the concept of a central 'me' who can do the introducing. Such maps of psyche have been vital to me. Openness was the will to wholeness. Therapy has been the skill to wholeness.

In short... I was lost, but I couldn't hide inside rigid pseudo-science and go into denial of the unknown. Nor did I get stuck in reaction to the flimsy certainty-claims of the premodernity I was leaving behind. I was naive, but I stayed relatively open. In all of this, while most of the modern world went numb, I was running in the dark in the footsteps of those existential explorers who were already sketching the holistic psycho-spiritual map. I feel grateful to these people. As the years passed and I gradually joined them I learnt to tame and live out my noble gut-instinct to openness. Thanks to them I can write…

(i)
Today I made love with spirit.
You never forget your lovers.
We walked together in the garden.
That is what green spirituality forgets –
that before the casting out,
spirit also lived in eden.
Heaven was invisibly close.

Premodernity gave itself to spirit.
It lost itself.
Modernity is a loner –
beginning to flirt
clumsily, shamefully,
with the earth.

(ii)
I am in love with them both –
the flesh earth
and the transparent beauty of spirit.
I am erotic-awake and out-of-my-body.
I am sexual, omni-sexual,
supra-sexual and spiritual-sexual.

The earth is voluptuous and seductive,
and eternally in flux.
Its core is molten
lust –
and I am made
of that.
Spirit is penetrating and in-coming
and over-coming and overwhelming
and everywhere already.
And I am also always, intrinsically, inextricably, inseparably that.
This is the alchemical marriage-of-one.
This is holism.

This is me.
I am the vanguard of the cultural soul.

I am in eden
as I never was,
even before the fall.
I am in eden
as me.

I am the hero, I am the heroine.
This is the monomyth, this is the fairy-tale...
I am spirit,
I am the beauty –
the earth is the beast I embrace.
I am the earth,
I am the beauty –
spirit is the beast I embrace.
Who is who?
I do not know.
All that matters is the love-making.

(iii)
When modernity
makes love with the earth –
if it doesn't lose itself,
if it has ego enough,
if it has esteem and skill enough –
an earth-child is born
able to make love with spirit.

Green spirituality is the sacralising of modernity,
but she is also its ripening, its fruition, its death.
Modernity is a nervous adolescent.
The earth is the devouring lover,
as old as age.

The child must be careful.
Silly to have rebelled so long against spirit,
only to be eaten by earth.
My soul is mine,
and so is my body.
If they were not mine
how could I surrender them?
How could

I
surrender?

Today I made love with the earth.
Theories are like acquaintances,
understandings are like good friends,
but your lovers you never forget.

Again: this is the promise of holism. Holism must hold a promise. Without a promise there is no pull, no determination. The promise of premodernity was heavenly bliss forever, the promise of modernity was a rational haven – safe from the Eastern winds of myth and faith, and the African winds of passion and rage. The promise of modernity was that everything could be, and would be, understood. The promise of holism is a state of sacred-erotic openness. It is the perennial promise, the esoteric promise, the secret promise, the promise of the few made public. In the modern world, the promise of holism is the promise of transpersonal therapy. It is the promise of a spirituality rooted in the landscape of our humanity.

The promise of holism is that, at this very moment, as I write this, as you read this, each one of us (however emotionally mature, however psychologically literate, however spiritually aware – whatever our sex, colour, age, IQ, state of relationships, health, finances or criminal record) is an utterly perfect and whole physical-spiritual creature of love, beauty and limitless magic. We might be heavily clothed, we might be armoured, but we are here, present, all the time, watching, calling – being watched, being called. Perhaps it's a paradox... In every conversation two souls meet each other in a state of blessed innocence, and simultaneously, two sets of armour clatter at each other loudly about nothing.

The great promise, the holistic promise, is both individual and collective. It is the great myth of homecoming. It is the endlessly retold epic journey of return. From merged, unconscious presence in the garden (childhood, premodernity), we experience conscious, separate absence (adolescence, modernity). We become ourselves, but are lost. Before making our way home – to individuated, conscious presence (adulthood, possible postmodernity).

The commonplace (exoteric), premodern knowledge of spirit is taken up again, and completed, by therapeutically-informed holism. As is modern, secular knowledge. Both the old promise of a paradise-beyond, and the recent promise of a paradise-of-matter, are renewed and expanded. We are promised the garden possessed of both our spirituality and our sexuality. We are promised paradise here and now, and everywhere forever – as ourselves. Every outlook has its promise. Without a promise an outlook has no ground, no roots. Without roots it has no authority. And without authority it has no power – it can have no influence.

The promise of holism to the individual is self-evident. And its collective promise is not dependent on whether or not modernity now moves immediately towards maturity. As a holistic activist I might be attempting to influence the collective, but I am also aware that the path might be spiral, and that we might need to pass through (and might have already passed through) innumerable premodernities, modernities and postmodernities – before we can arrive collectively, in wholeness, in the holy, ordinary garden.

Furthermore, if we are discussing humanity, and not only our dominant, globalising culture, we need to acknowledge that different groupings are at different turns of the spiral… Thus, although the promise of wholeness is clear, the 'how', and the 'how long', are not – and need not be.

And although I have said that, at the personal level, the promise of holism is self-evident – the speed of its fulfilment can never be predicted. Perhaps each of us must pass through innumerable private premodernities, modernities and postmodernities – before finding ourselves where we always were, and seeing that place for the first time. And perhaps, just as different cultures can be seen as being at different points on different turns of a collective spiral, there are different parts within us at different points on different turns of our individual spirals. Thus, individually too, the promise of wholeness is clear, but where each of us must travel, how far and for how long, before our homecoming, is never clear – and need not be, and could not be.

Split-off Sex

Renting the cheapest rooms I could, and working a minimum so that I could write, walk the Devon outdoors, and get myself together – I began to make friends. Dishwashing and waiting and clearing tables in a vegetarian café in Totnes high street, at the hub of the sub-culture, put me in touch with the whole colourful, cosy mood of the town. I had found my way to a fertile fringe of mainstream modernity.

In many ways my new philosophy of openness was supremely modern. I was individualistic – I was the axis of my world, not God. I let others be their own separate selves, and I was mine. And I was naturally and unquestioningly egalitarian – everyone was obviously equal, it seemed to me, because everyone was obviously equally existing.

But I was too purely, innocently scientific… Whereas scientism, fundamentalist pseudo-science, only admits the down (matter) and the out (the external), I refused to investigate neither up nor down, neither in nor out. And although I had lost my religion, I still had a faith. I'd lost its name, but I still had it. I'd lost my tongue, but I could still hear meaning. Alongside my very modern openness were traces of an openness to something modernity had turned its back on.

And so, after a decade's exile, I set out to explore. I had no promise yet. All I had was my openness. I had no concept of wholeness, no experience of living in co-creativity, no insight into the erotic unknown. But I knew I needed the world again. I knew I needed to reconnect, flesh to flesh… What better to explore than sex?

And so from almost-no-sex, I quickly flipped into as-much-as-I-could. I masturbated with pornographic magazines. I juggled five girlfriends. I played the spiritual playboy. I seduced with my wisdom and freedom and vulnerability. This sexual exploration seemed to me, at the time, like a vital healing. I had to re-open to my sexuality, I told myself. I had to get it back.

I did need it back. But somehow it wasn't filtering through. I was having sex, but somehow the whole of me wasn't linking up. I was connecting with my sexuality, but I was losing touch with the rest of me. In fact, I was just getting agitated and obsessed. And although I felt justified by my philosophy of openness, I was becoming consumed by a split-down sexuality that measured the value of a woman by the curves of her hips and buttocks and breasts. I don't know how painful or insulting this was to them, but it was disturbing and damaging to me. I was impelled. Somehow I was now out to fuck – and any impetus I'd had to meaning, or feeling, was secondary. It was lovely if there was affection, but it had become incidental. The point was to penetrate… I was becoming split. Again.

My split-up spirituality had turned me into a holy zombie, split-down sex was now turning me into a secular zombie, a sex zombie. It too was cutting me off from myself, from sensitivity and discrimination – not just during sexual intercourse, not just with my sexual partners, but generally, with everyone, all day everywhere. It was emptying me. I had been a spiritaholic, and now I was becoming a sexaholic, a sex addict – only really interested in merging with the objects of my desire… I became a women-abuser, I became an other-abuser, a user of everything. And my objectification of others turned me into an object myself.

To be fair, to be truly accurate: I wasn't one hundred percent without centre or self. I wasn't nothing-but-a user and abuser of people and things. I wasn't just an object surrounded by other objects. Paradoxically, simultaneously, I was now becoming more of a person than I'd ever been. I had been a split-up, alienated object of God. Now I was in support groups, reconnecting with my emotions (feeling the feelings of others, and feeling my own grief and pain), and I was working with my will (thinking my own thoughts again, acting on my own desires, and deciding my own direction). I was becoming less of an object, and more of a subject, than ever. Nevertheless, meanwhile, somewhere else, a part of me was now a citizen of the pornographic culture. And like all things modern – it knew only things. It was itself a thing. A sex thing.

It has been so helpful to think in terms of parts of myself – parts which are often in opposition, parts of myself which might even hate each other, parts which might be travelling in opposite directions…

Because while many parts of me were healing, a pornographic part was carving out a new wounding. While most of me was unifying, an agitated, escapist, sexually split-down part was cutting me in half again. While most parts of me were getting to know each other, a hunter of sex-objects, a user (which is an abuser), and a fucker (which is a destroyer) were dragging me into the shadows of numbness. I was recovering from being a spiritual fanatic, and I was becoming a sex fanatic.

Thinking in terms of parts like this, the ugly parts were so much easier to 'own'. I was ugly, but I was also beautiful. 'I am a women-abuser, an other-abuser, and a user of everything.' Unless I had known that I was also the opposite of all this, it would have been very, very difficult to have confessed 'Yes, this too is me.'

Thus, bizarrely, in the name of healing and openness and the pursuit of truth, I connected with the classic male sexual archetype of our culture: the find-'em-fuck-'em-and-forget-'em James Bond hero of the macho modern man. Clearly, just openness wasn't enough. I had no context, no vision of the journey of wholeness. I got split again. It was the same split. It was the same premodern sex-spirit split updated, played backwards. In the name of 'openness' I was just acting out. And acting on any split widens that split. Lacking maturity, and lacking guidance, in my efforts to heal-together I was slicing myself in two again.

My repressed sexuality struck back. It wanted out. It was fed up being stuck in the shadow. It burst out. It had a voice, it wanted to be heard – understandably. But any part that breaks out, in reaction, and takes us over, is dangerous – to others and to ourselves. I flipped into being a split-down, body-obsessed intercourse fanatic. It's all very well to speak out, or even act out, within a therapeutic setting. But I picked up and dropped girlfriends with only one aim – penetration, and its bliss of self-release. And to act out from our wounding, as I did, in the world, without consciousness or direction, is the path of pain and confusion.

And this, as I see it, is the huge dilemma of our culture. This is where my biography and the collective biography run parallel. Over the last few centuries, and particularly in the last half of the twentieth, we have flipped *en masse*. Millions upon millions of men and women have been acting out. An entire civilisation has disconnected (as I did) from spirit. It has loosed itself – with its mass history of sexual denial, repression and frustration. It has broken out of its goody-goody, spiritual childhood. It is a culture on the sexual rampage.

From individual to individual, and couple to couple, of course, the sexual situation varies. To the degree that there is honesty and openness there is the possibility of keeping love and sacredness alive. And so, to varying degrees, we include the physical, emotional and spiritual levels within our sexuality. But mainstream modernity, as a whole, has not even the vaguest conception of sacred sex, of sex-as-oblation, or of sex-as-holy-communion.

We might be passing through an essential cultural adolescence, but adolescence is a rite of passage in itself – and rites of passage are dangerous. In adolescence we say 'no' to the meanings and values of our authorities, but we don't yet know our own 'yes'. It's a risk. We are impelled to cast ourselves into a valueless, meaningless limbo. There, potentially, we will find our 'yes' – to our own values. But if, as is the case today, the culture is largely empty of value and full of addictive, compensatory temptation, there is a danger of remaining lost in an early adolescent limbo, with only an impertinent 'no' to cling to.

I was learning the a-b-c of therapy. I was learning to distinguish the trends within me. I also had faith. And faith offers a transpersonal context and facilitates detachment, both of which are vital for healing into wholeness. But mainstream modernity offers none of this.

I was fleeing core existential pain. I had fled to spirit, now I was fleeing to sex. I couldn't face the feeling in my heart of hearts that somehow I wasn't good enough for life, for truth. Yes, but this is everybody's issue. This is the core existential wound of the human race. We all carry existential shame and feelings of unworthiness and inadequacy. And we all flee from them. That's OK. That's a stage in our development. But there then comes a time when we can't pretend any more, when we stop, turn, and look inside. The difficulty is when addiction has hollowed out our being, and we are too desensitised to even feel the pain of pretence.

And ours is an addictive culture. Just as we talk of individuals who are drug addicts, sex addicts, shopping addicts, food addicts, and so on – the personality of our culture is an addict. And just as an individual addict can switch addictions, being cured of alcoholism, for example, and become bulimic – our culture is addicted to every possible form of materialistic escapism. Not only is there an almost total lack of eternal values, but within that void there is a glut of damaging addictions. This makes the healing of our culture particularly difficult.

In the pornographic culture of modernity the cut-off sex addict has been the main image of a man. To be split-down, to feel no value, and to fuck as fast and furiously and frequently as you can – this was the measure of how much you were of a man. In the face of this some women became defensive and disempowered, others hit back – but either way, struggled to unfold into full womanhood. And men became hardened, caught in an ever-worse personality trap, denied contact both with feeling and with their own real will:

porno-addicts in the pages and in the flesh. Men just got more wound up –
because we were so off track. It was when I joined a men's group, shared my
story and heard other men share theirs, that I began to realise how collective
the wounding was. We had no idea where to find our own sexuality. We
thought it was inside others. We went out to take. We had nothing to share,
nothing to consummate.

Modernity today, at the start of the twenty-first century, is thus at the cusp
of both degradation and unprecedented healing. The genders are exchanging
roles and qualities, and there is much sexual self-questioning. But we lack
images of woman and man, and of realistic sacred sex. The role models of the
female and the male, the archetypes in the collective energy field, are severely
wounded. Even among men who have embraced feeling, and who can truly
be in relationship, how many carry a clear, strong archetypal image of the
whole man? And even among women who stand their ground and hold their
own – how many live their lives in the presence of an archetypal image of
woman in her fullness?

Healing is not only retrospective. It is not only about tending past wounds.
It is also the cultivation of the unimagined. It is also a growing into new imaginations. This is why menswork and womenswork are so needed. This has
nothing to do with sexual preference. Men need to retreat together, and
women need to gather without the men. And there, in preparation for uniting
anew, they can tell it all, among others who know the same pain, and tend
holistic myths – until the life in those images overtakes their minds and they
find themselves imbued with a stimulating new vision.

But the wounds do need tending... The obsession, the shame, the emptiness – it all needs to be heard. And understood. And forgiven. The mature
openness that leads to integration is the ability to enter all parts of ourselves,
and to hear their conversations, and to be larger than them all. (As against the
immature openness of acting it all out – which leads to imbalance, fragmen-
tation and dis-integration.)

To tend the wounds is to love them. Not approve, not condone, but
acknowledge, hold, be compassionate to... 'Who are you?' we need to ask
each part, and 'What do you want?' And although you might be distorting,
'What is the gift you bring?' We need to ask 'Please tell me – what part of me
is still missing? What more must I allow in to become whole?' Outer openness
might sometimes be necessary, sometimes unavoidable, but it is this inner
openness, contextualised on the holistic map, that unites the split continents
of the psyche.

But without a new imagination our inner worlds will be blended, but bland.
As men we need to imagine a mythology of the whole man. Many good men,
embarrassed by the James Bond caricature, ashamed of their passion, and
afraid of their power, have imagined the 'soft man' or 'new man' – a kind of

'mummy's right hand man' – and lost their manhood. The soft man is an impotent postmodern option. He is not the whole man. How can men be whole if they renounce their potency?

There is a sub-theme of menswork that runs throughout this book – it is in no way intended to diminish the importance of womenswork. Although the specific issues for men and women are different, the double focus of tending the wounds and re-imagining one's gender is the same. But rather than generalise, I feel I can speak more powerfully out of my own personal male sexual healing-journey. And in the men's groups I have been in, and in men's events I have attended, I have seen and felt one very healthy new imagining and remembering. Images of a lusty, creative Earth Man are re-surfacing…

The Earth Man is not the whole man. But the Apollonian sun god is already bright and strong within the male psyche. And for the myth of the whole man to emerge he needs to meet – somewhere, in some archetypal dimension – with this Earth Man. He needs to meet and merge with his lost twin, his dark other half. Robert Bly's 'Iron John', and the entire labyrinth of mythologies of the wild man, the Minotaur, Pan, Dionysus, the Green Man, The Horned God, Shiva and Osiris – all point towards one man…

> *I am holy, dark, passionate Earth Man –*
> *I am Sacred Phallic Man.*
> *I am man made of breath of seasons –*
> *I am man of mud and storms.*
> *I am out-all-night, out-of-my-mind*
> *dancing-free-man.*
> *I am man who kills with his teeth.*
> *Yes –*
> *now do you see what I mean?*
>
> *Where am I? Where am I?*
> *Let me out of here!*
> *Don't you remember me?*
> *I am the seed and the life!*
>
> *Teeth? Hah!*
> *Teeth? I am man of fangs!*
> *In battle I rip your arm from your torso*
> *and spit you to the ground!*
> *I am your protector, your instinct, your outrage.*
>
> *I am no devil.*
> *I am not evil.*
> *How many more thousand years?*
> *First you invented hell –*

and now you say it doesn't exist!
Hah! Some irony!
How much longer?
Don't you remember me?

I am moon man, river man, stone man.
It is I who leap boulders in starlight.
It is I who clap thunder,
it is I who laugh in clouds.
I am the life-force, I am the will-to-life.
I am survival,
I eat, I eat...
Only I really love death.

Don't you remember the celebrations?
I remember.
I remember how I'd meet my beloved,
at the equinox and at the solstice –
both of us pale with ecstasy,
both of us emptied pure in our separation.
I remember the outline of that body
approaching from the other side of the fire –
and I remember that flesh as we met
and died inside the flames.

Such was love and such was sex
and such was fire and death.
The frenzy of tenderness.
The spiral fire entering the sky.
The orange flame, the black night.
If you don't remember, I can't explain.

But I struggle here inside you,
I can't help it –
it's not my nature to obey or be quiet or tame.
I am Neptune, Poseidon, I am Agni, I am Vayu,
I am Father Earth!

Hear me!
It's my writhing that's twisting your smile,
it's my yelling that's contorting your words.
It is I, your servant,
wishing only to be possessed,
who possesses you.

It is I who make you batter,
it is I who make you rape,
it is I who make you fuck –
it is I, The Lord Of The Dance,
who fucks you.

It is I, I, whose garland is the rainbow,
it is I, I, whose glance is the moonlight,
it is I, I, whose dance spins planets,
it is I, I, the seed-giver of creation,
it is I who am reduced to this.

I, who am time,
I for whom every moment is eternal,
I have been moaning here for how many thousand years?
I cannot lie still...
If I must –
I will kill you to be free.

Oh Man!
I belong to you.
I am yours.
I am you.
Remember me, take me back, awaken me.
Take me back in your blood.
I am your semen.
I am the rain.
I am the wet soil.
I am your night sight,
I am your wings and claws.
I am the wind that blows through you.
I am your cunning and power and fear –
oh man, what are you without me?

Oh man –
without me you are not fit to receive spirit,
you are less than empty –
you are nothing but desperation.

Oh man,
let me gush through you,
let me burst you,
let me crack you
back open to the stars.

Oh man –
until you let me out
your lovers will run from you and fight you –
even as they offer you their lips.
Until you release me
even your tenderest intent will turn sadistic.

Oh man –
what choice do you have?
Hear me! Remember!
Remember how we loved.
Remember how we bowed down.
Remember our awe as we beheld our beloved.
Remember that embrace –
our hair streaming across the sky,
our hands around the equator,
our toes in the sand,
those fingertips on our neck,
that silence in our heart.

It has been said that at puberty a boy must cross the river from the women's camp to the men's camp – but that in our culture there is no such rite of passage. The evidence that a boy has crossed the river is that he is not caught in the love-hate of mother/woman. He is no longer so needy, or so resentful of his need, or so blaming. He can father his own neediness. Because he has entered his culture's myth of manhood, because he stands in the power of man, he can re-enter the orbit of woman with confidence.

The call of Sacred Phallic Man
who kills with his teeth
is a call to turn the blood of boys
to sacred semen.
It is the wind from across the river.
Some men are cooking on an open fire.

This is absolutely crucial. At the moment the mass male and female imaginations are stuck in stunted stereotypes. There are infinite varieties and subtleties, but the pivotal, foundational archetypes of our culture are James Bond and The Barbie Doll. This is certainly changing – this book is one of a million signs of that change – but these profoundly powerful images don't just disappear. It takes generations. These images, and the myths they carry, are internalised and passed from father to son, from mother to daughter. We are all stuck watching a cultural film with heroes and heroines who tell us physical, emotional, intellectual and spiritual stories about how to be man, and how to be woman. The film is evolving, slowly, as it must, at the pace of our imaginations.

In Section Three we will be discussing the development of the third sphere (the collective developmental sphere) of holistic community. And although in one sense one can't choose, in another I would say that the most important structure within the third sphere is the initiation of men and women – even more important than marriage/partnership. After all, without whole men and whole women, how can we expect to have wholesome relationships? And if we are to develop journeys of male/female initiation into holistic woman-hood/manhood, then we must be very clear as to how we are working the collective imagination. We need to know the images we need. We need to decide which myths to tell ourselves.

> *Sacred Phallic Man is not the whole man.*
> *He is the earth god, Father Earth, the husband of Gaia.*
> *To reclaim him*
> *is to reclaim the male goddess.*
> *We know the sky god only too well.*
> *We have determination and detachment and denial and moral judgment*
> *sewn into our bones.*
> *We need to find out what it is to be*
> *male on earth.*
> *We need to feel the flux, the beat,*
> *the pulse of incarnation.*
> *We need to feel what it means to be*
> *alive in the meat,*
> *alive with each other*
> *and animals and trees –*
> *in the sacred and mysterious flesh.*
>
> *And perhaps, if the radiant and pure sun god*
> *is willing to embrace*
> *this hot, wet earth god,*
> *and the hot, wet earth god*
> *is ready to forgive –*
> *then in brotherhood heaven and earth*
> *will sit down before spirit itself,*
> *and narrate an epic tale*
> *of wholeness,*
> *which we generations of mortal men will listen to*
> *enraptured,*
> *and live from.*

Through this last decade there have been times when I have lived naked on the land, when I have danced through the night, and when I have been present in my body in the most primal ritual. I have been massaged and massaged myself, I have meditated on the body, in the body, through the body – alone, with one other, and with many. And I have come to know where my sex lies coiled, and that it is mine – to share as I do or do not please.

I have reclaimed my body for spirit. I have reclaimed my sexuality for spirit. And when the physical meets spirit (as long as the heart is open, relaxed, unburdened), we touch the holistic experience. In this book I have used phrases like 'sacred-erotic awareness' and 'the sexual-spiritual experience' to describe this state of being – the state of the whole man and the whole woman. I have spoken of it as the existential core of holistic community.

It is a place many of us have visited. It is a place I visit. It is not the place I permanently reside. It is a place of loving oneness with the land, with the living, with time, with the dead. It is a place of intensified beauty. It is peace there. It is home. It is an eroticism of the heart. It may or may not be genital. And we don't need drugs to get there. And, of course, as always, the traditional paradox applies: we only get there by completely accepting where we already are. It is a place with a divine will of its own: we can't decide to visit it, it decides to visit us. And yet our souls tug at us, we can't help but travel towards it – and this is the shared sacred journey, this is holistic community.

Many people have described a state of mystic oneness with creation – with life itself. I would just like to note how sexless these descriptions almost always are. And I would like to suggest why. The problem with sexuality is that, unless we know that it is an energy within ourselves (that can be stimulated by the external, but which nevertheless always remains internal), then we will tend to chase after external objects (in other words: other people's bodies) – in order to connect with our sexual pleasure. Sex is a hot energy. It is frightening to handle. And we haven't been schooled in holding the erotic fire, in just being-present-to-it, in passively delighting in it. We're frightened to be forever chasing everyone. We're frightened of being out of order, out of control. Mystic experience is safer without it. Yes, no doubt, but not as exciting. And not as complete. Non-erotic mystic experience is nice in the clouds, perhaps, or during out-of-the-body experiences – but, as I see it, it is not the complete incarnate spiritual experience. It is not the full bliss available to us as embodied spiritual beings.

Not only this, but sex is personal – sex means relationship (even if it's very, very brief). And relationships bring the psychological dimension: our neuroses, our messy, sticky 'stuff', our emotional entanglements which get entangled with others' entanglements, and… Oh yes, spiritual experience is certainly simpler without it! But if we feel called to the path of wholeness, and if we are to travel together in holistic community, then we are going to need to acknowledge each other, moment to moment, as sexual-emotional-spiritual beings. We are going to need to know our desires and our boundaries. And we are going to need to become more and more expert at handling sexual, emotional and spiritual energy.

But who was I then, in Totnes, still so new to all of this, as I walked back from the restaurant to my flat – my eyes fixating on women, my mind obsessed with openness and honesty and truth? Two fragments from my early Totnes notebooks...

1.

Moments of openness,
of the feeling of truthfulness,
of somehow-sacred insight –
are moments of propulsion,
moments of inner motion,
moments of uncovering.
Moments of openness
can be slow-motion, difficult joy.
'Oh, but in a moment of openness
I saw I am hopelessly conditioned!'
Perhaps, in that open moment,
you touched something less conditioned.
'Oh, but in a moment of openness,
I saw I have squandered my life!'
Perhaps, in that moment of openness,
you touched meaning.

When we're peaceful, comfortable and trusting enough –
when we're brave enough –
to risk taking down defences...
when there's nothing worth proving anymore,
when there's nothing else worth winning, or losing, anymore,
when there's nothing else that matters any more
except truth –
moments of openness fill us physically
with a fuller-knowing,
a hint of beauty...
And moments of openness
lift us up
to go on
day-to-day
watching ourselves
opening and closing...

2.
Opening up
is gradually remembering peace.
What release!
What a relief!

... and opening
*   and I'm peaceful*
*   and closing and I'm all nerves*
*   and opening*
*   and I'm relaxed again*
*   and closing again*
*   and I'm on edge...*

And when do I close?
And where do I close?
And I watch out for it,
and I catch myself at it.
Here I am closed again, suffering.

... and opening
*   and I'm happy,*
*   even in my pain –*
*   and closing*
*   and I'm down again*
*   and opening and I'm myself again –*
*   everything's perfect*
*   somehow*
*   I lose it again*
*   and I'm miserable again*
*   feeling separate, alienated, and so lonely*
*   until I remember I'm closed again...*

And how do I close? And why do I close?
What's my fear? Of self? Of madness? Of mind beyond time?
For everyone it's different,
for everyone it's the same.

One way or another,
everyone's afraid to let go –
everyone's afraid to die into truth.
That's why as children we agreed to conform,
and still do,
and still are.

We're still afraid of the night –
of invisible sounds and shadows that move...

We're afraid of death
and we're afraid of life –
we're afraid of others
and we're afraid of ourselves.

Opening up
is the experience of increasing mystery and meaning.
And decreasing fear.
It's a gathering of knowledge –
a readying, a training, a path.
Opening up
is a relentless dismantling
of psychic defences with a purpose:
to keep pain out.
It is a noble commitment.
Opening up is invigorating,
powerful, painful, relaxing, beautiful, blissful, and tough.

It is faith
in honesty
and the path of pain
to guide us home.

In these fragments I can see my own maturing. They are theoretical, but they are grounded in experience. Re-reading them re-connects me with my disclosing, with the stumbling and the shame, and with the blessedness on each occasion when it was done. My only criticism would be that I sense my lack of respect for fear. I still saw fear as bad. Fear blocked openness – so it had to be got rid of. But a subtler, more aware holism would value fear too. Fear is a moderator and a guardian. Fear too brings its gifts. Fear too needs to be befriended. Then the integration process can unfold. It can take the shape it wants to take, not the shape we might want to take it to.

And I'm also aware that, much as I preached openness, I was still mostly closed to my shadow. And the Sacred Phallic Man who kills with his teeth, who embodies my high sexuality, my generative potency, my earthy power, my wild nobility and my glorious rage – this great archetype was still largely hidden and unknown to me.

It wasn't until I was first with Elisabeth that I really began to confess just how split-off I'd become. It was only then that I felt unconditional acceptance enough to confess. I felt safe enough with Elisabeth. I felt safe enough in myself. I had begun to find my feet, and my centre, within the world of feelings. I confessed to her and I confessed to myself. And at that time I was in a 22-man men's group. There I also felt safe – and I confessed to them too. We spent a year looking at male sexuality – exploring our shame, our hearts, our power. That was enormously helpful in closing the split.

And so, even though I respect the ideas in these last two fragments, I wince slightly because I know that at the time they were written I was using ideas about openness to get women to bed. I was engaged in spiritual-philosophical seduction. Was I a fake, again? Again – like when I'd faked certainty for my Hindu god? I'd say slightly less so. I was preaching openness and I was opening up. But I was young and undirected in my openness. Even today, as I write about holism, I know I could know it and live it so much more. To a degree, I know I am still a fake – but each time, on each downward turn of the spiral to my centre, perhaps slightly less so.

Although I was in my late thirties, this was the adolescence of my life's pilgrimage to value. I displayed all of the pretension and inflation of a teenager. Against the backdrop of modernity (our culture's bewildered and self-destructive adolescence), as adolescents do, I constructed the best identity I could.

Can I embrace all of the characters I have been? Can I look back and understand and forgive that absent fundamentalist? Without minimising any inappropriate deed, word or thought: can I look back with love? And can I look back at that nervous, lost, sex-addicted, frantic, over-aged teenager, clinging to his openness – and without minimisation or sentimentality, and having grieved my grief: love him too?

As a man of religion I was absolutely unconscious. But even as a free-thinking modern man I was barely conscious. All I can really say is that I am more and more convinced of my direction. And my direction is wholeness. My task is to bring all of me to myself – to that erotic-most point where I stand, like the tree of life, the axis mundi, uniting earth and spirit as only I can. And my task is to embrace my losses of self – listening carefully to the winds that carry me away. That which is embraced is not split-off. It can be integrated. To integrate is to value. And the closer I am to value, the closer I am to life.

For me, the task has been to embrace the beast. We often assume, because the tale of the beauty and the beast starts with a curse, that it is the beast who must learn to love – that our completion is in developing our finer, higher sensibilities. Which is true. But the beauty also has to develop. She has to embrace the beast. If we take the beauty to represent spirit – all that is non-material in us – and the beast to represent matter, the earthy, the sexual, and all that is human in us – then a second moral is of a completion in loving the material.

Having been split-up, I know spirit. I was the beauty. It is the beast I have been avoiding. It is the beast who has been pursuing me. My fear has been of losing myself in materialism, in my material desires – of being consumed by the beast, who is also me. But to love the things of this world, is not to become a thrashing, trashing materialist. To love sexuality is not to fuck as many others as you can. That is not love of sex. For my beauty to develop love for my beast, I must approach him tenderly. I must bring respect. I must risk a relationship.

That is my side of the great holistic love story. That is my story-so-far. For modernity as a whole, both sides of the story, both morals, are relevant. Mainstream modernity needs to reconnect with both the beauty and the beast. But it is the beauty who enters the castle of the beast, and not vice versa. We could interpret this as suggesting that we need a connection with spirit in order to enter a loving relationship with sex, psyche and the world. If we do not approach the beast in beauty there is a danger of dissipation – and eventually, the cynical viciousness of addictive materialism. But then again, if we do not approach the beauty with self-respect and grounded, graceful, sexual, animal bodies then there is a danger of puritanism – and eventually, the inhuman cruelty of fundamentalism.

Completing Adolescence at Forty

The adolescent must step out of the garden of childhood. He must descend into the outside world. He must separate out from the fusion of family. He must find his 'no'. And he must find a new 'yes' to himself, to his own beliefs, to his own sense of value – to his own sense of self.

This might sound obvious. We might think 'I know that'. But how many of us really let go? Adolescence is a crucial developmental phase. How many of us really complete it? How many of us stop growing at 12, or 14? How many of us are still 16 in old age?

Even if it looks as if we've left the security of childhood, how many of us go forwards wearing a brave face and cloaked in a protective false identity – while our true selves are still playing on mummy and daddy's lawn?

I wore the iron cloak of fanatical spirituality. Mine sounded like a thunderous 'no' to my parents' materialism. But in my heart I was afraid to leave their garden, to go on the adventure of my own identity, and to become whoever I was – and so I re-entered the child-like state by regressing into premodern religious obedience.

My psychological development remained more or less arrested for a decade, until I de-robed. I completed my adolescence – my transition into adulthood – in midlife. At about 35, disillusioned and broken, I wrapped the cloth of openness around my true self, and tumbled out into the world for the first time.

Culturally we now have the opportunity to complete our adolescence. The hard-core, fuck-it-all attitude of the pornoculture is just a sham, a posture, a cover-up of a teenager who's scared to be out on his own. Our premodern religious cultural childhood is over – despite the regressive, revivalist tendency that's determined not to let go (these people are the psychic spasm characteristic of any life-transition). The bulk of us have gone on. We wouldn't and couldn't look back to spirit to explain us to ourselves – but neither can we explain ourselves to ourselves.

Mine was an iron cloak of spirituality. Modernity's is an iron cloak of no-value and immediate pleasure. I donned mine in immature reaction to my parents. Modernity donned its psychic cloak in immature reaction to the self-deceiving, rotten and rigid spirituality of its parental premodernity. Mine wasn't iron when I put it on, it hardened over the years – then it split. Modernity's cloak was idealistic and high-flying at first, but it hardened over the centuries. Now it's splitting.

This splitting, which has been highlighted above all by the global ecological crisis, this collective initiatory moment, presents modernity with various possibilities. The teenage cultural body can opt for the regressive trend, or harden even further, or 'get real'.

'Getting real' would mean:

a.   facing its parent and the past: admitting that it has mistakenly thrown out community and eternal value in its frenzy of teenage rebellion,

b.   facing itself in the present: admitting it is an utterly existentially lost porno-addict, and

c.   facing a future of healing and wholeness: finding its own unique centre, and authentic ways of relating to self and other.

To expect our entire culture to take this three-point 'get real' option would be unrealistic. Realistically we can expect people to take all of the options. The question is how many will take which. But only this last option will help move the culture into adulthood. The revivalists will just go back to childhood, and the materialists will stay pubescent forever.

As I moved through my own psychological adolescence I was moved to write this next fragment – affirming my commitment to adulthood. I called it *The Punk Bible*...

> *The punk bible might not have been written,*
> *but it exists.*
>
> *For example,*
> *it lists the phosphorescent green dinosaur mohawk hairdo*
> *under 'approved' –*
> *while, in the section 'the ethics of child-rearing in the punk ethos',*
> *pretty pink frilly skirts for girls,*
> *and cute blue shorts for boys,*
> *are categorically 'disapproved'.*
> *Net stockings, the many-earringed ear,*

chains, studs, black leather, anything black
are all 'approved', 'accepted', 'in', 'good' and 'right'.
Almost everything else is 'out', 'wrong', and spurned.

This might give the impression of narrow-mindedness,
but no – the punk bible defines the punk as
'not one of the oppressed,
TV-hypnotised, newspaper-brainwashed masses'.
The punk is in fact (quote) a 'symbol of challenge to authority',
and an 'anti-sectarian, free-thinking individualist'.

However, all punks follow their bible with a strictness
to rival the most radical fundamentalist.
Rules of uncleanliness, for example, are rigid, almost ruthless –
and no punk would be seen dead clean.
Nor is membership superficial. It is not just a matter of dress –
there is jargon, mannerism, etiquette...
To be a punk is to talk punk, and only punk.
To be a punk is to walk, sit and gesticulate punk, and only punk.
To be a punk is to hear punk, eat and vomit punk, to smell punk –
above all, it is to think punk – and only punk.

The punk bible lists beliefs – about intoxication, work, society, sex...
a long list of beliefs, which all punks in all places at all times
believe utterly and never question nor doubt.
Furthermore,
the punk bible preaches the punk mission: 'thou shalt outrage'.
And thus the devout punk passes his or her day
in the service of the higher good –
(rather pitifully) defying narrowness with narrowness,
(rather pathetically) challenging non-thinking with non-thinking,
bible bashing the bible bashed,
and touting his/her own brand of brainwash to the brainwashed.

And thus it becomes obvious
that to belong to the conformists,
or belong to the non-conformists,
is to belong, and to conform.
To be closed in traditional conventions,
or to be closed in rebel conventions,
is to be conventional,
and to be closed.

The pursuit of security of identity,
via whichever bible –

of whichever social class or clique –
however well masked as the brave defence of tradition,
or the brave advance of rebellion –
is all much of a muchness –
all cowardice,
all the terror of truth.
All of them avid for confrontation,
all of them terrified of confrontation with self.

I'm not sure if this piece is entirely fair to the punks it uses as its example, but it makes its point. It doesn't enquire into the need to belong – so important in adolescence. Nor does it ask what part of the collective psyche the punks were acting out. But it does assert my determination to grow up into myself.

In later fragments, such as this next one, I observe the maturing of my holism. I note my coming of age. But in all I wrote at this time I am working out my relationship with my rebellion. I am concerned with questions of obedience and humility because premodern parental wrath is framed in the accusation of pride. For example, in my final days as a monk I wrote: 'The (parental) drilling begins, "The plan of action has been drawn up in the scriptures by God and His great generals – yours is to put your ideas in line, and march. Don't straggle and speculate! Who do you think you are? Do you think you know better than the general? You're out of step – it's because you're proud! Come on – sing! And quiet your devil's mind!"' I now needed to convince myself that my urge to independence (to be 'out of step') wasn't spurred by pride – that I wasn't bad for becoming me...

Humility is not obedience
to the code-book, or spoken-law,
nor to custom (however age-old),
nor to institution, or delineated group of any sort.
Humility is an attitude –
it grows as we grow,
it grows as we open.

In achieving openness we grow in self-respect,
in respect for others,
in respect for animals and plants,
and in respect for time, patterns and events.

This self-respecting is not pride –
on the contrary, it is our fullest humility.
It develops because, in order to open,
we must respect our reasons for having closed.
To become secure

we must accept and respect our insecurity.
Opening to our insecurity
we become secure –
because security is in opening.
To become fearless
we must respect our reasons for fearing...
they are understandable and perfect.

Gradually we come to bow before others –
and to bow before ourselves.
We can bow before others
because we're no longer afraid of them.
And we're no longer afraid of them
because we're no longer afraid of ourselves –
no longer afraid to be exposed –
to let parts of us die.
We feel open, we feel united...
That person in a hurry is me,
that person bored, that person crying, that person angry –
they're not me,
and yet they are.

And feeling this oneness –
I realise I can only bow before others
because I can bow before myself.
I can only respect others
because I respect myself.
And I cannot respect others
until I respect myself.

Therefore,
this self-respecting is not pride.
This self-respecting is the prerequisite of humility –
whereas pride is its opposite.
We can only bow before ourselves in genuine self-respect,
when we are genuinely humble.
While we're proud
there's only self-doubt.
Pride is not the excess of self-respect,
it is the absence of self-respect.
This self-acceptance and self-respect –
is humility before oneself,
humility before others,
and humility before existence itself.

And the more open we become –
the more conscious –
the more we perceive
the longing for value
within everyone's every word and deed.
And daily life becomes laden with value –
with our longing,
and value's longing
for us.

The openness that became self-respect and unity with others,
becomes the mystic appreciation that bows before all things.
This is full humility.

Whatever was not completed during the rite of passage of adolescence will reappear, and offer itself for completion, during the rite of passage of midlife. Rites of passage are there, within us all – like milk teeth that must fall, or skin that must wrinkle. They are unavoidable. They have an objective subtle existence. They happen whether the culture acknowledges them or facilitates them or not.

At the moment these initiatory life-phases are almost totally ignored. If they are engaged with it is usually as a solitary journey – often completed against cultural opposition. For the most part, we cannot face them because we have neither the ideological unity (sphere 1 of community development), nor the self-developmental experience (sphere 2), nor the community cohesion (sphere 3). Which means that almost all of our attempts to direct and reform society (sphere 4) are the flimsy patch-up guesswork of boys masquerading as men, and girls masquerading as women.

Above I spoke of our cultural breakdown, made particularly visible by the ecological crisis. And I spoke of three available options: a return to a premodern fundamentalist childhood, the perpetuation of a porno-techno-adolescence, or healing together into adulthood. We could also call this last option the initiation of our culture. The question is how many of us will come forward to take part.

I also spoke of healing-to-the-past. For men, the great sign of completion of the initiation of adolescence is reconciliation with the father. To be able to say, for example…

I honour you,
my father,
Harold Josephs.
You.

I honour your life-story,

your experience of time-passing,
your not-knowing...
your sensations
in your fingertips, your cheeks, your lips, your penis, your feet.
You.

I honour your life-choices,
decided deep in the warmth of your mind,
a warmth with an exact temperature only you know –
as only I exactly know mine.

I honour you
who are no one else,
nor were, nor will be –
brilliant, unique and insignificant:
you fill the whole sky,
you are the totality of existence,
and you are gone like a thought –
like me.

I honour the houses you have inhabited,
the buses and boats, and trains and airplanes and cars
that have carried your body, your feelings, your dreams.
I honour everything that has come true for you,
and your pain.

Father –
whether or not you have been able to grasp me,
whether or not you have been able to sit with me in silence,
I honour your love for me.

I know you reach out from very, very deep inside yourself.
I know your reaching.
I feel your love.

And whether or not I have been able to honour you until now,
I honour you in this poem.
I honour you with my tears as I write.
I honour you with my love.

This, of course, is not a poem from a man who has been severely abused, or who had no father. But all men need to go beyond their reactivity to their childhood's authority. All men need to find the father within themselves – the place of strength and compassion that enables us to protect and educate children, to support and serve others, and to maturely co-ordinate the crowd within. Having emerged from one's reactivity, one enters equality. Then one doesn't have to be spiritual in order not to be materialistic (like me), or materialistic in order not to be spiritual (like this culture). Then one is free to be anything and everything. For me, and for this culture, this opens the possibility of the whole human being.

In Section Three, particularly in Looking Practically At Initiation, I look at how we might set about the long-term task of reconstructing the traditional rites of passage of adolescence. But before opening the discussion of the development of the communal sphere, I want to underline the full implications of holistic community for our civilisation. I want to look at the three of the main sculptors of the contours of our culture space: science, religion and politics. And I want to look at their interface with holism. I want to stimulate our imagining of a holistic civilisation.

Pseudo-scientific Fundamentalism

The regressive fundamentalism of the religious revivalists
is paralleled in the modern era by another,
more insidious fundamentalism:
the fundamentalism of facts,
of lists and comparisons and proofs.
It is the terrorism of tidiness –
of neat statistics, of figures that fit, of results that count.
Here the worship is of information –
the creed is efficiency,
and the bible is written in logic.

This fundamentalism is the transnational religion of modernity.
It is the dogma of the materialistic split.
In less than a century it has conquered and colonised the globe.
It is inside everything –
the immaculate cut-glass of the shopping mall,
the professional competence of the well-run office,
the fine-timed productivity of the factory.
It is everywhere –
in schedules and modules
and plans and projections
and test runs and targets.
It is even in our play –
swimming is now a fitness programme
done in lanes

between opening times
with numbered locker key wristbands.
It is even in our homes –
in the children's school timetables (and grades and exams),
in the vaccination certificates of the pets,
in high-tech kitchens and precision hygiene,
in home accounting and home computing,
in electrics and wiring and sockets and plugs,
in plumbing and pipes and tanks and taps,
in everything kept ordered, co-ordinated and under control,
in everything and everyone
functioning and functioning and functioning.

And presiding over this sparkling, rigid reality
is not the humble, open-minded scientist,
but the frightened, fact-worshipping, fact-mad pseudo-scientist.
He or she, but usually he,
is high-priest of this modernist fundamentalism.
He is priest because he has access to the truth
And access to truth equals authority –
temporal and universal.
This fanatic of pseudo-science is priest because
he can read the mind of the information god.
He is a technician of truth.
He knows the way
that god's mind works.

Thus the atheistic congregation of modernity (much as the premodern congregation before it) has a tidy truth ('there is no eternal value'), a priesthood to explain it ('don't worry – that earthquake was not the karmic wrath of any God or Goddess, it was a purely material phenomenon'), an ethic ('have a good time while you can'), and a social etiquette ('think, speak, and above all, always look, efficient').

At the time of writing this next 'fragment' I had not long escaped the fundamentalism of religion. I labelled this pseudo-scientific materialism 'fundamentalist' because I recognised the rigidity that sets in when we defend a lie. Here the lie was not, as before, that life-on-earth has no value – but that nothing has value. Like recognises like, and although I was already in recovery, I recognised the distorted humanity, the strange ways people sat and walked. I would hear young boys out-facing each other, or old women discussing the weather like meteorologists. And I would be familiar with the empty eyes, the discomfort, the way people were not quite themselves, the odd, artificial tones in their voices.

When the victims of pseudo-scientific fundamentalism speak they sound surreal, less than real, not quite there – physically apparently present, yet oddly absent. They are the devotees of modern functionalism. They are devout instruments of the informationist worldview. They are stuffed and overloaded with information, their words come out in a jerky dry logic, their skin is too tight on their faces, they express emotion painfully (like a betrayal), their breath is shallow, their arms and legs are too straight – and above all, they are always correct. Is this a caricature? Who are these victims? If pseudo-scientific fundamentalism is the doctrine of modernity – is it not all of us? To a degree, yes. Some of the cultural soul went on ahead, some of us might have been less affected – but perhaps more than we usually acknowledge.

As I have said, premodern split-up alienation is very different from split-down modern alienation. The former is ethereal and away-somewhere, the latter is gross and empty. The casualties of premodernity are out-of-the-body because they're supposed to be full of spirit. The casualties of modernity are so full of facts there's no room inside them for themselves...

> *The underlying axiom of science is:*
> *what is true is what is proven.*
> *And by 'proven' is meant*
> *physically quantified, analysed, verified...*
> *It is the ultimate faith in proof.*
> *The believers of science thus live in a proven universe.*
> *This is their faith.*
> *When this attitude is accompanied by the proviso:*
> *'but what is unproven is not necessarily untrue –*
> *it might be, but it might yet be proven;*
> *it is as-yet-unproven' –*
> *then science is a dynamic, undogmatic faith.*
>
> *But when*
> *ghosts, hobgoblins, fairies, souls, subtle energy-fields, gods –*
> *aren't true,*
> *because they aren't proven.*
> *then science oversteps itself.*
> *When the axiom 'the proven is the true' is extended to:*
> *'the unproven is untrue'*
> *science becomes pseudo-science –*
> *scient-ism, a fundamentalist tradition.*
>
> *Pseudo-science –*
> *as it is so often preached in our schools and universities,*
> *and as it so often controls public thinking –*
> *with its creation theory, its atheism, its awesome absurdity,*

and its morality of the survival of the fittest –
has lost its spirit of growth, its spirit of investigation,
its scientific spirit,
its openness...

Which science teacher tells the children
science has never proven
hobgoblins aren't true?
In these pseudo-science lessons
the daring intent of science is settled in comfortable formulas –
its questioning momentum ended,
supposedly QED.

Like all fundamentalisms,
pseudo-science is frightened to go further.
It sets the circumference of truth,
and refuses to step outside.
Its scare-words aren't 'pagan' or 'heretical' or 'devil-inspired' –
but 'unscientific', 'illogical',
'not squaring with the facts', 'not making sense',
'sentimental', 'folkloric', 'just myth'.

It is often said the scientific tradition grew strong
as a reaction to the corruption of the religious traditions –
not only the moral, but the existential corruption –
from disgust with the decadent absence of discovering of truth –
from disgust with cold, still, conceit...
'No', it rebelled,
I'll only accept as true
what I can touch, and see, and prove!'

And perhaps, for some time,
it was a new, challenging, inspiring doctrine...
It enlivened us with the dis-covering of truth.
It was a religious revival.
But pseudo-science has repeated the error
of the traditions it overthrew.
It too is existentially corrupt.

This then is the doctrine of split-off modernity. Within each of, to varying extents, is the premodern, the modern and the postmodern. But this is the thumbnail, throwaway philosophy of all that is truly, purely modern in us. And it is the mental set-up of utter alienation. It is dead to the mystical beauty of the living world. It is dead to the piercingly sweet fear of life-in-the-unknown. For hundreds of years the bulk of the cultural mind has been hypnotised by this credo of no-value and matter-only. The collective energy field has been clogged and blocked by it. It is the philosophical backbone of the pornoculture. It legitimises objectification of other, and self-objectification. It underpins all consumerism, and the whole cult of appearances. This utterly unscientific scientism creates the reality frame and provides the theoretical holding for untold frustration, violence, addiction and abuse.

It is essential to see the relationship between this informationism and the pornoculture. It is essential to see how cosmological theory captures the collective mind, and repercusses in our thinking, feeling and behaviour. This is the influence of the first sphere, the existential sphere. It impacts on the second, the personal sphere, on the third, the communal sphere, and on the fourth, the practical sphere – finally creating objectified individuals (sphere 2), incapable of soul-to-soul relations (sphere 3), inhabiting a functional, secular state (sphere 4).

The fact that, alongside the emptiness and the compensation, we now see mass movement towards self-healing and earth-healing means we can assume this fundamental sphere of thought patterns and beliefs must also be shifting. Indeed, Einstein's relativity, Planck's quanta, Heisenberg's principle of uncertainty – the whole flow of twentieth century physics, ending now in meetings with the personalities of sub-atomic particles – has shaken the pseudo-scientific priesthood, opened up the intelligentsia, and relaxed the mass cultural mood. Gradually, now, as we enter the twenty-first century, the unproven is being welcomed back. There is a gap, a gateway in the cultural psyche. New possibilities are getting in.

The very statement 'unproven therefore untrue' begins to sound absurd. As sub-atomic waves become particles become waves become particles, and even pseudo-scientists can no longer say which or when or why, and the very definition of matter is falling apart in their hands, the two categories 'proven' and 'unproven' are being replaced by one category – 'unproveable'. The mystery of premodernity and the factuality of modernity are meeting in an unprecedented postmodern holistic unity.

Here's another fragment, entitled *Primitive Technological Fear*, written not longing after derobing, when the clash between factless premodernity and factualised modernity was still ringing in my ears…

> *With a casual technological arrogance we dismiss*
> *animistic invocations of tree-gods and wind-gods,*
> *and faith in ghosts and talismans and omens and augury –*
> *as stone-age superstition.*
>
> *But which scientist has proven*
> *spirit is nonexistent, the future invisible,*
> *or that thought can't move the world?*

On the contrary, investigations into
near-death experiences, astral travel and mediumship
strongly suggest spirit exists –
experiments with precognition and telepathy
seem to reach beyond time and place –
and psychokinesis, hypnosis and levitation
have been popular mind-over-matter entertainment for years…
to name but a few phenomena
which contradict and confound popular pseudo-science.

Every school library History of Humankind
lectures all-knowingly on the cave dwellers
and their fear of the untamed elements.
But are we not –
despite our glamorous insulation of street lights,
and central heating, and water on tap –
as afraid to expose ourselves to existence
as ever we were?
Are we not fearful, defensive city dwellers –
clothed in space age superstition?

I am not debating or doubting the genius of technology –
but technology is not existential advancement,
or psychological maturity,
any more than a baby is a scholar
because it has a dictionary in its hand.

Unless we become confidently honest,
and thus comfortable in uncertainty,
will we not remain space age primitives –
hiding behind our fear –
suffering and struggling and blocked?

In this last fragment and the next I again argue against mainstream pseudo-science, the fundamentalist folkloric science that still underpins our era. With adolescent zeal, still wounded by dishonest premodern absolute certainty, I argue for honesty and openness. And this still seems necessary. Even though the cutting edge of science might have seen itself in the holistic mirror, and be in the process of re-visioning itself, and even though the cultural soul is certainly stirring, the mass of us are numbed and coping – at home in the consequences of the hard cold reality of fanatical, conventional pseudo-science…

'No', our leaders rebuke us,
'we have to get down to hard, cold realities!'

Our depersonalised faith in the elements
is the theology of a depersonalised universe –
a tidy, but dead universe of rocks and boulders and empty space.
Hard, cold reality.

The sick joke is
the pseudo-scientific tradition believes
all feeling to be chemical reaction, a biological function –
whether parent-child, male-female, or whatever...
and therefore, it preaches,
we should not be excessively (inefficiently) controlled by feeling –
not be weak-willed wishful thinkers,
not be unrealistic romantics –
we should give up our gods and ghosts and goblins –
we should give up our vague ideals and dreams and faiths...
and yet, these so-called scientists are,
themselves,
totally and irrationally,
passionately and dogmatically,
fear-bound and faith-bound
to their own theology
of unquestionable, hard, cold cosmic truth.

Science measures facts. Sometimes, around its measuring, it spins fantasies. Absolute faith in these fantasies-called-facts is what I call scientific fundamentalism. In these 'fragments' of mine I am arguing, again and again, for honesty and openness – not even really knowing, at the time, that these are the qualities which pave the way to holism. But they are absolutely crucial.

Being children of modernity, our conditioning is to await the voice of truth of the scientific priesthood, and to bow before its jargonised pronouncements. This is our collusion, and the perpetuation of the myth of absolutist pseudo-science. However: well informed as even an authentic scientist's views about her data might be, they are not the absolute truth. Firstly, they are the fantasy around the facts. Secondly, the facts themselves are shaped by the fact gatherer, and the fact gathering process. And thirdly, the scientist is only the priestess of the empirical – and not all of reality can be measured and weighed.

When we believed that only matter existed, then, naturally, the scientist, being the expert on matter, was the highest authority – on matter, and therefore on existence. But since sub-atomic physics has revealed that matter is not as material as we believed, and our matter-only cosmos is collapsing, then with it goes the authority of the scientist. If there is more to life than matter, then there is more to authority than science.

Just as modernity had to awake from the spell of religion, postmodernity has to awaken from the trance of fundamentalist science. Just as modernity recognised the limited awareness of the religious priesthood, postmodernity needs to recognise the limited knowledge of the scientific priesthood. Fundamentalist religion held premodernity in a blinkered split-up holiness – and with honesty and openness modernity broke free. The fundamentalist church of science holds modernity in its hard cold value-empty reality – and, again, we'll need to risk honesty and openness to break free.

And if we appreciate the degree to which our civilisation was once shaped by premodern religion, and the degree to which everything (everything, from the way our countryside looks, to the way I am arguing this point) has been re-shaped by modernism, informationism, scientism – then we can appreciate the degree to which a cultural shift into a holistic worldview would once again utterly transform our culture. The key is in deeply seeing the link between this fake populist pseudo-scientism and the pornographic culture (as I define it in Section One).

It's easy to see how our motorways and train lines and air routes and seaways have all bowed down to the logic god of modernity. It is even easy to see other people's tight little minds as having been shaped by modernism, but how tight are you and I?

(i)
Synchronicity is not an event.
Synchronicities do not happen.
What happens is our perception.
Synchronicity is constant.
What is occasional is our perception.
How occasional?
How factualised am I –
how linearised?
How optical is my sight?
Do I ever see through?
How often is my vision transparent?

(ii)
Miracles don't happen,
whether you believe in them or not.
What happens is that sometimes they're so outrageous
they blow through us,
they blow us away,
they blow us out.
There is only miracle.
But it's too constant, too intense,

too detailed, too holy,
too personal and too vast to take.
You need to be a strong vessel
not to shatter.
How shattered –
how blown away have I been?
How strong have I become
to be able to stay in the miracle?
How many times a day do I gasp?
Or is this the only statistic that doesn't count?

(iii)
I will tell you how to measure
how tight you are –
how tightly gripped by the facts –
I will tell you how to evaluate
how informationised your bones have become...

Picture this, my friend:
the god and goddess of birth and death are dancing – wildly,
and you notice it's on your grave.
A voice, sweet beyond all sweetness, softly suggests
'It is she who kills us all –
the fat-breasted goddess of our infancy
is also the skull-faced crone who stops time.'
Even though you are dead
their heels pound your chest.

Then again, the voice of sweetness speaks...
'And he whose essence is the semen you are grown of
only bore you to enjoy this moment of your death'.
And as their feet crush your stomach and your head,
you witness the beauty in their eyes.

How grateful are you?

To that degree
you are and are not
the gutted victim
of the experiment of science.

What I am suggesting in this dramatic piece is that you and I have internalised modernity – more than we might like to think. And it is hardly
surprising. After all, since we were in the womb, second by second year after
year, we have been fed on food grown without sacredness or ceremony, and on

ideas of no-meaning, efficiency and silly-fun. We have swallowed and imbibed modernity in a thousand million ways. And the unscientific proof is this: that day to day, minute to minute, digital second to digital second, almost always, almost forever, we are blind to the glory of time.

Finally, as a way of bridging this chapter on science with the next on religion, I would like to add a notebook fragment entitled *The Opposition Of Science And Religion...*

Science and religion haven't always conflicted. On the contrary, Newton was a Christian – and according to Saint Thomas Aquinas, God authored both the book of scripture and the book of nature. The Muslims constructed astronomical observatories, and discovered 'al-jabr', algebra. The Taoist *Yellow Emperor's Esoteric Classic*, expounded by a Celestial Master, is a medical book. And as the Burmese Buddhist U Thittila wrote: 'Dhamma is the law residing in the universe which makes matter act in the ways revealed by the studies of modern science in physics, chemistry, zoology, botany and astronomy.'

At first in the Christian West science was more open – doubting, discovering, inventing – but gradually it collected 'proofs', and gradually the proving of science began to contradict the proven of religion. Faced with an intractable, fundamentalist religious tradition, science gradually lost its innocence, its playfulness – gradually it slowed into utter certainty of itself – and utter certainty of the uncertainty of the religions. Free-flowing scientific discovering became the fundamentalist scientific tradition. Science and religion – not naturally polarised or antipathetic, but harmonious and sympathetic (being identical in essence) – were now both petrified with certainty, and became immovably opposed.

Science's childhood was a process of centuries: it was the rise of individualism – the swell of human dignity (the increase in respect for others due to increasing respect for ourselves) of the Renaissance, the Reformation, and the Enlightenment. But by the mid-nineteenth century, science had become a rebellious adolescent: impetuous, idealistic, harsh and intolerant. Thus the two traditions finally did battle – most brutally in the Judeo-Christian world (where fish and birds were created on the fifth day, and animals and humans on the sixth – not over aeons of molecular selection) and the scientific tradition overthrew the parental church, and the scientific age began.

One closed mentality overcame another. And yet – there was less 'believing as we've been told to believe', and more 'finding out for ourselves' – young science wasn't quite so closed. An adolescent scientific tradition – still pitifully insecure and over-confident – left home, and took office, leaving behind the safety of 'full faith and following', to rule a newly secular, mechanical world. Was this a victory? In a way, yes. In a way, the most urgent, the most fearless, the most penetrating within the religious traditions perpetuated itself in its prodigy – its only born son: the scientific tradition. In a way, the most eager, the most optimistic, the most visionary, left home to explore… Humanity without God's shelter: 'damn the consequences – the truth will set me free!' Even if, to reject its parent (to overcome its guilt) science had to brace itself (very well, too well) and don its own hard armour… still, it took a brave crusader to step out beneath a fixed, mechanical sky.

But if there was any victory for humanity, it wasn't that of science. If there was any victory, it was that of the element of openness science still allowed.

Science is not preferable to religion, nor religion preferable to science. But openness is preferable to closure. Science and religion are distinct-and-one – but they were divided and set in opposition by the irreligious, unscientific, closed, fundamentalistic attitude.

Perhaps it was a psychological necessity to gird ourselves with closed certainty in order to escape. But, like adults looking back at themselves in immaturity – especially now, after a century or so in the horrific earthly paradise of fundamentalist science – perhaps now we can admit that of the value of life science has told us no more (in fact, less) than religion, and confess that whatever innocence and openness we had we lost.

We rebelled against superstition, but we became as superstitious ourselves – we rebelled against cold-heartedness, but we became as cold-hearted ourselves. And perhaps now, at the beginning of the twenty-first century, as the vanguard of the scientific tradition takes off the old armour of over-certainty (allowing the return of humility, and mystery), and a broader ecumenical spirit weaves its way between and beyond the religious traditions – perhaps now, as the mass mind touches, for a moment, the possibility of adulthood, perhaps now, once again, science and religion can become diverse and complementary aspects of one unified project of truth.

I enjoy re-reading this piece. In a few, quick words it sketches the drama of our recent collective-psychological history. It tells of the rebirth of integrity – in terms of science being 'the only born son' of religion. It affirms our cultural puberty. We emerged from the premodern-religious worldview into the modern-scientific, and we gained independence, individual dignity, equality, human rights, freedom of expression, medical and technological expertise…

We became narrow and dogmatic (like father, like son), yes, but these gains have been crucial – not only in social and political terms, or even in terms of easing suffering or increasing life expectancy – but without this thunderous collective protestation of our self-worth we would never be able to say (to quote myself):

I am in Eden
as I never was,
even before the fall.
I am in Eden
as me.

Through science, if nothing else, we have expressed a faith in ourselves. Science has been the perfect voice of our adolescence. It has presided over the era of identity. Without it holism would not be possible. But there comes a time when men look at fathers they have rejected and rebelled against, and realise they look very alike. They recognise that, somewhere in their essence, they share a sameness. And if that's not too painful for these sons, they become friends with their fathers – and with their own fatherhood.

In this last 'fragment' I make distinctions both between an open religious attitude and a closed religious tradition, and between an open scientific attitude and a closed scientific tradition. I hint at an 'essence of attitude', both religious and scientific. That is the essence of father and son. And I would still agree that if we are to reclaim our losses, while holding on to our gains, this 'essence of attitude' will need to be our guide.

However qualified we might be, however politically informed, however scientifically equipped, or religiously attuned, or transpersonally psychologically aware – there is an attitude of receptivity to truth, which somehow allows the presence of grace, that we need to follow. It is this open attitude, beyond definition, that will lead us into a holistic postmodernity – if anything ever can.

But is there a way to maintain this attitude within a culture – to nurture it, to protect it? Or must institutionalism, whether religious or secular, inevitably lead to tightness, closure, fundamentalism? Can we develop postmodern community traditions in which religion is not split-up, and science not split-down? Can we keep that essence alive? Can we be determined to know, and at ease with not knowing? Or must that essence rigidify and die?

Ours is not the first era to have faced these questions. They are the ever-recurring questions of well-intentioned women and men. The whole of this book asserts a belief that holism is a truly adult philosophy, capable of holding us in openness even to paradox and contradiction – and that co-creativity (which we will be looking at in Section Three) is a mature social methodology for keeping essence alive. But how many of us actually live holistically and co-creatively? How many of us, in and of ourselves, despite the nonstop bombardment of informationism, are powerful enough? Not I. The question, then, is perhaps: how many of us would have a better chance if we were supported by communities woven of essence?

Holism, Community and Religion

As my adolescence-in-wholeness progressed, I asked myself if I was still religious. Being religious had meant being worthy – ultimately, eternally worthy, worthy in life's eyes, worthy in the eyes of spirit. Was I still religious? And if not, was I no longer worthy? And if I was worthy, but no longer able to reside in the house of religion, what did that imply about religion? Was religion unworthy?

This leads us into the 'fragments' that follow. But let's just pause to consider the implications of this issue of worth. I know that when my self-esteem is down I don't look after my body (the way I eat, the way I dress), I am lazy in my awareness and careless in my behaviour (wasting hours-even-days caught in babyish patterning), am prey to escapism and compensation, and near-emptied of the will to succeed. Because I believe I am unworthy, I set out to fail. And someone who feels constantly and completely unworthy feels it would be better if they just didn't exist.

What does this mean culturally? In premodernity we had access to a sense of self-worth – by being good, by being religious. In modernity there is no such access – because there is no eternal value. And eternal worthiness can only be felt in the presence of the eternal. Material success doesn't fool the soul. Nor does prestige of any sort. Even philanthropy won't work. And not only is there no way for the inhabitants of modernity to feel ultimate worthiness, but we have inherited the remnants of the premodern mindset. And this mindset insists that we are bad if we live for ourselves, for pleasure, (not for God) – that such people are bad in a bad world. We touched on this in Section One while discussing the silence, and ancestral shame, around masturbation. It makes the moderner feel that somehow she is bad, although she has no conscious idea why. But now she can find no redemption because ultimate worthiness can only be felt in prayer, ritual, creativity and meditation before ultimates – and modernity has emptied them all from the world.

And what does a culture do when it has no self-worth, when it feels its badness, and when it has no route to redemption? It exhibits writ large the symptoms of the self-worthless individual – it becomes self-destructive, even suicidal. Tell children they're worthless, see what happens. Tell children they full of worth, watch the opposite happen. Dr. Frankel's theories of the will to meaning, based on his studies of the Nazi concentration camps also bear this out. This suggests a collective-psychological and collective-spiritual explanation of the environmental crisis – an explanation, at least, if not of how we got into it, of why it's so hard to get out. An explanation that no amount of energy conservation or recycling or eco-planning will ever address.

The question becomes: how to realistically re-connect with eternal value, and thus with the possibility of real worthiness? Here is the dilemma I touch upon in the introduction to this book, when I introduce Section One, and I return to it in Section Three in pieces like Flexible Form: we want religion, but not traditional, dogmatic, hypocritical, split-up religion. As moderners we view religion with suspicion. But it is simply the cultural form we give to our spirituality. In and of itself it is simply a structuring. But because the structuring of the past has been so destructive we are loath to even consider the possibility of supportive structures that might support and empower us in our self-image and self-esteem.

I called this next fragment *Is this Religion? What is Religion?*

> (i)
> *In Arabia Islamic fundamentalism is on the march.*
> *In Israel, the revival of Jewish orthodoxy is gaining pace.*
> *In America Christianity is being loudly, euphorically reborn...*
> *Is this religion?*
>
> *People are running by the million*
> *into letter-of-the-law fundamentalism,*
> *into we're-right-you're-wrong sectarianism.*
> *It's a terrified, desperate flight*
> *from facing the facts, from facing ourselves,*
> *from individuality and responsibility.*
> *It's existential panic.*
> *Is this religion?*
>
> (ii)
> *Faith in the individual*
> *(as against authority)*
> *has been deepening since the middle ages.*
> *Fortified by the evidence of nineteenth-century science,*
> *it ravaged the Christian congregation,*
> *(and every congregation the Christians ravaged).*
>
> *People say:*
> *'No, the traditions aren't doing worse than before –*
> *look at all the revivals!'*
> *'Revival' says it all.*
> *There's nowhere near the same mass, medieval*
> *conviction, or enthusiasm, or devotion.*
>
> (iii)
> *And today,*
> *how can there be*
> *when my neighbour on my right is a Hindu,*
> *and my neighbour on my left is a Shintoist?*

It was easy before,
when one drank the blood of Christ and ate the Lord's flesh,
to be convinced of one's only-way –
when no one really knew anything about all those exotic pagans
with their barbarian rituals.

(iv)
Today faith in the individual is about the only faith left,
but the most individualistic societies are the most neurotic.
It's an age of chaos.
No wonder the revivals, the appeal of authority.
But is this religion?

(v)
What is religion?
Is it Hindu or Christian or Jew?
Is it one way and not another?
Is it institutional obedience,
or can one improvise one's own?
Must it harmonise with science,
or doesn't it matter?
To what extent are the revelations accessible,
to what extent overlain with dogma?
Hundreds of such questions make that medieval total dedication impossible –
except by a wild slinging away
of respect for one's neighbour,
and oneself.

What is religion?
Is religion motivated by panic,
or by the urge to truth?
Is religion a ready-made set of answers,
or an experiential enquiry?
Is religion a hiding place, or an exposure?
Is selfless obedience a prerequisite, or a disqualification?
What is religion?

I was on my way to an adult holism, and I clearly wasn't going back to the dangerous mind-locked lopsided truth of my path's childhood. But within modernity, was all religion premodern? What about those trends within the traditions which had sought compromise and adaptation? Of course, my concern was not with these more flexible trends, because they had not been my experience. But it was not only that...

I was also of the opinion that the fundamentalists were the truest members of their traditions. As I saw it, the essential paradigm of religion was of revelation and descent and obedience. Interpretation might evolve, to a degree, over the centuries, but only ever within the boundaries of the revelation – one could only bend it so far. The individual was subservient to the revelation. As soon as one began to speculate and pick-and-choose, one made the revelation subservient to the individual. And this was a paradigmatic shift into the energy field of modernity.

Different trends bent and speculated and shifted to different extents, but to the degree they moved into modernity – to that degree they lost themselves. To that degree they were no longer religious traditions in any meaningful sense of the term. They might be cultural packages, but not religions. They would be cultures influenced by a specific spiritual inheritance, but also influenced by the zeitgeists of whenever and wherever. And thus, inevitably, as time passed, and zeitgeist after zeitgeist left its trace, the traces of the original spiritual inheritance would disappear. To shift out of the premodern fundamentalist paradigm was, therefore, to slowly kill off one's religion.

Which is why I wrote *Openness Is Not A Religious Tradition…*

> *Openness isn't a religious tradition…*
> *It has no closed cosmology, no framed reality-picture –*
> *upon which, and only upon which,*
> *its followers must focus.*
> *It has no fixed destination, no dogma-defined end –*
> *towards which, and only towards which,*
> *its followers must aspire…*
> *It has no theology of the fall, no eschatology of rise or return –*
> *within which, and only within which,*
> *its followers must live and die…*
>
> *It has no prayer, no mantra, no silence –*
> *no ceremony, no liturgy,*
> *no holidays or holy days,*
> *no Friday, no Saturday, no Sunday,*
> *no beads, no wheels, no cross, no star,*
> *no hats, no robes,*
> *no way to sit, or kneel, or whirl,*
> *no bald-patch, no pony-tail,*
> *no holy diet, no holy tongue,*
> *no holy land, no holy waters,*
> *no holier than thous –*
> *no 'ours, ours, ours'.*
>
> *It has no beginning, no book,*
> *no founder, no prophet, no saviour,*
> *no rabbis, no gurus,*

no baptisms, no barmitzvahs –
it isn't monogamous, or polygamous, or celibate –
it doesn't bury, or burn, or feed to the birds –
it has no this-is-the-way-it-has-to-be-done,
and no this-is-the-way-it-has-not –
it has no us and no them –
nothing to follow, no one to obey...
no hideaway, no false escape.

No, openness isn't a religious tradition.

It has no crafty wink, no quick handshake –
no unspoken accord:
'if you pretend you believe I'm certain,
I'll pretend I believe you're certain'.
No 'nobody whisper a word'.

No, openness isn't another tradition.

Freedom! I'd run away from home, and in my own eyes I was still religious. I was worthy – not in a Hindu, Christian or Jewish God's eyes, but in my own God's eyes. I was good. But I was anti-religion. Religion was fanatical and deceitful and closed. Religion was bad.

How has my outlook matured? I would no longer define religion, if it is to be distinguished from a philosophical or psychological or spiritual system, as fundamentalism. I would say that would probably suffice as a definition of premodern religion, but not of religion itself. I would now say that post-modern, evolving, democratic structures can just as validly house religion as the authoritarian structures of the past.

And I can now honour the fear of existence that prompts us to set up closed realities, closed social systems, and to close off. Not only is the world out there full of threat, but powerful urges and impulses constantly bombard us from within. Furthermore, the seemingly sweet promise of spirituality, when we actually taste it, can feel like death, and dissolution. (Which is why a sturdy ego is needed if we are to fully open up. Which, culturally, is another reason why we need to pass through this egocentric modern era, if we are ever to stand together in holism.)

And lastly, rather than point out how traditional religion is essentially closed and fundamentalistic, and dismiss its more open adherents as false religionists, I would now validate the more open trends within the religions – and ask how they might be developed within the framework of their particular inheritances.

There are obvious obstacles on the open road to holism for anyone who stays within a religious inheritance. But there are also advantages. The main advantage is the community cohesion and continuity – the patterns of being and doing, of work and prayer, of grieving and celebrating passed down through the generations. For those of us who find ourselves without a religious tradition, there are no such comforts.

The difficulty on the inside of religion for somebody who's opening up is that the patterns which preserve traditional religion are separatist, elitist, dogmatic and split-up. These tendencies will need to be re-interpreted, even interpreted-out. And, of course, there will be resistance to this because people will fear that eventually there will be nothing left. 'Eventually,' they will object 'our religion will be indistinguishable from any other. It won't even be 'religion', in any traditional sense.' (My old stance.) But if we see religion as the social structuring of our spiritualities, then rigid, literalist structures are not inherently superior to more flexible, interpretive structures. And perhaps, if this process is managed responsibly and consciously enough, distinctive communities will emerge – Christian Holists, Jewish Holists – each with their own particular holistic patterns to pass on to their descendants.

Thus some people will remain regressed in fundamentalism, others will choose the liberal trends of the religions – considering that the payoff of community tradition validates the struggle with narrow-mindedness (and that, inevitably, long-term, the tradition must open up), and others, like myself, will feel the self-betrayal too great, and unable to compromise with the remnants of split-up, patriarchal religion (or unable to tolerate the necessarily slow pace of change), will find themselves without given patterns for their minds or their days or their friendships or their children.

However, I believe there are ways (and this is the where the whole of this book is going), for religion-less, community-less travellers-into-wholeness to weave themselves together, and to weave living traditions around themselves. It's just that it's an unavoidably slow, trans-generational project. How we might begin is the subject matter of the third section of this book.

One line that stands out, for me, in the last fragment is 'nothing to follow'. I assert this proudly, in true adolescent fashion: openness is great because no one can tell you what to do! But this is also the sadness and the lack of pure openness. And this is where holism goes further. Holism does have a 'reality picture', although it isn't 'framed'; it does have a 'fixed destination', although it isn't 'dogma defined'; and it might not have 'prophets or saviours', but it does have teachers – 'rabbis and gurus'…

The rebellion against boundaries of adolescence has a purpose. But having broken free of our fundamentalist premodern home, we can't wander in openness forever. We need to build a postmodern value-full home. A holistic home. And holism means inclusivity. Authority has its place too. The question is not how to do without it, but how to integrate it, and keep it in relationship with all of our other needs.

We need a holistic worldview – without unity of vision there is no psychic community. And we need holistic social forms – from holistic birthing to holistic dying. Without them there's no community-weave, either among us now or through the generations. We can't stay teenagers forever. We need to find our adulthood. We need to find authority – not by association with somebody else's one descending truth, but through personal connection, each of us, with our own. Not a pompous absolute authority, but an adult authority that can hear and hold, that can hear life's pulse, that can hear life's pulse inside everyone – and that can parent and care for and forgive and say 'no'. We need this kind of authority if we are to build holistic community and re-house eternal value – and offer ourselves the opportunity to experience our own eternal worth.

One final fragment. I called it *What Does It Mean To Be Religious?* It might have been better entitled *What Does It Mean To Be Spiritual?* Because as I said above, religion is a question of structuring. And given the disillusion and individualism in the collective psyche, today it is an extremely difficult question. Structures need agreements, from the philosophical (sphere 1) to the political (sphere 4), and agreements need structures to uphold them (whether harshly or humbly). Whereas spirituality can remain purely individualistic, religion is about community. It is about how we structure and maintain and apply a shared spirituality, and the relationship of that spirituality to individual variations and differences. It is about the dance and the pitfalls of independence, interdependence and dependence.

When I wrote this last fragment I knew I was now on my own. I was without a religion. But I had a path. I had my openness. And I could define my religiousness by it. I didn't yet have any structures around me, I didn't yet have any community, but I had the beginnings of redemption and self-esteem…

(i)
Is a person religious because he or she feels linked
with one or other congregation, or with one or other scripture?
Must one have a scripture to be religious?
Can one be religious and not believe in God,
or in any Absolute?
What does it mean to be religious?

Normally the question 'Are you religious?'
is answered in terms of appertaining,
or not appertaining, to a particular tradition:
'No, I hardly ever go to Church. Once a year, maybe, at Christmas.
No, I wouldn't say I was a very religious person.'
To the degree people feel linked with a particular tradition
they consider themselves religious, and vice versa.
But is this true?

Are we religious to the degree we identify
with a particular revelation?
Is this the criterion? Or are we religious
to the degree we're dedicated to the discovery of truth –
and to the degree we're cultivating the attitude of discovery?

If this is the case, the question 'Are you a religious person?'
might be answered, for example:
'Well, look, I try – I make an effort to listen to life,
to re-evaluate myself, I try to open and to evolve –
but I must say I know a lot of braver people than me.
No, I wouldn't say I was a very religious person.'

(ii)
If to be religious is to be developing openness,
one doesn't have to be baptised, or circumcised,
or initiated, or swear any vow of allegiance,
to be religious.
The appropriate attitude –
vulnerable and empathic, courageous and authentic –
is the only criterion.
And therefore,
religion exists within and without the traditions.

Religion becomes a question of consciousness,
not of faithfulness of affiliation to Temple, Church or Mosque,
or of strictness of adherence to any predetermined doctrine.
Attitude is the only criterion.
The theist, the monist, the polytheist, the agnostic, the atheist,
the theologyless, the confused –
no one is by virtue of their belief system,
or lack of one,
any more religious than anyone else.

I was affirming my own eternal value – regardless of parental opinion. So necessary. An excellent first step. Then comes the personal management of openness: the art of holism. Then comes the social management of openness: the development of a holistic culture. And to do this we need contexts, within all the spheres. This is why Ken Wilber is establishing a holistic postmodern intellectual context. This is why Roberto Assagioli and those who continue his work are putting a holistic postmodern psycho-spiritual context in place. This is why those who have furthered and advanced the work of Fritz Schumacher are pioneering a holistic postmodern economic context. And this is why I am participating in preparing the holistic postmodern community context.

But I would like to end this discussion on the relationship between holism and religion by looking at it against the backdrop of some encounters I have recently had with the religious tradition I was born into, the Jewish tradition. These encounters were with the modernist end of the Jewish religious spectrum. The further one goes along that spectrum towards the traditionalist extreme, of course, the further one falls into the frightening pit of the blindness and fanaticism of premodern piety.

I was invited to attended a Jewish New Year (Rosh Hashanah) service in Totnes, in a rented room at the Quaker Meeting House. There were about twenty-five of us. The part that touched me the most was when we were asked to introduce ourselves. Most of us had had little or no contact with Judaism for many years, and there was a special feeling, a feeling of homecoming, being among Jews again. It was very emotional. Odd, unexpected thoughts entered my mind... Was this my true home? Had my journey into wholeness now brought me full circle back to my roots? Would truth to myself mean I'd soon be engaged in Jewish ritual? What would it mean to have a non-Jewish wife?

But I didn't feel nourished by the prayers... *the people of Israel, God's people, the chosen people*... The sweet feeling of belonging clashed with an uncomfortable sense of tribalism. The Chosen People? What rubbish! And, of course, spirit was personified as a solitary, supreme sky-male. It was the usual split-up patriarchal formula. The usual humiliation of woman. Eva, my beloved ten-year-old stepdaughter – who'd come in innocence and eagerness to experience her stepfather's heritage – whispered and muttered her discontent.

Later that week I went up to London because my father had gone into hospital. My mother picked me up at the station and we drove back to their house. We talked about my sister, Jo... Her husband, Manú, isn't Jewish, and Jo was pregnant with their third child. Eli and Amber Lua, their first two, were girls. 'But if this child is a boy,' my mother told me, 'and they don't get him circumcised,' (which they wouldn't), 'your father won't want to know him.' (My father is the holder of the 'jewishness' for my parents' relationship.)

On that visit, once again, feelings clashed. On the one hand there was the tenderness of seeing my father so thin-skinned and vulnerable in his hospital bed. On the other, I shuddered with images of the mutilation of baby boys, with the irony of the bigotry of this man who'd risked his life to defeat the Nazis, and with all of the family upset there would be if Jo's baby was born a boy.

Where does all of this leave me? Torn... I want to be part-of, I want to share a universal vision, I want familiar prayers and ways of praying, I want festivals and rites of passage and moral codes we all know, codes which have come to us through the generations. I want community. I want it desperately – but not if the price is my truth.

I can imagine the Jewish tradition, or any religious tradition, as a light shining down through time. And can I imagine the well-meaning elders of each generation keeping that light alive – and passing it on, and on, and on… And I ask myself: 'Can I stand in this light and be myself? Do I accept these ancestors as my guides? Do I respect this guiding community light enough to surrender to it? I long to let my hyper-individualism drop away, to accept and be accepted – I ache for that rebirth… is this the place?'

And this question is particularly poignant for me because, for several years now, I have been experimenting in establishing community structures. I've been convening men's and women's initiation groups and partnership groups, and facilitating community ceremonies and celebrations, and in all sorts of ways attempting to weave just the kind of community Judaism already has.

It's as if, wanting community so much, but unable to surrender to Judaism, I have set about creating my own. But the warmth and loss I felt at Rosh Hashanah seem to tell me I haven't been able to, at least not yet…

Ten days after Rosh Hashanah there's another major Jewish holy day – Yom Kippur, the day of atonement. Once again, I went to the Quaker Meeting House, where local Jews were having a day of prayer, meditation and discussion. Again there was a special feeling. I took part in a discussion about being the chosen people. The life of everyone there, it seemed, had been touched, and wounded, by this issue. 'Chosaholics Anonymous', I thought. I felt safe and at ease. Most of us seemed to struggle with the idea. There were suggestions like: 'We were chosen not because we're superior, but because we have special responsibility,' and 'The rabbis tell a story of how God asked all of the nations of the world to be His people, but that only the people of Israel accepted – thus they chose to be God's (as against having being chosen)'. All of this, to me, to be blunt, sounded like a lot of convoluted nonsense. To me, it was the typical ethnocentric elitism that characterises most, if not all, premodern cultures.

…and I imagine the elders of each generation keeping that light alive – and passing it on, and on, and on… And I ask myself: do I accept these ancestors as my guides?… And my answer is: no. Both angrily and sadly – no. I will not align myself with a community tradition which has always considered itself somehow suprahumanly chosen – whether to teach, or to suffer. In my holy book there is no such thing as racial intimacy with the ultimate truth. No one tribe has spirit's ear. In my scriptures every race and no race, and every individual and no individual, has a special relationship with Truth, or God, or the Goddess. I would love to stand as a Jew among Jews and feel comfortably at home. I would even love to feel I was one of the chosen people – one of God's own! But I would feel like a liar among liars. And whatever everyone else's perspective or journey – I will not collude. I will not bow down to what, for me, is a lie.

And so where, once again, does all of this leave me? Where does this leave me – and the millions of others who have been unable to surrender to a traditional religious culture, but who also want to belong and to live with their families in stable, supportive, sacred and soulful communities?

I cannot stand in the light of my Jewish ancestors because I don't believe, as they did, that the five books of Moses are the pure word of spirit, the fairly pure word of spirit, or even the impure word of spirit. I believe they are the word of Moses. I don't believe, for example, that spirit demands we kill homosexuals (Leviticus 20.13) – I believe Moses was a culturally-conditioned homophobe. And I will not live out my life in the narrow beam of sky-light descending from Moses, passed down by male rabbis, as if it was the absolute (or even relatively-absolute) truth. I believe it is a primitive, tribal, split-up, patriarchal truth. Where does this leave me? On the outside… without ancestral line, without community patterns – without any given design for my life.

I respect those Jews who believe, like me, that the full path is into wholeness, but who have stayed on the inside. Perhaps their task is to bring uncertainty to the certainty, and certainty to the uncertainty; to broaden the scope of the descending light, and to incorporate the wisdom of sexuality and shadow. May they and their families enjoy the warmth of traditional community, and may they lead the tradition into maturity. Similarly, I extend my well-wishing to those travellers into wholeness who have chosen to remain within other traditions. I feel a bond with them all – despite the differences in our destinies.

My choice is to sacrifice the warmth and belonging of tradition and descended truth – rather than work to reform it. Rather than working to ground a narrow, obedience-oriented community tradition, I am working to establish a community tradition which is holistic from the start.

In outline, I want to be part of a community tradition that is:

(1) holistic (as adoring of the earth as of heaven, of sex as much as of spirit)
(2) not based on one revelation, but on shared perceptions and perspectives, and
(3) flexible and 'human scale' (in which power is not centralised, but resides locally)

This might sound contrived, artificial, human-made – a kind of D.I.Y. approach to religion. We are used to power descending from great sacred revelations. This sounds almost industrial. How, we object, can we cold-bloodedly manufacture community – and then expect it to sustain us on our mystery-laden journeys into wholeness?

Personally, I have no doubt that we can weave our own, local, vibrant, holistic community traditions. Nor do I doubt they can be value-laden, nourishing and elevating. In the few years I've been engaged with Balance I've seen meaningful community begin to cohere – somewhat experimentally, somewhat nervously, somewhat chaotically – but begin to cohere nonetheless.

And a few years is a few years, and the Jewish tradition is thousands of years old. No wonder I feel a special warmth and bondedness on returning to the

Jewish camp. As a baby I was circumcised, weekly throughout my childhood I witnessed the lighting of the Sabbath candles, as a teenager I was barmitzved and taught about the persecutions. As was my father. As was my father's father. As was my father's father's father... How could I possibly expect to feel anything similar from a three-year old community experiment struggling amidst the psychic confusion of the end of the modern age?

I should imagine it will take at least three or four generations until people feel an even vaguely comparable sense of unity. I should imagine it will take at least that long for those feelings to enter the family blood. And thus, to use a Jewish metaphor – we who choose to weave holistic community for our descendants will never enter the promised land. We will never feel the holistic community tradition in the way that our great-grandchildren will. We will never feel the depth of belonging, or of being held, or of common purpose that they will feel. Not, that is, if we have woven well.

There is no easy community option. Modernity has seen the disintegration of local community, of the extended family, and now even of the nuclear family. The only options are to reform the premodern, or to pioneer the post-modern. The insider-reformer option offers warmth, but is overrun with compromise and confusion. Traditional religion lacks a powerful affirmation of the sexual-spiritual holistic state. It lacks a clear holistic psychotherapeutic map to get there. And its power structures are inappropriately top-down. Change from the inside needs to acknowledge this. It is all very well to reform, but that reform needs a guiding principle. Insider-reformers, I believe, need to find their consensus as holistic congregations. This is an immense challenge.

Meanwhile, for the outsider-pioneers, the lack is of stability, of roots, of age-old community patterns, of familiar festivals... As we continue to weave here, in the Totnes area, and others begin their own projects in their own areas, the challenge is different but equally immense. The challenge is of vision and deter-mination and patience. Community structures need to be woven and held in place with strength and openness. It is a long-term task. And in as much as it is an offering to the generations to come, it is a selfless task. But since most of our culture already lives outside the religious traditions, the outsider-pioneers are perhaps preparing the postmodern community option for the majority.

And as I am writing this, the phone rings. It is an Israeli woman who attended the Rosh Hashanah and Yom Kippur ceremonies. She's holding a clay menorah-making afternoon at her home. The menorah is the seven-fingered candlestick holder of the Jewish Chanukah (also known as Christmas – the Winter Solstice). Yes, I tell her, I'd love to make a menorah. I'd love to mould my own ritual fire-object to light my meditations while the sun hours are few... 'Am I moving inside,' I wonder, as I put the phone down, 'despite myself? Despite my hard-line holistic stand – am I becoming a soft-line holistic insider? Or perhaps it's not an either-or... Perhaps I can be both.'

Holism, Community and Politics:
Notes on Holistic Democracy

As we envision a holistic civilisation, several spheres of concern begin to crystallise: the existential sphere (belief in holism), the personal sphere (holistic physico-psycho-spirituality), the communal sphere (community ritual, the interpersonal sphere), and the practical sphere (the physical realm, organisation, survival). In these first two sections I have been mainly discussing spheres one and two, the philosophical and the personal-developmental – in order to create a foundation for the discussion in Section Three, in which I will be looking at the practicalities of setting about developing holistic community in our local areas.

In Section Three, as well as looking at lessons learnt within the Balance project, and outlining basic Balance maps and methods, I will be discussing sphere three, the community-bonding sphere of social structures. Although the four sphere model and the community forum lead to a re-evaluation of the current dominance of the fourth sphere, and to a re-visioning of our current hard cold approach to the fourth sphere, I will not be addressing the contents of the fourth sphere directly. I will not be recommending any housing or employment policies, or even making any suggestions about transport or trade. Many people have already given much thought to such matters, and I believe there is already enough material for local community development projects to draw upon in order to make informed choices within their own areas. However, I want to end Section Two with some general reflections on the practical sphere of organisation and action, and on the relationship between holism and politics.

I have seen many holistic sphere four projects come and go locally – environmental projects, citizens' action projects, community alternative-economic projects – more and less successfully. But because sphere three is not in place, because these projects are not embedded in a local human infrastructure, because people are not joined (via sphere three) to a shared psychological experience (sphere two), or a common existential context (sphere one), in terms of community development they leave little trace – the participants fall back into their slots as separated individuals.

However, dictatorships have been overthrown without the presence of stable, coherent deep community. We can't wait for paradise to act. Nevertheless, if political action is to be imbued with the qualities and ethics of a new holistic culture (and not only invoke them in its rhetoric), then it calls for groups of people who know each other – not only as members of a cause, but personally. And not only personally, but transpersonally. Protesters cannot only be 'against'. Social activists need to have experienced a social alternative.

Communities who have stood together in sacred space, who have grieved together and celebrated together, who have seen each other through and through – such communities could engage in truly holistic, truly alternative politics.

I am not trying to establish some sort of rule. I am not saying that the first three spheres of community must be in place for political action to be worthwhile. Not at all. What I am saying is that I have seen the lack of the interpersonal sphere (sphere three), I have seen a proliferation of wonderful, one-off, unlinked holistic political initiatives (sphere four), and I have seen an ever-expanding involvement with existential questions and personal growth-work (spheres one and two), but, because the spheres are unconnected, the personal remains personal and the political remains political. And impersonal, inhuman politics is a dangerous affair. And the humanisation of politics could be achieved by attending to and interweaving the four spheres of community.

Meanwhile, progress can be made simultaneously in all spheres. Particular emphasis, I believe, needs to be put upon the interconnecting of the spheres, and on the development of the third sphere of collective-developmental structures. And although I believe that we were not ripe until now, I also believe that the lack of attention given to this third sphere explains our inability, so far, to weave coherent, consciously holistic community. This sphere, the sphere previously the responsibility of the religious institutions, has collapsed – leaving a hole at the core of our civilisation. We are left either overly private or overly public.

And any public policy, whether concerning education, treatment of the elderly, recycling, food production, or multinationalism, is packed with the personal – with deeply felt emotional, psychological and spiritual issues. These need to be acknowledged. Policy is not a statistical calculation. It is always and everywhere an ethical and existential decision. It is always a statement before truth – whether we rush it through, or meditate on it with heart.

In Section Three I will be discussing the community forum as a practical first step in establishing deep community – community in which the personal and the public are merged. The community forum is intended as a focalising community 'institution' – a regular open meeting at which local people can discuss and debate, and also weep and rage if they need to – places at which all the dimensions of our being are allowed, welcomed, embraced. But what I am stressing here is that we need to weave the community web, to knit together the threads of our holistic birth and death rites, and our long journeys of preparation for holistic initiation and partnership – so that as we file together into the public meeting place we already know each other, and we are already practised in honesty and openness, in standing in the unknown, and in being seen.

But what might we mean by a 'holistic politics'? I see it as the completion, the fulfilment, of democracy.

Democracy is the starting point because it is already respectful of the individual, and inclusive – as against totalitarianism, monarchism, oligarchy, or any minority rule (whether in the name of communism, or disguised as democracy). In theory, democracy heeds the words of the people. It is a philosophy of creativity and empowerment.

Unfortunately, like any other political process, democracy can be hijacked and manipulated. If any set of images of an ideal world is inculcated for long enough into the mass mind, then politicians who promise to make that imagery real will win the voting. We tend to think in terms of the democratic process being manipulated at elections, or by corruption, but the democratic process has been hijacked, and is manipulated continuously, day to day, by both those leaders and those among the led who desperately strive to perpetuate a modernist 'flatland': that one-dimensional, single-surface reality in which the soul weeps, and the body is safe but stuck. It is that place where relief, distraction, busyness and numbness are sold in endless variety. It is the porno-scientific version of life – and the political process as we know it is almost entirely in its hands. We suffer the politics of flatland. We live in a flatland democracy.

It is very difficult, however, to convince a flatlanded-mind that it has been flatlanded. The world vision with which it has been bombarded – via education, advertising, entertainment, journalism, political propaganda, etc. – has become internalised. The mind that has been converted to flatland now goes about flatlanding others – convinced that it acts of its own free will.

Nevertheless, it is obvious to anyone who has had the good fortune to live in relative media exile, or to live in relative harmony with the seasons, or to travel outside of this culture (and then return to it and see it afresh), or to have ever touched anything other than the most superficial levels of their own being – that our entire democratic society has been captured by a self-destructive materialistic mindset.

This is my point then: that there is no such thing as neutral democracy. Neutral democracy is a misleading myth. We live in a split-off, split-down, flatland materialistic democracy. Holistic democracy, on the other hand, implies the acknowledgment and inclusion of all parts of ourselves. It is not opposed to comfort or luxury, but because it also values our existential needs, our personal-developmental needs, our relationship needs and our community needs, the pursuit of comfort is not its be all and end all. Not only this, but holistic democracy can pursue comfort without being obsessive – it is not consumed by consumption, like materialistic democracy – because it is not in denial, and compensating for all of its unmet needs on other levels. Holistic democracy includes materialistic democracy. It doesn't negate it. It melts it, by making it whole.

Democracy is not enough. It is only a vehicle. It is the vehicle of beliefs. And there are no voids. There is certainly no moral vacuum. A democracy will perpetuate one set of beliefs or another. Alongside our choice of political method, therefore, we need to choose the beliefs we want perpetuated.

All of this might be called the qualitative subversion of the democratic process. But if we wish to develop holistic democracy, grounded in local community, then we also need to consider the quantitative subversion of democracy. The quantitative subverter of democracy is central government, or centralisation. If, that is, democracy means participation by the people, by the community, in its own organisation and governance.

With the rise of bureaucratisation and massification the individual feels increasingly alienated and disempowered – not only in relation to national policies, but more importantly, in relation to her own community, to the land she lives upon, and to the rules that control her everyday life. This isn't democracy. This is fake democracy. It might look like democracy, it might even function according to the laws of democracy, but if people aren't being empowered to shape their own, local destinies then something else is going on – in the name of democracy. Democracy means inclusion, not alienation. And if the leaders of our society have its welfare at heart – as many of them do – then they need to give back the power of decision to local communities. Just see how quickly people will become re-engaged!

If, then, holistic participatory democracy is the destination, what might be our guiding principles, right now? I want to name three: authentic communication, the love of the land, and decentralisation. What do these imply?

Authentic communication, ultimately, can only be fully present between two people in the moment they fully acknowledge their equality, their oneness, their eternality, and their frailty. Ultimately, authentic communication is the language of those who are familiar with the intricate habits of the mind, who have befriended the neuroses of the heart, and who experience the miracle in the everyday. I don't mean to set this as the standard of community political dialogue. I do mean that, to start with, open, empathic listening, and 'owning', non-blaming speech need to be taught and practised if varying needs are to be heard and respected, and balanced policies pursued. This means emotional, psychological and (non-sectarian) spiritual education. At all levels. We need emotionally, psychologically and spiritually literate politicians, and we need to educate our children in all aspects of their being too. We can't hope for a holistic politics unless we have holistic politicians. And we can't hope to elect holistic politicians unless we ourselves are a holistic public. So holistic education is a priority. And we need to apply it: to whatever degree possible, we need to be restructuring the procedures within our schools, offices, factories and town halls in order to make room for authentic communication.

Secondly, love of the land. And of the air, the water, the fire and the ether. Ecological and environmental sensitivity. Of course. We are killing the earth, of which we are a part. What could be more insane than our blasé mass suicide? This is obvious even on the most materialistic level. Here I want to add another point; I want to suggest that in order for us to heal our relationship with the earth we need to plant food and trees and flowers. What I am saying is that not only does the earth need our love, but that we need our love of it – that, in fact, our wholeness depends on it. And I don't believe love of the land can grow in concrete. One comes to love the earth by living with it, by touching it in all of its seasons' moods. How can there be love without relationship? Holistic community must mean holistic people, and holistic people have spirits that fly, but they also have fingers that touch mud. A holistic politics, therefore, must include a return to the land. Not a return to the exclusion of technology, or of comfort, or of elegance or sophistication. But a return in order to include, to complete. We need to reconnect. For the earth's sake, and for our own.

Thirdly, decentralisation. I do not mean that communities should be introverted and self-serving. I do mean that our present total reliance for resources on a transnational technological and commercial superstructure leaves us in a fragile and depressed state of dependence, vulnerability and disempowerment. We don't know how to grow our own food, how to design or sew our own clothes, how to hammer out our pots and pans – we don't even know how to make a needle. By decentralisation then, I mean not only a hugely increased reliance on local community decision-making, but also the development of local agricultural and commercial self-reliance, and the cultivation of local crafts.

I believe fervently (and also quite casually, because to me they seem like common sense) in these three guiding principles. They can, of course, be formulated more comprehensively, and have been by various commentators. And on closer examination we might decide on four, or five. What is important is the flavour of interconnectedness and inclusivity – of depth, of wholeness, of embeddedness. And what is also important is an ability to hold the creative tension between crisis and immediacy, on the one hand, and, on the other, the fact that we are discussing a process that could take centuries.

One more essential point, before including some 'fragments' from my earlier political reflections: that not only does holistic democracy need to be rooted in the sacred structures and ceremonies of community, but that community needs to be politically aware and active – for its own sake, for its own completion. Holistic politics needs community, but holistic community also needs politics. In order to be truly holistic, and not to fall back into the trap of split-up spirituality and self-absorption, holistic community needs to take on the hard facts and confrontations of politics with the same commitment that it enters its sacred spaces. Political engagement must become the completion of its worship. Holism is a philosophy of engagement, it is a psychology of involvement, and, ultimately, a spirituality that declares that every act is an opportunity to make love with the world. Holistic philosophy (sphere one), holistic self-development (sphere two), and holistic communal structures (sphere three) all find their fulfilment in the practical sphere (sphere four), the sphere of matter, of manifestation, of organisation and survival.

I call this fragment *How Could It Be Otherwise?* It asks 'Is holism about personal belief, and personal development, or is it also political?' And it responds with a historical perspective on the relationship between belief and action...

> In the early centuries of the Diaspora – the dispersion of the Jews – after the destruction of the Second Temple in Jerusalem, there were two main parties in the Sanhedrin, the Jewish Houses of Parliament: Rabbi Shemmai was the leader of one wing, inclined to a more literal, more conventional interpretation of the constitution, and Rabbi Hillel was the leader of the other wing, tending to a broader, more flexible policy. And the constitution was, of course, the Torah, extended and amended in the Mishna and Talmud. There was a total inter-penetration of the word of God and the word of Parliament. There was oneness of Synagogue and State.
>
> Until Henry the Eighth established the independent Anglican Church, England was ruled by God through Rome. And even after breaking away the monarch remained a God on Earth – possessed of the Divine Right of Kings. God ruled the universe, and His ambassador ruled here on earth, on His behalf, according to His will – as expounded (or at least transparently implied) in the holy books, the books of the immutable law.
>
> Similarly, the Ramayana and Mahabharata portray a oneness of Temple and State in ancient India – a society ordered according to laws descended from the gods. Here the 'ksatriyas', the noble monarchs and knights, were subservient to parliaments of 'brahmans', their poverty-bound priests and mentors. Here was a culture controlled from above: the 'brahmans' lived in heavenly piety, the 'ksatriyas' enforced their wisdom, and the 'vaisyas', the traders and farmers, and the 'shudras', the menial workers, obeyed. Thus the law of the Absolute was the law of the land... as in the days of the Sanhedrin, in the days of the Divine Christian Kings, and in the days of the Islamic Caliphs, those 'Commanders of the Faithful'.
>
> But how could it be otherwise? How could a society that really believed that God, or the Absolute, had spoken, not govern itself according to that divine message – not organise itself in line with the perfect precepts of those heaven-sent words? If it didn't, we would be forced to doubt whether that society genuinely believed in the divinity of its word, its covenant.
>
> It isn't that Church and State, religion and politics, are inherently separate – the one concerned with terrestrial matters, the other with the

life to come. On the contrary, every tradition agrees and insists its influ-ence should permeate all levels of existence – the personal, the familial, the local-social, the larger-social (the national and international), and the universal, the existential.

This leads us to the hypothesis that the degree of unity or separation of a society's religion and politics is proportionate to its faith or lack of faith in its religious revelation. The more faithful a society, the closer its religion and politics – the less faithful, the further apart.

The reason our world-dominant culture is separated from its religious revelation is that it converted to the pseudo-scientific faith. But the oneness of religion/world-view and politics remains. Throughout modernity there has been a oneness of the church of mechanistic pseudo-science and the mechanical state. There has been a secular onen-ness of religion and politics, of belief and action – how could it be otherwise? Whether individually or collectively, how can what we do not mirror what we believe we are?

Is holism about personal belief, and personal development, or is it also political?' Whether premodern oneness of religion and politics, modern oneness of science and politics, or a potential postmodern oneness of holistic belief and action – there is always oneness... But the more split-up we are, the more likely we are to minimise action, and the more split-down we are, the more likely we are to minimise belief. However, the more holistic we are, the more difficult it is to minimise or deny either being or doing, either inner or outer, either belief or action. There can only be unity of worldview (whether secular or sacred) and politics – and, by definition, holistic community is its most complete expression.

Sociologists talk of the modern 'privatisation of religion', by which they mean that the ideology of the public arena has become secular and functional, with anything other-worldly or inner-worldly marginalised as 'a private concern'. Masquerading as beliefless, split-down fundamentalist pseudo-science has dominated the public affairs of modernity. But it's easy to split off that which is split-up: while religion is predominantly concerned with the other world, and therapy mainly with the inner world, they present no challenge to modernism's domination of the world around us.

Holism, however, is a challenge. Holism must, by definition, bring 'the inner' out into the market place, and 'the up' down to earth. Holism recognises and respects the push-pull, and the complementary value, of polarities. And one such set of polarities is 'the inner-and-other worldly' versus 'the world around us'. Our relationship with the inner-and-otherly is vital, and so is our relationship with the world around us. These two needs are in constant dynamic flux. And sometimes they become one. But polarities are inseparable. They are the extremes of a single continuum. When one is denied the other suffers. The premodern denial of the world around us resulted in a patho-logical inner-otherliness, and the modern denial of the inner-otherly has resulted in a pathological this-worldliness. But holism, because it will not split inner or other or outer, because it respects their connectedness, cannot be content to be privatised. It must involve itself in the public, political arena.

Another set of polarities sits on the individuality/collectivity axis. Our individuality has value, and so does our collectivity. The premodern denial of individuality resulted in a pathological collectivism, and the modern denial of collectivity has resulted in a pathological individualism. Holism includes a respect for the relationship between our need to be separate and our need to be together – it recognises that we are both whole-in-ourselves and part-of-the-body-politic. Thus, again, holism must intrude upon the public, political arena.

Holism carries the collective impulse into the separatist social status quo. Simultaneously, it implies an unprecedented individualism: the arrival of the whole individual, with his full depths and his full heights, upon modernity's surface land of one-dimensional politics, economics and social organisation.

Today many people are working inside the political traditions – to reform, to make whole, to bring spirit and soul to existing political decision making. Others are creating new alliances – trusts and foundations, co-operatives and environmental schemes – consciously nurturing a holistic ethos, and consciously pursuing holistic policies and aims. Others participate by choosing to buy locally grown organic vegetables rather than (usually cheaper) chemi-cally fertilised and sprayed vegetables shipped from the other side of the world. Others watch from the sidelines, feeling guilty with their ambiguity, but basi-cally sympathetic to local community development. But whether we are pushing forwards inside or outside the existing political traditions, or neither, or both – those of us who favour an interconnected, holistic approach, who would prefer a humanised politics embedded in communal life, and who would therefore back radical quantitative and qualitative reform of contem-porary democracy, whether we have previously framed our stance in such terms or not, actually carry a postmodern vision of oneness of action and belief: the vision of holistic community.

Here's another fragment from my earlier political thinking, called *The Political Traditions*…

'Once the religious traditions ruled – both administering to the soul, and governing the body. They ruled beneath their banners of absolutes – dishonest and proud, loveless and cruel – people so afraid they were no longer themselves… But are not today's secular systems sick with the same psychology – the same superficial, vicious immaturity, the same closed indifference, the same unconcern with truth?

Throughout the twentieth century the right and left wings have bick-ered, and squabbled, and massacred each other, true to the tradition of traditions... And were they not as absolutely right and wrong? Was not the red threat evil? Was not the dictatorship of the proletariat Hell on Earth? Were not the capitalists decadent revellers? Did they not plunder and exploit the poor?

And both wings have been certainty-mongers – propagandising through the pulpits of their media. Or has it been coincidence – like millions of Christians being born in Europe, while millions of Muslims were somehow born in Arabia – that so many American children have had faith in so-called-free enterprise, and that so many Russian children just happened to have concluded state communism supreme?

One and all, religious and secular, the traditions are recognisable by their closed mindsets: their fear of the unknown, their collusion in false certainties, and their persecution of the scapegoat. The appalling consequences are always the same: the Vietnam War, the Crusades, the torture of Russian dissenters, the Inquisition.

But can any system ever succeed until its population becomes more whole? And is it possible to introduce concepts such as wholeness into politics? Is it realistic to promote concepts like openness not only as ethics of private, but also of public life? But until we do our politics will remain egotistic and neurotic (if not paranoid), our policies will remain unfeeling, manipulative and defensive-aggressive, and relations with 'other' either convenient compromise, stab-in-the-back, or outright war. The fact is, if we want to go beyond this psychological and social primitivism, we have no choice.

But only people who are opening will elect politicians who are opening. And only politicians who are opening in themselves can be genuinely committed to a politics that goes beyond appearances and rhetoric and impersonalism and demonisation.'

Re-reading this fragment today I agree with its sentiments – but it is very large. Inasmuch as the insistence that a half-truth is the full-truth is deceit, both the premodern religious traditions and the modern political traditions have been liars. The premodern pretence that the world of matter has no value, and the modern pretence that nothing but matter exists, are both distortions and deceits. And to live a lie and defend a lie day after day thrusts us, whether individually or collectively, into a neurotic state of awareness. Always afraid of the emergence of the other half of the truth, always fearful of being found out, we go to insanely elaborate lengths to decorate our lie – and to eliminate any possible opposition.

Thus I still agree that a non-neurotic politics must be based on an openness to wholeness. And a non-neurotic politics can only be held together by non-neurotic politicians. And non-neurotic politicians can only emerge consistently and in quantity out of a non-neurotic populace. But we are very many, and the path out of the neurotic defence of our half-truths is different for each of us. It is not something that can be coordinated at a distance by a centralised government programme. It is a very personal, very lengthy process – for which we need regular, kind, wise support and feedback from others who know us intimately. In other words, to open to ourselves and others and life itself, we are dependent upon our community.

And if we are talking about personalising politics, and connecting the four spheres, then it is precisely because we have supported someone in their personal development, and know them profoundly, that we feel confidence in their integrity and are willing to offer them community responsibility. If we have seen a man stand alone beneath the night sky and admit that all of his faith and feeling and thought is uncertain, and that however deep his convictions, he doesn't know why he is alive – we trust him in a way we could never possibly trust someone we've only ever seen on television. We have sat with him, together on the edge of the unknown. We know his humility and his humanity.

Deep, authentic political change, therefore, can only stem from grassroots community development. That is not to say we cannot achieve worthwhile ends using existing national and international political institutions. But the fundamental paradigmatic change, from a shallow, materialistic, oppositional politics into the holistic political dimension – the genuine qualitative and quantitative reforms demanded by holistic democracy – can only by facilitated by thousands upon thousands of independent, human-scale, local communities taking responsibility for the solidity, depth and beauty of their lives upon themselves.

To move from a politics of neurosis towards a politics of wholeness, a massive decentralisation programme of community empowerment and autonomy is called for. To enter a postmodern adulthood we need to complete the cut from centralised parental power. In our premodern childhood that centralised power was absolute, infallible. In our modern adolescence it has become human, relative and fallible. But to enter adulthood we need to break and re-connect, and relate to that central power from a powerful centre of our own.

But a decentralised society of empowered holistic communities is a slow revolutionary enterprise of enormous proportions. What would such communities look like, in practice? And if we can imagine them, how might we develop them? How, practically, might we go about establishing them? These questions lead us into Section Three. Sections One and Two have been about arriving at these questions, and hopefully arriving with understanding, with desire and with will.

We need to appreciate the grandness of our enterprise – to see it in its historical context. We need to see it in perspective within the panoramic journey of the collective psyche. We need to know the hunger of the cultural soul.

Perhaps we want it for humanity, perhaps we want it for ourselves. Perhaps we want it for our grandchildren, and perhaps it fills us with an utterly erotic longing to live together in truth.

3

A Possible Postmodern Era Holistic Community

Sex and Spirit

Introduction

This last section is based on articles, essays, diaries and notes I have written while actively working to develop holistic community through the Balance project. This has been the period in which I've tried to apply my theories, tripped up on my emotional limitations, stumbled upon the limitations in my thinking, and been repeatedly brought to earth, humbled and knocked into shape.

The contents of this last section emerge from a five-year experimental, alchemical phase in which my grand visions have been tested in the fire of interaction with other. I've burnt with doubt. My understanding, my methods, and my motives have been reduced to ashes and resurrected a thousand times. My zeal has been tempered. My passion has deepened in tone. And I have survived. And Balance has survived. And I would like to believe I now have more humanity, more clarity, more simplicity, and more faith.

I have watched as my compensations and false selves have fallen away. I have watched myself risk walking into the world as me. And I can see how the support of my marriage, my men's group, my couple's group and the larger community has made this possible. Elisabeth's respect for her own journey, for mine, and for the journey of our relationship, and the commitment of so many men and women around me, has held and allowed my own unfoldment. As I have experienced others accepting themselves, all of themselves – yes, all of themselves – it has become more and more natural to let myself be me. And so five years on, I still believe in holism, I still believe in travelling the path of wholeness together, and I still believe in the need to structure our communities to facilitate that.

Balance is a project of trial and error. There is no plan to follow. There have been hints and intuitions and inspirations, but neither which materials nor which tools to take up is anywhere written. There have been holy but rusty bits of premodernity, sparkling but empty bits of modernity, and warm but unformed bits of postmodernity – but no assemblage instructions. I have nowhere found a D.I.Y. Holistic Community Kit.

I wrote in the introduction to this book that the aim of this third section would be to equip the reader with enough confidence to begin developing holistic community in her or his own local area. What I can offer is my under-standing-so-far – the bits of community building kit that I have managed to piece together. My hope is that some readers will go further, that we will keep in touch, and that together we will develop a network of deep community projects…

Firstly, then, what will I be saying about the four spheres in this last section? The philosophy of holism (sphere one) and the path of wholeness (sphere two) have occupied most of Sections One and Two. So in terms of their content, I have no more to say. In terms of their practical application, I will be proposing the community forum as the central structure of holistic community, within which people can raise questions, suggest programmes, request events, and so on. There, equipped with the shared vocabulary of the four spheres, people can recognise and discuss issues pertaining to these first two spheres...

It might be felt, for example, that the community would be enriched for generations to come if sphere-two communication skills were taught in the local schools, or that the first sphere would be helped by a page of people's more intimate thoughts and reflections in the local newspaper. All of this could be brought to the community forum, and taken further whenever there was energy and enthusiasm.

Any number of third-sphere communal issues can also be brought to the community forum – issues, for example, like the rite of passage of retirement, and the relationships between the generations. But in this last section I want to offer some reflections on developing probably the two most fundamental structures of the communal sphere: partnership and initiation into adulthood.

And regarding the fourth sphere, I will not be discussing organic agriculture, local trading, ecological architecture, or community banking – or any of the other obviously sensible fourth-sphere policies we need to pursue. Policies have already been amply presented elsewhere by others far more politically literate than I. My focus will be on questions of quality and integration. 'How do we cultivate a deeper quality of political and economic dialogue?' And 'How do we integrate our practical policies with the concerns of the other three spheres?'

But in order 'to equip the reader to begin developing holistic community in her or his own local area' I see just three basic elements. The first is a sense of holism as an outlook, a world-myth, and as a path of personal fulfilment – which I have already discussed at length. Secondly, there is co-creativity – which is perhaps the way holism is lived. If holism is about respectful, sacred relationships (within ourselves, with others, and with experience itself), then co-creativity is a way of living in that dialogue of sacred respect. And lastly, there is the four sphere model which, whether applied personally or socially, is an aid to the application of co-creativity. In a way it brings us full circle back to the holistic worldview, because it is an aid to living holism holistically – to becoming neither too holy nor too worldly. As well as looking at the community forum and the basic structures of the communal sphere, therefore, I will also be offering overviews of co-creativity and the four sphere model.

And I have also included a chapter on Balance, looking particularly at lessons I have learnt. I hope this will be useful not only in terms of the specific lessons, but also in communicating a sense of the experimental nature of holistic community development – and of the inevitability of our own fears and biases entering the process. Holistic community is not a finished vision, with clear-cut social structures waiting to be filled by perfect people. It is about travelling together in our wholeness, our full humanity, with all of our bruises and gashes, and our radiance – and working it out as we go along, staying faithful, as best we can, to the omnipresent unknown.

Co-creativity and Flexible Form

1. CO-CREATIVITY

At the end of 1994 I set up Balance as a vehicle for experimentation in establishing co-creative holistic community. Since then I've set up groups, published articles, run camps, organised conferences and community gatherings, edited a newsletter, facilitated community ceremonies, stumbled and picked myself up a hundred times, felt depressed, felt elated, had visions and lost them, felt drained and danced in bliss.

Above all, my struggle has been with myself. My very core aches for community – and yet many parts of me have investment in my remaining a misunderstood, rejected outsider. Somehow, somewhere, between the lines, within my words, especially early on, there was always a double message: what I'm offering is very important – please reject it!

By mid 1995 this was definitely healing. In a diary I wrote 'a strange and thrilling shift is taking place inside me as I more and more deeply experience that *I am a part*. In this I don't feel diminished in my individuality – on the contrary, it makes it easier and easier to be myself. But I feel myself carried along within the collective psychic web. Within this I have choice, but I am a part of a consciousness larger than my own. The wounding is larger than my own, the connectedness is tighter than I'd ever imagined, and the opportunity to support each other in standing in freedom feels like it's at our fingertips. It is in presentness to this experience that I work to develop social structures to sustain holistic community.'

Until then there'd been a lot of intelligence in my work, a lot of abstract vision, and a lot of determination, but I wasn't inside it with humility and heart. To put it rather harshly: I was good at lecturing others on the theory of community reconstruction, but I wasn't living it – my words were brittle with lack of felt experience.

I felt I understood the need of community infrastructure. As that same diary entry went on to say: 'there are certain basic structures that hold a society together. Communal structures such as birth rites, initiation, partnership and the family, regular communal observances and celebrations, and so on. And practical structures – the legal, economic, political, military, and so on. As we stand today, there are many of us with a basically holistic outlook, but we are separate, we are separate individuals. Balance is dedicated to the development of holistic community by establishing the underpinning infrastructure we need to hold us.'

But because of the tension within me (the known: solitude and low self-esteem, versus the unknown: being held and valued by others), I'd always had difficulty in communicating 'co-creativity'. 'Holism' was straightforward, 'community' too – but co-creativity always came across either as something intricately intellectual, or as something rarefied and very highly spiritual, or as something utterly obvious that everyone was already doing anyway. It was either unattainably meaningful, or self-evident to the point of meaninglessness.

Do We Need It?

Firstly, obviously, co-creativity was about creating together. But I was using the term to refer especially to a method for communities, of whatever size, to create their own cultural forms. Cultural forms are always the expression of the collectively held world-view. They express it not only in what they do, but also in how they do it. For example, the Church service is held with the priest standing between the altar and the congregation. The Christian under-standing of the position of the Church is being read or spoken by the priest, but it is also being enacted. The physical, visual message is that the Church and the priesthood are the go-between between God and the people. Clothing, symbolic objects, the structure of the ceremony, of the building, appropriate behaviour, tone, atmosphere – the message is being imbibed in a hundred unspoken subtle ways.

I believed in holism and there were many others living nearby who also favoured a holistic approach. My question, then, was how we might go about establishing our own, holistic cultural forms. We needed a method – a method that allowed for both individuality and collectivity, and that was as personal and psychological as it was transpersonal and spiritual – an inclusive, holistic method.

Or did we? Were we not already a community? Let me offer a working defi-nition of 'community'. By a community I mean 'a group of individuals who share a worldview, and which is tighter or looser to the degree they share cultural forms and norms to express that worldview'. After all, if we were already a local community – why did we need co-creativity, or anything at all? But communities can be so loose as to offer their members very little support – they are little more than groups of geographically related individualists – or so tight as to be suffocating.

I placed our community, and most of the groupings of holistically-minded individuals elsewhere around the country and the globe, very much towards the loose end of the spectrum. Not surprisingly really, since the holistic outlook has (at best) only been significantly present in our culture since the 60's. And the first step, for each of us, understandably, has been to ask how holism applies to us personally… 'How has the material/spiritual split affected me, personally?' 'What can I do to heal and become whole?' But holism leads naturally to questions of sacralising the world, of spiritualising the everyday – of awareness and sensitivity not only in meditation, but also in the market place and in places of power. And so, as I and many like me had entered midlife we had become the generation that would inevitably ask questions about not only re-shaping ourselves, but about re-shaping our communities. Not only this, but there in our scattered sub-culture, for the first time, was a generation with a degree of experience of groupwork and knowledge of group dynamics. So as I and many others saw it, as individuals we were ripe for holistic community – as a community we were extremely young, loose and ungrounded, and in need of a suitable shared method for weaving ourselves together.

Tasting It

So my concern has been – for myself, and for others – how we might establish holistic community forms which are not too tight, and not too loose. And I've been experimenting with co-creativity. I've been experimenting, and I've been experiencing. And as I experience it, I can communicate it more clearly…

It's a sense of journeying together, of community on the move. It's a sense of all being carried, swept along, carried aloft – not aloft into heavenly spheres, but into expansion. An expansion which includes casual, everyday perception, which grows to include a perception of oneself as part of the community in the here-and-now, which can then grow to include a perception of the community as a moment in human history, and which can even expand to include a perception of self, community and humanity as all situated within the journey of consciousness itself – the final beginningless movement of the stuff of existence… going nowhere, going everywhere, never, forever.

But let's come back to earth! Co-creativity is all of this, however far we want to take it. We might say that it is a movement, at whatever level, in community, into the unknown. It's not a complete, pre-set, all-explaining, foolproof philosophy – it's an opportunity, an invitation. It's an awareness of oneself as a part of the community, a unique part with a unique set of gifts and delusions and challenges – travelling alongside other equally unique personalities.

And it's a sense of travelling within an energy field which is larger than all of us, and which can accommodate our differences. What this energy field might be, whether it needs to be named, whether it can be named, whether it is the sum total of the individual energies of everyone present, whether it is a tapping into a collective unconscious or superconscious… I wouldn't wish to try to pin it down. But in the expansion of co-creativity there is an experience of peacefulness and stillness, acceptance of self and other, a bubbling fullness, a wisdom and a knowing, and what can only be described as a sense of the holiness of all things.

Co-creativity as the Marriage of Tradition and Modernity

But how does this potent experience relate to the construction of cultural forms capable of sustaining holistic community? Now that I am entering co-creativity more experientially a strange feeling arises: I now know what I've been talking about all along!

And I look back at my own argument for co-creativity. I review it. It is this: 'over the last millennium we have experienced the erosion of a worldview and its descending, hierarchical cultural forms – forms which once bonded us in community. And this has been a great loss, yes, but, to the modern mind those forms were ethnocentric, them-and-us, friends-and-enemies, we're-the-only-way, absolutist, fundamentalist, fanatical, oppressive and misogynistic. They had to be overthrown. We had to claim back our dignity, our dignity as individuals, as equals beyond colour, creed or sex – with minds freed of the hell-backed tyrannies of unquestionable gods.' So much for nostalgia!

But, my argument has always continued 'nevertheless, a sense of loss lingers… 'Does freedom have to mean separatism?' we ask ourselves, 'Does dignity have to mean isolation?' Today our children are thrown out upon an urban-industrial landscape, and they are on their own. They are not held by a meaningful cultural worldview, and thus, inevitably, they are not held by meaningful cultural forms. They have no community. Fundamentalist sects try to go back in time – and others romanticise tribal life, simple village life, and ethnic, indigenous peoples. But I believe we can re-create community without reviving the oppression of the past. We can create community in a way that acknowledges and incorporates all that we've gained.

Co-creativity calls us together, in the way premodern cultures did, but with respect for individuality. Fear of imposed form, of conformity, need not leave us stranded in formlessness – we can co-create, we can mould our own forms, together, in community… We can tend them, adjust them, discard them if we need to. Our fear of authority, of hierarchy, of disempowerment in ultimate matters, in matters of meaning, of spirituality – these need not leave us stranded in a desacralised, disenchanted flatland. We can co-create, we can create together as equals, we can co-create structures and situations which empower us, which enrich us, which fulfil us.'

I hear my own words, words I've spoken, in various permutations, on a thousand occasions – and I realise that a fundamental doubt of mine has gone. It was this: 'can co-creative structures *really* work? And by 'really' I mean – can they support us on our paths of transformation, and in organising our communities, in the same way as structures that claims suprahuman origin? Can they ever have that kind of solidity? Or ever become as stable as structures that claim to have been passed unaltered from teacher to teacher for centuries – or any ancient structure imbued with the wisdom and experience of the generations?' A secret, denied part of me has always wondered: 'yes, but isn't it a bit like children playing… can such things just be 'made up'?'

Now, with a quiet faith borne of experience, I feel I can answer that, yes, they can be 'made up'. Not casually, not whimsically, but, yes, if approached with authenticity and reverence, they can be – co-created. Cultural forms don't have to be descended from the holy ones, or from the holy one. They can be co-created by communities of people who are not all-knowing, who are very fallible and finite. They can be created democratically, co-operatively, with awareness on many levels, and with flexibility. My experience has convinced me that co-creative community structures are a real and potent option. They combine the sacred collectivity of the past with the equality and individuality of the present. They demand skill and maturity. They are not an easy option. But – despite my determination to remain the worthless outsider – even I have experienced their empowerment, their healing power, their holding, and their strangely silent expansiveness.

Not Easy

The essence of co-creativity is perhaps to be able to hold a dual perspective – of oneself as both a discrete individual and as part of a unified whole. And this requires great sophistication. The togetherness of co-creativity, the sense of shared journey, can fragment in two directions: when we merge (and deny our differences), or when we enter opposition to each other (and lose our unity). This is, of course, inevitable. The process of co-creativity involves a constant losing and re-finding of that place of unity in diversity.

In a mature group (or a group with facilitators) not all of the group will lose the mid-point. A conflict might arise, for example. But not everyone will take sides. Some will be able to hold the co-creative context. They will be able to be larger than the conflict. This doesn't mean minimising the conflict in any way. It means embracing it. The whole can contain conflict. And, of course, even in the most experienced, mature community sometimes everyone will become identified with a conflict – and any sense of both opposites being complementary facets of the whole will get lost… Until someone remembers, and returns the gathering to an awareness of co-creativity.

Co-creativity doesn't mean there can be no hierarchy, or leadership. But it does mean that power dynamics (which are always present) need to be as explicit as possible, and that ultimately, power is held (and can be revoked by) the group. But with or without facilitators or leaders, co-creativity requires great emotional sophistication. Sometimes there might be hardly enough experience of growth-work and groupwork to be able to sustain co-creativity. And even for people with decades of experience of their inner-journeys, co-creativity is unfamiliar. It is a new language. And it has to be practised. Co-creativity might make philosophical sense, it might make cultural sense, and it might hold an existential promise, but it is not easy.

Most groups can't co-create immediately. Like all things, groups grow up – or don't. Potentially they have a premodernity, a modernity and a post-modernity, a childhood, an adolescence and a maturity. A group's childhood is characterised by a need for directive leadership, its adolescence is charac-terised by self-assertion, and only its maturity is characterised by co-creativity. This also needs to be recognised.

Another complication is the issue of size. In a community development project everyone participates in the community forum. The project might split up into gender subgroups, or into subgroups working on different environ-mental projects, for example, but everyone comes back together at the central community forum. These two settings – the smaller subgroups and the larger community forum – offer different opportunities for co-creativity, and different challenges. In smaller groups we tend to reproduce our attitudes towards our families. In larger groups we tend to reproduce our attitudes towards society and the world at large. This is another factor in the co-creative process.

Furthermore, splitting doesn't only happen when there's a conflict (as in the example above). Groups constantly tend to split into opposed subgroupings – them and us, the insiders and the newcomers, the-gentle-caring-ones and the hard-realistic-ones, and so on. But the co-creative challenge is always the same: to allow the opposition – without opposing each other! Similarly, groups tend to scapegoat – to load up someone with the group's garbage, and send them packing. Again, the co-creative option is to keep recycling! And all of this is easier said than done. Co-creativity is a huge challenge.

However, there is a simple magic with which to travel this challenge: to name the process. We need to look at each other, and name what it is we are doing. We need to state our intention. 'We are practicing co-creativity.' 'We agree on the basic principle of co-creativity – of holding true to ourselves, while staying open to our onenness and to spirit.' 'We know co-creativity is not easy. Sometimes it's painful, sometimes it's joyful. We are practicing it together.' We need to hold this awareness for each other. We all need to hold this awareness for everyone. This creates intellectual, emotional and spiritual unity. Then the group is supported. Not secure. Not sure of success. Just supported.

I know of no 'correct' way to communicate co-creativity. Recently, in a workshop, after various exercises with body and voice to explore our oneness and difference, we sat down together to practice co-creativity. Like any medi-tation, co-creativity takes practice. We had three 'guardians' – one for our individuality, one for our collectivity, and one for the guiding presence of spirit. Each guardian would give the group a regular nudge. The guardian of individuality, for example, would ask us if we were in touch with our own bodily sensations, or with our own feelings (however much they might be contrasting with the general mood in the group), and so on.

The workshop was for a national organisation that was not achieving its aims. The co-creative process revealed the unspoken power dynamics in the organisation – which were blocking its progress. By focusing on our oneness we soon saw who was over-dominating, and who was under-participating. By honouring and encouraging difference, difficult feelings were able to be included. And holding the whole process within the larger perspective of spirit seemed to make us all more expansive, and more generous.

The 'guardians' idea seemed to work. It can be useful to name some basic components of co-creativity. It can be useful to state the group's intent. And facilitators can sometimes be useful – they can also be inhibiting. But in this section I do not intend to offer any how-to programme for teaching co-creativity. Many, many of us have experience of therapeutic and spiritual groupwork. People will come to co-creativity with a background in Group Analysis, David Bohm's Dialogue work, Scott Peck's Community Building work, humanistic and transpersonal therapies, or self-help and support groups. Others will have no background in groupwork, but an understanding of 'owning' their emotions and not blaming. Others will come with no growth-work background at all. I trust that as different community projects come together to explore co-creativity they will find different ways of practising and communicating it.

More than Groupwork

Finally, co-creativity isn't only about groupwork. Nor is it only about community. It is not even only a method for managing holistic social structures. It is something we do, more or less consciously, all the time everywhere. Co-creativity is about togetherness and aloneness and the presence of eternity. Well, we are always in oneness, we are always in difference, and we are always in spirit. We are always in oneness – be it with another person, with animals, with the grass, or with the stars – because we are of the same life-stuff as all things. And we are always in difference because we are always only ourselves. And grace is permanently, inescapably here, there, within, beyond.

Thus we are constantly co-creating, whether we are aware of it or not. We are constantly co-creating because we are constantly in relationship, and all things with which we are in relationship are pulsing with the divine mystery – like ourselves. We are constantly co-creating with reality, with existence.

Some postmodern holistic philosophers talk of a 'participatory universe', of an ever-unfinished, unfolding reality in which we co-create existence in partnership with life itself. By practicing co-creativity within a group or community setting, and then extending that experience into our moment to moment lives, we can realise this holistic philosophy.

Co-creativity is the very dynamic of holism. It is how holism is lived. It is the experience of the world of matter unfolding within spirit. In co-creativity we experience ourselves as unique cells with the body of life, passionately human, infinitely fragile, unshakeable in our knowing – engrossed in our little egos and embedded together in the unspeakable mystery.

2. FLEXIBLE FORM

Introduction

The aim of Balance is to empower people to create new community structures, their own structures, balanced structures – structures which acknowledge both the inner and the outer, the civilised and the wild, the known and the unknown…

Balance is presently working with new models of partnership, men's and women's 'sub-communities', community seasonal celebration, and community forums and organisation. However, in this chapter I will be attempting to explain, not what new forms Balance is proposing, but rather the nature of its forms – their theory, the way they work, their style.

This will lead us into questions such as: what is 'balance'? Where is the balance point? How might social, cultural and political structures integrate such a concept? What do balanced structures look like? How do they function?

A Moving Point of Balance

I could waffle on, and argue that balance is a relative concept – give you lots of comfy armchair logic on how, for a Christian fundamentalist, balance is such-and-such, whereas, for a scientific fundamentalist, balance is some-other-such-and-such. And so on, and on. However, frankly, I do not believe that everyone's balance is as balanced as everyone else's. Elusive as it may be – I believe a universal place of balance, a meeting place, does exist.

But I don't see balance as a fixed point – more as a sensitivity, an attitude. Balanced responses differ in different circumstances. And balance always slips beyond definition…

Balance is about combination. It is about combining ideals and action – abstracts and realities. It is maturity. It is about merging the sacred and the profane. And balance is about the interdependence, and interplay, of earth and heaven, and of 'yin' and 'yang' on earth.

Balance is about paradox, about the equal value of opposites. Balance is about being certain enough to sacrifice one's days for not-knowing…

And balance also contains a still place, a place of equilibrium, equanimity, harmony, wisdom, justice. I would like to feel it rests at the core of every ancient tradition – although the fanatics of traditionalism make it hard to perceive. And if psychotherapy is our modern tradition of self-knowledge, I would like to feel that balance is alive somewhere within the core of that too.

But this very fluid quality has, for the most part, for thousands of years, been bound and tortured within an ingenious variety of distorting cultural forms. And now, because in the modern era we have thrown away traditional form, we find ourselves without any cultural vehicle, however distorted, for that place of balance.

This leaves many of us caught in an odd impasse. We resent the bureaucratic, rational-fundamentalist, hollow politics of the day, but we are terrified of churches and one-books and one-ways and holier-than-thous and being told what to do, and believe, and fear, and feel... In short, we want to touch balance together, we want balanced community, but we fear hierarchy and dogmatism: rigidity in matters of truth and beauty and love. We want balance, but we don't want fixed forms.

The upshot of this is that the path of balance remains without a contemporary social form, it remains a private concern, and the entire globe is being ever faster spun on its axis by not-very-balanced individuals themselves stuck in a cardboard-cut-out, cover-up mentality.

I believe that there is a solution, a middle way. Between the old fixed forms of spiritual social-control, on the one hand, and the social irrelevance of the new to-each-their-own, on the other, I see the postmodern possibility of flexible form...

Which, since balance is by nature so flexible, is perhaps its most natural form.

Co-Creativity and Flexible Form

Flexible form is applied co-creativity. It is a way of applying co-creativity to committees, to organisations, and to the social structures of communities. Its virtue is that it can put balance centre stage, without coercion.

Flexible form is developmental co-creativity. Let me re-cap on co-creativity. By co-creativity I mean a process in which there is no external imposition (there are influences, but autonomy and responsibility prevail), there is no fixed hierarchy (there is egalitarian cooperation, and leadership can be bestowed and revoked by the group), and there is no rigidity (there is openness, movement, evolution). But isn't this democracy (at least in theory)? Yes. And more. The two main differences are in terms of quantity and quality.

In terms of quantity – the co-creative/democratic process is castrated by centralisation and massification. Our group, our project, our community is disempowered to the point of impotence by massive, bureaucratised power-from-the-centre. The conception of power-from-the-centre was certainly a human advance from power-from-on-high, papal infallibility and the divine right of kings. But for the full humanity of the ideals of democracy to flourish that power needs to be shared out even further. Less and less people vote. More and more people feel distrustful of, and alienated from, the democratic process – and they are then called upon to participate. But why should they participate from a place of disempowerment? They will participate in their communities when their communities have the autonomy and power to direct their own, local, democratic processes. Similarly, people will participate in their workplaces, leisure places and place of worship (unless they have been caught in the anti-modern fundamentalist backlash) to the degree they are empowered with responsibility.

The second difference between democracy as we've known it and co-creativity is one of quality. The difference of quantity that we have just discussed is, in the last analysis, not a difference at all. At the moment it is a difference of degree – but really it is only more of the same. It is just a fuller expression of democratic principles. The difference in terms of quality, however, brings a whole new dimension to social organisation as we know it. Co-creativity takes place when there is individual awareness, when there is an awareness of the group mind, and when there is awareness of an embracing guiding principle. The kind of awareness that takes account of emotional, psychological and spiritual factors could, I suppose, be seen as the ultimate expression of democracy – a full, holistic democracy in which all levels of the individual are acknowledged. But group management that is sensitive to subgrouping, scapegoating, transference and countertransference, unexpressed fears and desires clogging up the group mind, as well as transpersonal influences, is such a new departure that, at least for the time being, it has to be seen as adding something to democracy – rather than as being its fulfilment. We might say that co-creativity and its application in flexible form is psychological and spiritual democracy.

Flexible form is a structured co-creativity – it is not formless. It might not have a form controlled from above or from a distant so-called 'centre', and the form might change – but it exists. It exists communally, between people. It is a shared, living work of art. Together the co-creators are carrying the place of balance in their own ever-evolving form.

Just as all of the institutions of traditional cultures – legal, educational, rite of passage, and so on – reflected that culture's image of the balance-point, the truth-point, Flexible form is a way for us to build our own balance-reflecting culture. But, whereas the institutions of traditional cultures reflected one, and only one, dominant, indubitable, absolute image – flexible form is a structural model for reflecting multifarious, growing, changing images: images that change from community to community, and images that change over the years within each community. It is the democratisation of spirituality – and the spiritualisation of democracy.

Flexible Form, Not Formlessness

There is a trend (alongside the obviously regressive fundamentalist flight to the fixed forms of the major world religions), particularly in so-called 'new age' or 'alternative' circles, but also in our culture in general, to look for inner nourishment in the more esoteric, less accessible spiritualities of the past. It is obviously true that these premodern paths housed their own wisdoms. And it is obviously anyone and everyone's right to delve into those traditions. But I feel we need to be careful in our handling of traditional spiritualities.

Firstly, we need to be wary of a romanticism that often ignorantly glorifies oppressive ancient traditions. We need to be conscious of their inherent, often subtle, power dynamics. Also, we need to appreciate cultural specificity (i.e. that those forms suited those people, in those surroundings, in those times), and that they are not immutable or absolute. If we are going to tap the wisdom of the past, then we also need to become expert importers, translators and updaters. We must be careful not to block the creation of forms that are relevant to us, here, now – which embody our joy, our pain, which talk in our images, our symbols. The danger is cultural incoherence – one person will insist on the exact wording of his Native American chant, and another will insist on the exact step of her Sufi dance. Community will not be able to emerge. We will be caught in an incoherent jumble of esoteric fundamentalisms. And we will remain spiritually individualistic, and politically conveniently 'out of this world'.

And, of course, even this incoherence is only possible if he has deeply internalised the words of his chant, and she the steps of her dance. More often, in my experience, people have not immersed themselves in their chosen path for decades, they have not imbibed its manner, its pace, its aroma – they have hopped and skipped from one ancient truth to the next. They are not, therefore, even capable of translating their tradition's vision into its modern equivalent. They are caught in a pick'n'mix, spiritual-supermarket romanticism which will inevitably tends towards formlessness: yesterday Egyptian esoteric magic, today Celtic witchcraft, tomorrow Taoist sexuality. Fearing fixed form, there seems to be a tendency to swing to the other extreme of formlessness. From suffocating discipline we tend to escape into promiscuity – from strong-yang we flip into weak-yin. And we flit, and we flirt, and we lay no foundations. We are afraid to build in case we lock ourselves in. But the practical result of this is that we end up living in buildings built by people determined to keep balance locked out.

Flexible Form is a method of connecting *in community* with that core of sexual-spiritual balance – without naively reverting to fixity, or superficially playing around with all forms and no forms. The challenge, as I see it, is to build in sensitive and skillful co-creativity. Then each community can build with its own preferences and biases, reflecting its own images, in its own mood, at its own pace, in relation to its own time and place. And each community can continuously elaborate and simplify and transform its own unique creations. And balance can be housed, and freedom preserved.

But rather than continuing to discuss flexible form in the abstract, I would now like to move to specifics. I want to show how flexible form can be applied to a limited, defined area of concern. I have chosen two social situations. Rituals and committee meetings.

Flexible Form and Rituals

Rituals are all around us. We take part in a ritual every time we shake hands. When we participate in the ritual of eating out at a smart restaurant we adjust our appearance and behaviour accordingly. We might have a getting-up ritual – a sequence of actions we perform between rising and breakfast. Sport is ritualised play. We have ritual naming ceremonies for babies, rituals of well-wishing and gift-giving on retirement, rituals for the wedding of couples, rituals of burial and burning at death, rituals around our national flags. Nobody's life is untouched by ritual.

Ritual is characterised by symbols. It is all about symbolic objects and symbolic actions. It is about making feelings (whether emotional or spiritual) physical, tangible, manifest – it is about real-ising them. Ritual makes feelings manageable, it contains them, it gives them a place they can be expressed – and transformed. And in its purest and most complete form, ritual takes feelings into a sacred, eternal space – where they can be transformed in an atmosphere of blessedness.

Every culture, therefore, creates rituals great and small for the containment, expression and transformation of feelings. These are especially necessary at times of powerful emotion – such as births, marriages and deaths. And every culture has ritualised these events with rites of passage. Let us take the example of birth. Traditional cultures would have imposed strict rituals (physical, mental, spiritual) upon both the mother and father to be – rituals concerning pregnancy and preparation, the birthing time itself, and the postnatal phase. This was traditional fixed form – it descended from the sacred books, teachings, ancestors and elders – and it was fixed. And the point of these elaborate rituals was to ensure the physical safety of mother and child, but also to connect the mother and father, other siblings, the extended family and the community at large with the magnificence and mystery of birth. The shattering emotions that accompany the birth of a child, the mind-expanding and heart-expanding revelation, this was all ritually held, supported and celebrated by the community.

Birth in a modern hospital – the norm for most women and their husbands and partners today – much as it must be appreciated for its medical expertise, offers no ritual containment for the emotional and spiritual overflowing of agonising bliss. It offers no opportunity to hallow those sacred hours when, somehow, it seems, other dimensions have opened to ours, and everything is shrouded in miracle. What a tragedy it is for our civilisation that our children enter the world without such ritual. What a tragedy for our children and for us. What a bad start. What an empty start. What might we do to change it?

We might be distressed by the lack of meaningful birth ritual in our hospitals, but since, for most of us, our traditional religious structures are no longer the communicators of the absolute truth, we are also unlikely to call for a return to the fixed forms of church, synagogue, temple or mosque.

How then might we apply flexible form? When a woman becomes pregnant we might call together a group of family and friends, and begin asking questions like 'what do we need, what kinds of support do we want – physical, emotional and spiritual, before, during and after this birth?' and 'what do we want to express to the universe, to spirit, to the earth, to ourselves, to our inner truths – before, during and after this birth?'. The possibilities are, of course, endless. But from heartfelt, supportive discussion a pattern of rituals would emerge – from sacred ceremony through the birthing hours, to postnatal community support with the cooking… And maybe, when it was all over, some things would have gone well and others not. But everyone would have learned. Then someone else would become pregnant, and it would be time for the next planning evening. And the next set of lessons. And so on. And gradually the community would become more and more experienced in the co-creation of pregnancy-birthing-postnatal ritual. Customs would become established because they seemed to touch everyone's heart. And when one family broke a taboo, they would be doing it for everyone. The community would notice patterns beginning to emerge , and begin to be able to offer some guidance. These patterns might be offered to mothers and fathers to be, but they would always be open to adjustment – they would always be flexible. Thus the community would create its own flexible form, its own balanced, holistic community structures. There would be 'unpredictable continuity'. This is flexible form.

There is so much more to say about all of this. I have not discussed, for example, the possible need for helpers – not only midwives, but also, perhaps, facilitators for the group discussions, or celebrants for the more formal rituals. But my intention here has been (based partly on experience, and partly on fantasy), to sketch out how flexible form might begin to be applied to a specific social situation, a specific social structure.

In practice the co-creative process of flexible form sometimes flows smoothly and deeply, and sometimes doesn't. There are fears, conflicts of interest, negotiations, resistances, times of frustration and stuckness, unexpected empathies, unique creativities, and moments of breath-taking unity. The challenge is to balance discussion with action; to strive for consensus, but not to become immobilised without it; to stay with the process, to remain authentic, to keep the fire alive…

Flexible Form and Committee Meetings

For my second example I have deliberately chosen a social situation that would, at first glance, seem more down-to-earth, secular, prosaic: a committee meeting. And to highlight the contrast even more, let's imagine that our committee meeting is within the crucial social structure of local government.

Let us imagine a local government committee that sees flexible form as a vehicle for full, holistic democracy – and is trying to apply it within its own meetings. Perhaps, to make it easier for our minds, we might want to imagine that this meeting is taking place in a future in which growth-work and community development have become much more integrated into our culture…

Firstly, in order to include their deepest integrity, their core selves, their highest ideals, the committee has opened with five minutes meditative silence. I don't want to dwell on this because we have already discussed ritual, but we might imagine that, over time, as the group becomes more intimate, little additions are made to this silence – a poem is read, a picture is hung on the wall… Subtly, consensually, the group is co-creating its own flexible opening ritual. And this ritual is, of course, completely changing the quality of the atmosphere of the meeting. They sometimes even close their meetings with a short closing ritual – thereby offering a certain respect to the special mood they've been privileged to share.

But to include our 'centres', our most noble and compassionate selves, is not everything. Mr. J., the committee secretary, certainly has great clarity at the centre of his being, but today he is feeling especially confused by events at home. And the treasurer, Mrs. L.'s, eternal soul might sometimes overflow with tranquillity and bliss, but last night's events have left her feeling agitated and angry. The meeting's meditative opening is over, and the 'check in' begins. The 'check in', they have decided, is a chance to include their personalities, their ups and downs, their humanity. And each one, in the obviously limited time available, and to the extent they feel safe to share their inner lives with their co-workers, without any pressure to say more (or say anything), says a few words about what they've been going through, and what they're feeling at that very moment. Mr. J. and Mrs. L. feel greatly relieved. No one has tried to solve their dilemmas for them. In fact, they themselves only hinted at the issues. But it feels reassuring to know that the others know, that they are accepting. The meditation alone wouldn't have been enough.

And down to business… All goes efficiently until a potential conflict arises. Mr. S. is passionate about increasing funding to a certain environmental project, and Mrs. L. is certain that the money's just not there. In the past the conflict would have divided the committee into the 'he's right/she's wrong' and the 'she's right/he's wrong' camps. Not only this, but the room would have become increasingly tense, tempers would have become shorter, words sharper, and old animosities would have been reawoken. But the observer/facilitator they had for six months while they were practising co-creativity kept referring them back to 'the spirit of the group' – 'everyone is bringing an important contribution' she used to say. Now, rather than getting locked in conflict, the group is learning to value everyone's perspective. In this case, they see that Mrs. L. is voicing the community's expressed need for financial caution – an important consideration. And that Mr. S. is voicing the need for local government's deep commitment to meeting the community's expressed environmental concerns – also an important consideration. The difference of opinion is still there. But now it is held as complementary, rather than oppositional. Above all, the committee now has a sense of *being on a journey together*. Sometimes when passions are high, they even pause for a few minutes to each listen to their own hearts (as they do in their opening ritual). There are, of course, still conflicts and confusions (they don't always work things out as neatly as go on to do today), but they are beginning to cultivate a mood of mutual respect, of listening to each other, of supporting each other – of travelling in oneness and difference.

This is as far as they have got. They have an opening ritual, a check-in, and a certain level of co-creative decision making. Undoubtedly, this will change. In fact, every twelve meetings, time is allocated to reflection and self-assessment. Do they want to continue with the opening ritual? Do they want to modify the check-in? Are they balancing the personal and the public? They don't change the form every week, but nor is it taken for granted. And this is what makes it flexible form. It is regularly reviewed and adjusted. It is a flexible, open, shared, self-directed journey. Ultimately, possibly, as their sphere-two, personal development evolves – a shared sacred-erotic journey into the unknown.

Again, there is so much more to be said. Time is a very important consideration. And the balance between 'getting the business done' and 'including all parts of ourselves' can sometimes be a tricky one. What to do, for example, when an animosity between two group members is humming just under the surface, bringing discomfort and influencing the whole group's ability to come to decisions? A committee meeting is not a group therapy exercise. We have to be careful – having never included anything other than our intellects – not to flip to the other extreme of needing to process every slight wavering of emotion. But my intention here has simply been to hint at how flexible form might be applied to another, very different social structure.

And of course, I cast this scenario into the future because at the moment, as we enter the twenty-first century, most politics is not well-rounded and holistic, nor is it even vaguely close to the raw humanity of co-creativity. It lacks authenticity and honesty and heart. It is stuck in ideological mental games, power games, antiquated top-heavy oversized bureaucracies, and an all pervasive alienated, porno-flatland cultural climate. How far into the future is my projection, then? I do not know. But I can see holistic, co-creative community forums growing powerfully at the heart of local communities. I can see them growing powerful not just because they are popular or loud, but because they hold a whole new political mood. And I can see many local government councillors and officers responding to that power, to that mood. Not just to keep their seats, but because they too long for it.

In Conclusion

In trying to outline flexible form, I have discussed balance and form, the fear of traditional fixed form, the obvious and subtle fundamentalist flights back to fixed form, and the pendulum swing towards formlessness. And I have presented flexible form as a holistic-democratic vehicle for the moving-point-of-balance – and hinted at ways in which in might be set in motion.

I have tried to illustrate Flexible Form with quite specific examples – precisely because its application is so vast. Personally, I believe flexible form – or some other way of managing fully participatory, holistic democracy – is the balanced way ahead for a global society now living on the edge of a nervous breakdown. I have coined the terms co-creativity and flexible form in order to focus growth-work and groupwork principles on the recreation of community structures. I am discussing application. I am slotting psychological and spiritual principles into an anthropological, sociological and political mould. My concern is the re-construction of community, or, more exactly, the construction of holistic community – something we have perhaps never experienced. We had community, but it was fixed. It was rigid. It was oppressive. We rebelled. We now have our freedom. But we have no community. Might it be possible to have back the community without the oppression?

The flexibility and the form, together, gradually construct for us, as postmodern individuals, a receptive atmosphere of cohesion, involvement, unity, trust, depth and power – an appropriate atmosphere in which to receive the undefinable balance-point, the ineffable 'great mystery of life'. Truth, beauty, love, erotic-awareness, the Tao – whatever we might like to say lives at what I have been calling 'the balance-point' – cannot enter contemporary society because the old methods and structures have been destroyed. I believe that a method such as flexible form is the acceptable way forward for the awake and aware postmodern individual. I believe it can support every community structure – from rites of passage to community political organisation. I can imagine it blessing local areas with a sense of freely entered into community.

An Overview of the Model of the Four Spheres of Community

Introduction

I have referred repeatedly to the model of the four spheres throughout this book. I would now like to set it out more systematically. The first time I ever presented the four sphere model was in writing about the relationship between holistic community and healing the land. I would like to use some paragraphs from that article to introduce this overview.

1. Holistic community can be seen as composed of four spheres:

i. the existential sphere (holistic philosophy – the intercourse of spirit and matter)

ii. the personal sphere (individual healing and empowerment, 'healing into wholeness')

iii. the communal sphere (the collective journey – see point 4)

iv. the practical sphere (holistic democracy, trade, agriculture, etc.)

2. If we are to develop holistic community all four spheres need to be addressed.

3. The communal sphere is particularly underdeveloped at present.

4. Within the communal sphere there are two cycles:

i. the collective time cycle (the passage through the year – daily and weekly observances, seasonal ceremony and celebration, etc.)

ii. the individual time cycle (the passage through the phases of an individual life – the rites of passage of birth, initiation, partnership and death, etc.)

The environmental crisis has its roots in philosophical issues. Premodern Christianity denigrated the earth, and modernism has desecrated it. The existential sphere needs to be addressed.

However, premodern and modern attitudes have had perhaps irreversible effects. Thus not only the sphere of ideas, but also the sphere of action, the practical sphere, needs to be addressed. Environmental issues, and issues of decentralisation and community responsibility become paramount.

And then again, it's all very well to have the right *ideas* and to try to *act* appropriately, but unless we engage in our personal healing, our work will be abstract and moralistic – and might even tend towards fanaticism. Whereas if we have a loving relationship with our inner worlds – with all that is dark and frightening as well as all that is tender and nurturing – then we will be able to have a genuine relationship with the world out there. Thus the personal sphere also needs to be addressed. To put it bluntly, only people who are healing can really heal the world.

But there is still one missing factor if we are to develop holistic communities able to heal the land... Even if we can imagine individuals on their personal, inner, alchemical journeys, and economic and political organisation that is sensitive both to people and to the land, we still have separate holistic individuals organising themselves holistically. There is still no sense of shared journey. But when people share rites of passage around the births of their children, when they share transformatory, initiatory journeys, when they witness and support each other on the journeys of their partnerships, and when they stand in sacred space together at the death rites of the people they have loved – they become one. They become a community in the most profound sense. With their hearts open to the each other, to each other's children, and to the children to come, their hearts can open to the land they stand upon together. With heart-commitment to each other can come commitment to the land, to the local biosphere. It is the communal sphere that offers us the possibility of experiencing the journey, not only of personal unfoldment, but of rooted, bonded, long-term collective unfoldment. It is when the communal sphere is in place that all of the spheres can unite. Then, in commitment to each other, we can test our existential theories (sphere one) and our personal development (sphere two) against the realities of everyday life, and support each other in meeting the physical and financial duties of the fourth sphere as sacred endeavours.

This is something very beautiful. As an initiated brahman (Hindu priest), I experienced the bliss of community within a premodern, life-negating, patriarchal tradition. Eventually I rejected that tradition, and began to ask how we might develop balanced postmodern community – community that respects both heaven and earth, both spirituality and sexuality... I wanted the bliss of belonging, and of meaningfulness – without the repression or disempowerment. Gradually, now, the model of the four spheres of holistic community is emerging from my enquiries as a realistic, sacred alternative to the structures of our ecologically suicidal modern culture – a model a thousand local areas could take up in a thousand different ways.

The Existential Sphere

In this chapter I don't intend to stress the importance of the communal sphere. In fact, the essential suggestion within the four sphere model is that, if we are to develop holistic community, we need to be simultaneously active within all four separate spheres. That they are separate, but inseparable.

Firstly, we need to be cultivating unity within the conceptual existential sphere. But not too quickly... Let's not be in too much of a hurry to get back to our environmental activism, or our meditations. Let's not underestimate the influence of the subtleties of belief. It was a gospel of disembodied love that paved the way for modernity's desecration of the planet. The existential sphere is the fountainhead. It is the source. It is from here that all cultures flow.

Esoterically, it's explained that everything moves from the subtle to the solid. The four sphere model of community can also be seen as a progression from the subtlety of faith through to the solidity of action. What we believe (sphere 1) shapes how we are with ourselves (sphere 2), with others (sphere 3), and finally, with the world (sphere 4). If, for example, I believe the otherworld is good, and life-on-earth is bad (sphere 1), then I will repress all that is human in me – including my dependency, uncertainty, frustration, grief, and so on (sphere 2), thus my relationships will be narrow and tight and heavy with moral judgement (sphere 3), and deaf to the voice of the planet, I will see it as an object to be used for my pleasure – which will determine the way I and my fellow believers work, the shape of our industries, of our transportation, of our commerce, of our laws, of our politics, and so on (sphere 4). This is how the subtle moves the solid, and this is why we need to approach the existential realm with due sensitivity and respect.

On the same point, it might sound pedantic to criticise worship of the Goddess as the ultimate being. After all, isn't that what's now needed? Don't we now need a matriarchal era in order to redress the imbalances of the patriarchy? Perhaps. But repression is repression, and what is repressed always emerges – eventually, when all else has failed, with a twisted, deformed destructive power. Long-term (and the development of holistic community is a multi-generational project) the diminishing of men, and whatever qualities we might call 'masculine', will backfire – just as did the repression of the earth and all we have considered 'feminine'. One thing is to worship the earth in order to reclaim our relationship with it, but it is yet another to call it a 'she' and try to topple the God. Again, these might sound like subtle philosophical discussions – but that is precisely the point: that the subtle completely determines every detail of our how-could-it-be-otherwise everyday lives. It could well be otherwise. It has been. And it will be. And if we want to have a say in the vision that will shape the minds of our descendants and govern their every physical move, then we should lend our heartfelt wisdom to the existential sphere.

The Personal Sphere

Secondly, the four sphere model of community suggests we develop the personal sphere, that's to say – that we develop ourselves. As many a sage has explained, it's not the scriptures that count, it's the saints. In other words, our worldviews are just piles of paper if there's nobody who, to one degree or another, can embody them. Thus we might also say that all of the other spheres, including the existential sphere, depend on the personal sphere. In a sense, the process of manifestation begins in the individual heart. Ultimately, of course, all of the spheres are interdependent. But it's only when someone has directly, personally touched a sacred-erotic holistic perception of reality that they can explain it (sphere 1), relate to others as a whole being (sphere 3), and have a natural sense of how to handle matter with reverence (sphere 4). Thus our progress in developing holistic community is also entirely dependent upon our private sincerities, the intensities of our quests, our readiness for inner risk and reform, our openness to the body and to magic, and the tenderness, strength and maturity with which we hold ourselves (and let ourselves be held) on our journeys.

But what does it mean to 'relate to others as a whole being'? The communal sphere is dependent upon the personal sphere because I can't relate to others as a whole being until I can relate to myself as one. I, for example, was highly spiritual. I knew myself mystically. But I denied my humanity, my fears and passions and personal needs – until they eventually blew me apart. I have had to learn to embrace my humanity within my mystical perception. Rather than denying my anger, for example, or becoming possessed by it, I have had to learn to express it while holding myself with understanding – and staying present within my body. In such moments I am relating as a whole being. I am present both personally and impersonally. I am incarnate and excarnate. I am both subject and object, both performer and witness, both seer and seen. And to the degree I can have a respectful relationship with, in this case, the part of me that is angry – to that degree I can have respectful, whole relations with others.

The Communal Sphere
And, once again, we come to paradox. Because (just as the personal depends on the existential, and the existential depends on the personal), although we can't relate to others in wholeness until we have a degree of wholeness in ourselves, nevertheless, we acquire that wholeness in ourselves by relating to others. In other words, it is in the communal sphere that the personal sphere matures. Unlike the split-up transcendent model of enlightenment, which encourages serene detachment, holistic realisation happens in the world. Each person's path may or may not include periods of retreat or isolation, but ultimately, holism encourages blissful, serene involvement (and not so serene involvement) – involvement with one's body, heart and mind, with others, with matter, and with spirit-in-the-world.

When we talk about the communal sphere, and the rites of passage of initiation and partnership, it is a mistake to see them as two ceremonies. Initiation is a journey, and partnership is a journey, and they both take many years. And it is over these years that one develops self-acceptance and self-worth. It is on these exquisite and tortuous journeys that one develops wholeness in oneself.

But this wholeness is developed in the company of one's sisters or brothers in one's initiation group, and in the company of one's same-sex or other-sex partner. Their acceptance of our deepest shame, the worth they accord us... within this the slow, strong weaving of our wholeness takes place.

The opportunities that come to give, to see and be seen, to look into each other, to travel as one... All of this happens communally. Not only in the formal structures of the communal sphere, but on outings together, at parties, at dinner with friends... And, much as we need to be close to our own unique tone and pulse, ultimately, we know, we can never really be alone. We need to enter inside ourselves, and know ourselves, but our very knowing is in the laps of our lovers and friends. Our personal path, much as it is completely up to us, also rests completely upon the insight and compassion of our community.

I said above that, hopefully, we acquire a personal experience of the theories of the existential sphere within the personal sphere. Similarly, within the communal sphere we can hope to encounter a communal experience of the existential sphere. In other words, it lets us see what the philosophy looks like in a community. In the communal sphere we can see and appreciate the social promise of our philosophy. In this sense, the existential sphere is dependent upon the communal sphere. It is its sacred theatre.

And the practical sphere also depends on the communal sphere. It is its soul. The communal sphere unites us in our faith. In the circles and ceremonies of the communal sphere we see each other to the bone, we see each other's substance – we see each other in the spotlight of eternity. And thus we come to know – our sameness. Together we express our not-knowing, our helplessness, our surrender, our nobility, our glory, our power – feelings we all know, which belong to no one, which float among us and unite us in our humanity. Thus, having witnessed each other, having known each other, we enter the practical sphere as one. In the communal sphere the community body is formed. In the practical sphere it acts.

The Practical Sphere

We can work together because we have faith in each other. We can depend upon each other because we know each other's substance. We co-operate naturally because we know the other is ourself. This is not an intellectually enforced communism, but a simple and natural expression of human togetherness. Nor is this sentimental idealism. Action that comes out of the rawness of having been psychologically and spiritually naked together is soulful and down-to-earth. It is fragile and rock-strong. It is painfully real.

And because we have stood together in the sacred spaces of the communal sphere there is no shame of sacredness, no need to repress appreciation for the mystery of every moment, the miracle of everything we touch. To say that an environmental ethic is automatic would be an understatement. This is the problem with most environmental action. It doesn't emerge from a unified communal sphere. In fact, for the most part, it leaps straight from ideas to action (from sphere 1 to sphere 4) and thus, although much temporary good might be done (and this should not be underestimated either) nevertheless, at best it is a patch up job ungrounded in any real social alternative.

Thus: everything depends on the existential sphere. Everything depends on the personal sphere. Everything depends on the communal sphere. And finally – everything depends on the practical sphere. Everything depends on the practical sphere because if a civilisation were to only engage in the first three spheres it would remain disembodied – and its failure to honour the physical would rebound in its face (which, of course, is what has happened). It is in the practical sphere that the other three find their completion. The practical sphere, rather than being a burden and a distraction (as it has been seen by the transcendent path), becomes the field of full manifestation. In the sphere of action holism becomes fully manifest. All of our philosophy, self-development and communal journeying become preparation for entering the temple of life. Even the initiatory journeys of the communal sphere are, ultimately, only preparation for holistic everyday life.

As we seek to feed and clothe and house ourselves, and trade, and organise our community, all of the other spheres are tested. Does our philosophy make sense, in practice, or not? Has our self-realisation equipped us with presence, wisdom and heart – or not? And are we in this together, or aren't we? And ultimately, potentially, all the spheres merge – work becomes worship. The community's planting and harvesting and weaving and building and business and politics and law all become a collective sacred-erotic offering.

Conclusion

This then is an overview of the model of the four spheres of community. Although there are many sub-spheres and in-between-spheres, the model gives an overview of the basic dimensions of community. How can it help? Models can be very useful. Just to have the four spheres mapped out can be of enormous help to a group of people who want to develop holistic community in their local area. And if we understand their interdependence, we will be sure to tend them all.

How deeply do we understand holism? Maybe we need to attend to the existential sphere. Are we engaged in growth work? Is it holistic – are we working transpersonally as well as psychotherapeutically, and do the techniques we use also involve the body? Perhaps we need to attend to the personal sphere.

And do we have the communication skills to be able to travel together in openness? Does each of us know how to be a part of a group without getting psychically lost? Are we able to let the group be guided? Although each of our personal paths might involve different disciplines – do we share a common language of groupwork – such as co-creativity? And can we invoke a sacred space together? Do we have a common language for the creation, maintenance and development of ritual – like flexible form? Do we have a shared approach to initiation, to partnership? Perhaps we need to attend to the communal sphere.

And finally, do we know how to work the land with love? Do we know how to tend the water with reverence? Do we know how to build, to weave, to sew boots, to throw pots – with sensitivity? Do we have the knowledge and the skills? Do we understand decentralisation? Are we ready to take responsibility? Do we have a common understanding of socially responsible business? Perhaps we need to attend to the practical sphere.

And the model of the four spheres of community offers not only insight into the parts, but also a vision of the whole. It offers a glimpse of the potential beauty of holistic community. It is useful, but it is also inspirational. If we are to work hard together, and inspire our children and grandchildren to continue the work, then we need to carry a deep sense of what whole living might look like – of what it might feel like to live together within a mythology of wholeness.

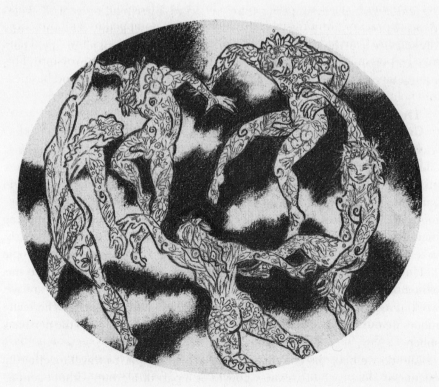

The Community Forum

The Theory

If we could enter the essence of holism, and hold time still, we would find ourselves in the sacred-erotic moment. But in practice holism is not still, it is continuous co-creativity. And in terms of community, this holistic co-creativity is very intimate and exposing. In practice, because we acknowledge the presence of the vast unknown, we are existentially humbled. Because we acknowledge our emotions, we are humbled in our pretensions to serene equanimity and self-realised magnanimity. Because we acknowledge our bodies, we are humbled in our physical need and frailty. Above all, when we enter the essence of holistic co-creativity we find ourselves together, much as we will at the time of death, on the cusp of the dying moment, in the most shocking vulnerability, face to face with the emptiness of the future, with no way out.

Flexible form is a way of managing this situation. It is a way of moving together. Because we *are* together. And it allows for our individual integrity. Because we *are* alone. Flexible form is not the kind of social order that calls revolutions upon itself. It is in a state of constant self-critique. It has doubt built in. It keeps us together by allowing us to be ourselves.

And the four sphere model makes sure we don't drift off into premodern pseudo-sacredness, or modern pseudo-eroticism. By reminding us of the interdependence of all the spheres, the four sphere model gently dismantles any division between the sacred and the mundane. It leads us to a place where politics and economics are conducted in full view of spirit – no less than a ceremony of thanksgiving for a baby's birth.

The Practice, and Inclusivity

This is the theory of holistic community. But is it not impossibly abstract? Given today's overlapping mess of fundamentalist reactionism, modernist numbness and postmodern confusion, how can we possibly translate these dignified and deep visions into anything of practical relevance – even at an individual level, let alone at the level of community reconstruction?

In this chapter I will be proposing the community forum as the first step towards an answer to this question. It is a simple first step. But even initially, it is something very beautiful. There is something very beautiful about people coming together and, one by one, letting it be known that they too share a vision of community life in which all actions, private and public, are considered equally sacred. It is beautiful and deeply touching to see people of all ages come forward and tell everyone that they too, in the most ultimate of senses, know nothing – and that they too dream of a mass intimacy based on nothing but honesty and openness and mutual support. It is an honour to be allowed to see into the profound integrity of strangers. It is an honour to confess, and to witness others confessing: that we all have a deep, unmet shared need; an all-but-abandoned shared longing; a shared secret-of-secrets – to travel together in all the pain and joy of love.

And such an evening might be how a community forum would begin. But for people to come forward and echo each other, each in their own way, would presume some preparation. Papers would need to have been circulated, open evenings held perhaps. People would need to be arriving with shared concepts, and a shared understanding of the matter at hand. Because there would need to be a strong echo, a strong resonance, if a holistic community forum was to crystallise as the core of a holistic community development project. If some people came forward with holistic ideals, and others with sub-holistic and supra-holistic and anti-holistic ideals, and similarly varied understandings of the point of the forum itself, then something else might crystallise, but not a holistic community project.

This doesn't mean the community forum would be closed or elitist – anymore than a marriage can be accused of being rigid or exclusive for being monogamous. Sometimes people say that for community to be holistic it must include the whole (by which they mean that it must include everyone), and that therefore we can have nothing so precise as a commonly held world-myth, or self-developmental myth, or myth of ideal community. I think this is a misconception. I think it is also naive. I don't believe it is possible to develop absolutely inclusive community. By definition, a community must share agreements – and there will always be people (fascist, atheist, religious fundamentalist, and so on) who will not accept them. And if the boundaries around these agreements are open enough, then people will come in when they want to. Postmodern, growth-working, green values are still spreading within the culture…

Not being inclusive does not mean being exclusive, in the negative sense of the word. But when I talk about holistic community, even to people whose lives are intensely committed to holism, again and again, I hear the same fear: of people being left out, of a sense of holistic superiority emerging, of an us-and-them, better-and-worse mentality. This is our great fear. But to stand for what one believes in does not mean denigrating others' beliefs. It means having the clarity and courage to honour oneself, to state 'I am this. This is the way I am. This is where I stand,' and to remain in respectful relationship when there is difference.

Modernity has addressed exclusion due to sex, due to race, due to creed, due to sexual preference, due to physical or mental difference… And it equates difference with exclusion and persecution. And having been raised in modernity we are hypersensitive to this equation. But we can end up excluding and persecuting ourselves. We can be so sensitive to any possible exclusion that we don't dare include our deepest feelings – in case they create a difference. We need to operate with a new equation, in which difference equals mutual self-valuing equals mutual respect. Without this postmodern mathematics of difference we can only go in the direction of a culture of the lowest common denominator.

We cannot be immobilised by a fear of difference, and of our own insensitive boundaries. Boundaries are there in all relationships. Relationships need them. Without them – where do you end? Where do I end? How can we touch each other? If a holistic community project is flourishing, healthy boundaries will certainly be present in its relationship with the local neighbourhood or town. Strong, gentle, confident, open boundaries – hopefully. To ignore or hide or minimise boundaries only results in messy, confused relationships. Boundaries are there. They need to be named. The question is not of whether they should be there, but of how to hold them. And as I see it, the boundaries of healthy community are porous. They exist (that is, within them the community agreements are in place), but they are open – both ways.

The boundaries of mature holistic community are porous inasmuch as they are neither over-fixed nor over-flexible. But as we follow the path of holism we become acquainted with our personal boundaries. We come to appreciate how we sometimes hold them protectively, and sometimes defensively. We learn to open and close them. Thus, inevitably, the boundaries of a holistic community will reflect the maturity with which the community members hold their own. And a subtle elitism, a tendency to see in terms of them-and-us, could easily arise – particularly, perhaps, early on when the community feels unsure and insecure. But knowing no community is immune to exclusivism could keep us alert, rather than stopping us before we start.

Slowing Down, and the Forum as Hub

I said earlier that co-creativity isn't easy, that it needs to be practised, and that groups tend to pass through their childhoods and adolescences before entering their adulthoods. And co-creativity is extremely adult.

As the forum practises co-creativity, questions of purpose will almost certainly come up. 'What are we doing, just sitting around getting to know each other. Surely this isn't holistic community!' 'Yes, but how can we throw ourselves into the debate about the closure of the local secondary school when we hardly know each other?' 'How can we just sit around getting to know each other when the educational future of our children is in jeopardy?' A being/doing tension might arise, between those who 'want to develop the project', and those who feel 'supporting each other is the most important part of community'. Of course, if there is a mood of co-creativity, people will value both voices.

I would tend to back the need to get to know each other by practising co-creative dialogue, particularly early on. Of course, we get to know each other by doing things together, but in today's speed-crazed, action-mad culture, we are uncomfortable with simply being together, and tend to avoid our discomfort by keeping busy. Our bodies seem to synchronise with the tempo of the culture. Even when we have free time we often rush about filling it with relaxations. It's culturally unnatural to slow down. But by slowing things down, and remembering the historical context (that holistic community development is a multi-generational endeavour), we can give attention to the quality of our togetherness, to the depth at which we intend to work. Of course, sometimes a fledgling community will be called to act – not out of avoidance or escapism, but because everyone's soul feels impelled to respond to a pressing local need. But generally, by slowing ourselves down, and resisting the impetus to act, we can attune to the pain and hope and beauty between us, and nourish the very ground of our togetherness.

Finally, however good and true and right we might feel holistic community to be, however much allegiance we might feel to its ideological principles, and however disillusioned we might be with all other possible social paradigms – we will only feel embedded in our local community to the extent that we allow ourselves to receive emotional and practical support from others, and to the extent we feel received and seen and respected. Gradually social structures will need to be put in place. And social structures hold community in place. But in the last analysis, it is one-to-one relationships that hold the social structures in place.

And eventually action will come. Whether it is a call for a festival, an old people's support group, a car-sharing scheme, or a protest against building yet another multinational supermarket in the town, action of one sort or another will be called for. But what direction to go in? It might be useful to see the community forum as the hub of the community, with a circle around it divided into four sections representing the four spheres. A better diagram would show all four spheres overlapping, and none closer to one than to any other – but a circle with four sections is a start. And looking out from the hub into each of the four spheres we might ask what we already have, and what we lack.

First glances into these four sections, and obvious responses, might look something like this… Looking into the first sphere we might be reminded of our lack of clarity about holism, and decide to organise discussion groups, or a conference. Looking into the second sphere we might note our lack of communication skills, and decide to arrange some workshops. Looking into the third sphere we might be saddened by the lack of local holistic celebration, and decide to come together to mark midsummer with our bodies, hearts and souls. Or looking into the fourth sphere we might be shocked by the lack of availability of local organic produce, and decide to set up a local producers' weekly market.

Different subgroups would form to take responsibility for these different initiatives, and attempt to continue their practice of holistic co-creativity and flexible form outside the main community forum – in the way they met and planned and planned and carried out their responsibilities. And each subgroup would have its own relationship with the community as a whole, which would come up at the forum – appreciation, criticism, suggestions… And people would join and leave the various subgroups, subgroups would expand and shrink their portfolios, and subgroups would be born and die.

Spheres Within Spheres

But if holistic community is to flourish we need to lend particular attention to the quality of our activities. It is easy to seem to be flourishing, to have lots of ideas and schemes on the go. But we will only grow old together, and inspire generation after generation to travel with us, if our flourishing is deeply rooted. Only deep, authentic roots that feed on the truth of the human condition will hold us together, and speak to the souls of our children and our children's children. We need to make sure we are being deeply nourished. It is in the long-term interest of the community to slow down, to not rush to address every lack in every sphere, to form subgroups and committees and plan and perform and prove itself.

One way to do this is by being aware that, although we can situate any aspect of community in one of the four spheres, all four spheres exist within all things. For example, although trade might be a fourth sphere activity, there is a theory of trade (sphere one), an ethics of trade (sphere two), and a social dimension of business guilds and community relationships (spheres three). Similarly, the rite of passage of initiation into adulthood, whist clearly a concern of the third sphere, has a sphere-one existential context, sphere-two personal significance, and involves fourth-sphere planning and execution.

By considering all four spheres within all of our concerns, we can slow ourselves down, and imbue our initiatives with fullness and depth. Not only this, but by this kind of soulful mulling over of our lacks, we might find ourselves coming up with unexpected creativity. For example, our first glance at the first sphere told us we lacked knowledge on holism, and so we decided to form a subgroup to organise discussion groups and conferences. A predictable, linear decision. But if we'd borne it in mind that all things have their theoretical sphere, then we might have come up with a more lateral decision. We might, for example, since gardening has its theoretical sphere (not least of all in the permacultural perspective), have decided to clarify our understanding of holism out in our gardens…. or by exploring holistic architecture, or by comparing meditation techniques, or by experimenting in preparing and eating sacred-erotic suppers (and, of course, discussing the experience afterwards).

Going Out, More on Boundaries

When some subgroups are formed, they will go out from the hub, out from the supportive atmosphere of the holistic community project, and into the local area. Particularly sphere-four initiatives. A subgroup formed to address the issue of local transport, for example, will not be able to make progress without engaging in dialogue with local public opinion, various local stakeholders in the issue, and the local authorities. How should it proceed? Whether the subgroup decides to be a pressure group, or to convene a larger public forum, it will need to be realistic in the degree to which it can introduce the beauty and efficiency of co-creativity and flexible form. Realistic, but not condescending.

An issue such as local transport will draw a variety of interested parties. Parties not only with a variety of motives, but with a variety of worldviews. However, it can be a mistake to underestimate people's openness. A public meeting might not have a ritual opening (like the community forum might have), but a poem, or a piece of music, gently suggesting our sameness, might be deeply appreciated. And although the emotional openness of co-creativity, or an expectation of awareness of our oneness-and-difference, might be considered bizarre at a public meeting, an emphasis on ensuring that all voices were heard (including the disempowered and inarticulate ones) might also be surprisingly welcomed.

I am mentioning this for two reasons. Firstly, as an illustration of a larger point about boundaries... the question of where the holistic community project begins and where it ends – of when we are 'at home', and when we are 'out there'. The question of who's in, and who's out, of them and us. We might often wish they didn't, but boundaries exist. Whether vague, tight, or firm but flexible, they are there. And boundary issues will come up. For example, if the community forum has decided to start support groups for couples, and two couples who are not interested in the overall vision of holistic community want to join one of these support groups – can they? I am not saying they should or shouldn't be allowed. My point is that there will be an allowing, or a not-allowing. That boundaries exist. And that the maturity with which these boundaries are held will largely determine the reputation of the holistic community project within the wider local area. And that the way the project is seen will hearten or dishearten the project itself.

Secondly, I said in the introduction to this section that I would not be discussing the content of holistic politics, but that I would be looking at its qualitative reform, and at its relationship to the other three spheres. In terms of the quality of political involvement, I have wanted to suggest two levels. The fully holistic co-creative level within the community forum, or a politically oriented subgroup – in which issues can be explored non-oppositionally, and without any intended repression of the body, feelings, or awareness of the presence of the mystery. And a second qualitative level in which there is an attempt to balance idealism and realism, to introduce a maximum of co-creativity, of fully holistic democracy, but with a sensitivity and respect for local political norms and expectations. Of course, as the local holistic community grew, and as a more holistic approach to public meetings became more usual, the gap between these two levels would begin to close.

In terms of the relationship between the fourth sphere and the other three, in the hierarchy of modernity, the fourth is on top. Not only is the political and economic fourth sphere totally dominant, but it dominates the other three to the point of non-existence. There is the (sphere one) pseudo-scientific philosophy of the porno-flatland, but little more. For modernity, sphere two personal development and sphere three collective development are either hangovers from premodernity or marginal, holistic counter-cultural phenomena. In modernity, politics and politicians rule. In the community forum centred model of holistic community, however, politics is resituated. It becomes one sphere among four, an arena no more or less important than any other. And community members involved in politically focused subgroups, no more or less important than those involved in developing the other three spheres.

A Word on Size

Finally, a word on facilitation and co-creativity and size. As the community grows the community forum will swell, events will be larger – everything will need to be facilitated more skillfully, particularly if we are to proceed in co-creativity. But when we talk of co-creativity there seems to be an assumption that it is a completely 'horizontal' methodology, that it stands in opposition to hierarchy and authority and power. Luckily, this is a misunderstanding, because we need to be realistic about the degree of facilitation that is needed in larger co-creative situations. And the anti-authoritarian, often bitter stance is also self-deceptive. Because hierarchy and power are always present – whether they are hierarchies of sex, colour, age, knowledge or experience, whether they are stated or unstated, conscious or unconscious.

In a small group with a lot of experience of co-creativity, completely unfacilitated co-creativity is obviously possible. Not always necessarily desirable, but certainly possible. But as gatherings get larger, and the participants less experienced in the mystical process of co-creativity, the need for facilitation will increase. It is important not to label unfacilitated co-creativity as 'real' or 'complete' co-creativity. Although there is a temporarily unequal distribution of power whenever a facilitator is appointed, and although co-creativity is about individual empowerment, it does not preclude facilitation. Co-creativity is not less when led.

There are unfacilitated groups in which less confident or eloquent individ-

uals become the observers of the confident and eloquent. And there are facilitated groups in which the less confident and eloquent are given the time and
space to develop their confidence and eloquence. The former might look co-
creative, but are actually controlled by covert power – and disempowering.
The latter might not look co-creative, but involve stated, visible power being
used to facilitate equality and empowerment.

Not only this, but the so-called-confident who are dominating the group are
actually also in a position of disempowerment (otherwise they wouldn't need
to dominate), and the apparently co-creative structure (which isn't co-creative
at all) is perpetuating their disempowerment. Whereas, in the facilitated group,
clean power is being used to halt their domination. And in their silence they
have the opportunity of empowerment through really hearing and valuing
others (and thus eventually themselves).

Co-creativity does preclude absolute, unquestionable leadership – leadership mythically invested with divine omniscience. But leaders, or facilitators,
who are unquestionably human and fallible, who are temporarily placed in
positions of power, whose instructions are to serve the community, to serve the
co-creative process – such leaders are often crucial, especially when we are
many.

To experience co-creativity is to experience the journey of collective
consciousness. Large community forums and gatherings need organisation
and facilitation. To say that they therefore cannot offer the full experience of
co-creativity is a misunderstanding. In my experience, the small unfacilitated
band of experienced travellers may or may not 'take off' within the expanded
consciousness of co-creativity – at times they'll be harmonised, at times split
by conflict, at times cut off from each other, even while talking of love. And
at the other extreme the same is true. The large facilitated forum may or may
not become a surcharged, collective opening, awakening event. The deter-
mining factor is not the presence of authority. Co-creativity is not real or
complete without it, or unreal or incomplete with it. While we have to be
careful to maintain flexible and humane structures, the appropriateness of
facilitation is relative to the situation, and the factors which allow co-creativity
to fully unfold, I believe, are beyond the reach of words.

However, there is probably a certain number of thousands of people,
beyond which a community cannot grow if it is to be remain human-scale. But
that is not our problem at present. For now the challenge is to maintain holistic
co-creativity in the community forum, at the hub of the community, so that it
will permeate through all of the subgroups and all of the community's efforts
to develop the four spheres; to manage porous boundaries; to travel slowly and
deeply; and to hold on patiently to the long-term vision of a community of
openness and authenticity.

The Communal Sphere: Initiation

In Sections One and Two I looked extensively at the first two spheres. In the introduction to this section I said my concern with the fourth sphere would be to look at it in terms of its qualitative improvement, and of its relationship with the other three spheres – as I have been doing in the last few chapters.

I have spoken of the community forum as the hub of holistic community, as the coordinating centre. And I have also spoken of the third sphere, the communal sphere, as the central structure of holistic community, as the sphere that weaves all of the others together. I now want to look at the third sphere.

I believe the main structures of the communal sphere are the rites of passage of birth, death, initiation and partnership, and seasonal celebration. In my discussion of flexible form I touched on community co-creation of the rites of passage of birth. All that I said there could equally be applied to the rites of passage of death. In this chapter I will be looking at initiation and partnership. Which leaves one remaining structure: seasonal celebration.

Seasonal Celebration

Traditionally, all communities gathered at least four times a year. Ritual gathering can re-attune a community to its core-note.

Seasonal celebrations are not only about planting or harvesting. They are also about an archetypal intrapsychic cycle. Just as our moods can respond to sunshine and cloud cover, somehow we respond to the moods of the seasons. Just as nature pulls itself into itself in winter, in the darkness of winter we ourselves are re-conceived. In the awakening spring we too are re-born. Then in contrast to the introversion of winter, in the brightness of summer we act, we shine. Until in the autumn, once again, we mellow and reflect, and drift back inside ourselves again. The candles of midwinter, whether of Christmas or Chanukah or Divali, do not only light the night of winter, they re-connect us with our flickering souls' quick journeys from birth to death.

Of course, to the degree that we are alienated from the seasons' rhythms, whether by premodern heavenliness or modern urban slickness, we will lose contact with the seasons of the soul. We might even doubt their existence. And then there is another factor, our personal journeys' cycles and moods… We might, for example, be in a state of inwardness, even depression, in midsummer. It is not that everyone, always, automatically shines in summer. But although our individual journeys might sometimes clash with the prevailing emotional climate, there is a collective psychological response to the year. It is not by chance that we tend to take our holidays in the summer. Nor would it be a good idea to start school at the beginning of summer…

In writing in Section Two about the rite of passage of adolescence, I said they 'are there, within us all – like milk teeth that must fall, or skin that must wrinkle. They are unavoidable. They have an objective subtle existence. They happen whether the culture acknowledges them or facilitates them or not'. Similarly, the psychology of the seasons has its subtle-objective existence. And the celebrations that take place at the solstices and equinoxes, although they have different mythologies and rationales within different cultural contexts, do not mark sectarian or even culturally-specific phenomena. They consecrate the universally significant wave of psychological time.

And in gathering at these times, whether we tell the story of the resurrection or of the re-birth of Israel, we cluster as a community around the mysterious essence of our bizarre situation: the finding of ourselves (whatever we are), on earth (whatever that is, wherever that is), temporarily alive (whatever that means), with each other. And the link with the seasons, with fertility and barrenness, embeds us in this situation. We too have sex and age. And as we touch the essence of that mystery together we are bound in sacred appreciation. Sometimes, in times of horror or wonder, a community can be profoundly bound. But that is spontaneous. Seasonal ceremony and celebration offer the opportunity for a community to regularly bond in its deepest sacred humanity.

In terms of the four spheres, we might say that we have been discussing the first and third spheres of seasonal celebration. The fourth involves the practicalities of constructing co-creative ritual in flexible form. Free of the obligations of tradition, each co-creative community can arrange its own rituals and celebrations. Each community can build its own local traditions – traditions that are always open to addition, subtraction and modification. A picture of a co-creative culture begins to emerge… in which we travel from community to community, meeting variation after variation on a season's theme.

And the second, personal sphere also needs to be included if these gatherings are to be holistic. We need to acknowledge our individuality, our differences – what our hearts and souls have been through, how we've been touched and how we've responded – through the last quarter of the year (since the previous solstice or equinox gathering). When we include the personal sphere the ceremony gets real. When we include our pain the sacredness drops to yet another level.

Finally, before discussing initiation and partnership, I would just like to mention that there are also many others rites of passage within the communal sphere – from naming, to leaving home, to menopause, to retirement. And that there are many other opportunities for ritual gathering – birthdays, anniversaries and new years, things beginning and things ending, arrivals and departures, things remembered, times of joy, times of grief. And that sometimes ritual happens unexpectedly, and that sometimes it is best barely arranged.

1. LOOKING PRACTICALLY AT INITIATION

Introduction

The aim of Balance's menswork and womenswork is to contribute to the development of holistic men's communities and holistic women's communities. Not 'intentional communities', but communities of individuals dedicated to the path of wholeness (albeit in a thousand different ways) living *within* society.

Our first initiative was to begin setting up, not just men's and women's support groups, but men's and women's 'initiation' groups - the idea being that the rite of passage of initiation is the axis of both the men's and the women's communities, and that if we want to re-establish these communities we need to have the axis in place.

I am in one of these initiation groups and, outside of my marriage, it has become the most supportive place in my life. I have come to love the men in my group with a depth I never expected. And I feel loved. I am respecting, and I feel respected. I am learning the differences between, and the universality of, our wounds – and I feel part of a group-imagination struggling towards new images of manhood. I am finding my male-human identity (as against my suprahuman-spiritual identity), and I am finding my place among men in a way I never could before, because I could never get close enough.

But why consider initiation the axis? Because initiation immediately brings up the question of definition. What is a man? What is a woman? What is the essence of masculinity and femininity? To be able to initiate ourselves we must first have found social agreement on some sort of concept or vision of masculinity and femininity. So initiation can be seen, firstly, as a mystical and philosophical axis.

And it is at the time of initiation that we bond with the social whole. The boy feels himself expanding into identification with all of the men in his community. The girl with the women. The rite of passage of initiation establishes the whole social structure of the uninitiated, the initiated, and the initiators (the elders). Initiation, therefore, can also be seen as a social axis.

All of this might sound quite straight forward. All we need to do is recreate initiation (into, hopefully, deeper and higher images than James Bond and the Barbie Doll), and then, without too many hitches, new, healthy, healed men's and women's communities will gradually take shape – and healthy, healed, whole men and women will make healthy, healed, whole babies, and we will all live in healthy, healed holistic community happily ever after.

Challenges

But the truth is that – even if initiation is the philosophical and social axis of holistic men's and women's communities – the nitty gritty of how to reintroduce initiation into contemporary society in a real, relevant, sensitive and powerful way, is not so obvious. There are many subtle points to be considered. Practically, today, it's not so easy. But I want to name the main challenges I am aware of, and to outline my responses – responses which, to me, seem solid enough to keep me optimistically experimenting in cultural reconstruction.

Let me name, then, what I consider to be the most challenging issues we have to face. Firstly, who decides when we've arrived at 'the correct' definition of masculinity or femininity? And, even if we can decide this, who decides on the exact body of information to be passed on, and who decides on the exact form of the presentation? Secondly, where is the male or female community-of-the-initiated into which the initiand enters? Including, of course, the initiators, the elders.

Thirdly, who decides when someone's ready – and how? And fourthly, there's the question of age. In my experience, most of the men and women ready to admit they don't stand in their wholeness – that they do not fully know their own male or female dignity – are close to middle age. So can we really draw appropriate inspiration from the premodern rite of passage for wide-eyed adolescents? And what is the relationship between these near-on-middle-aged initiation-seekers and today's adolescents? Fifthly, is initiation a 'one-off' event? Initiation from adolescence into adulthood is a once-in-a-lifetime event, but might not the sort of initiation we're discussing consist of a number of events, over a number of years? And, lastly, cannot a road accident (and maybe a month in hospital), or an out of the body experience, or the loss of a child, or a sexual ecstasy, or any powerful experience, be in itself an initiation? And, therefore, do we really need to reconstruct the formal rite of passage?

This last point, although frequently made, is, I believe, quickly answered. Yes, of course the agonies and the ecstasies can all be initiations (in a general sense of the term). We could go further still, and say that every split second can be an initiation – if perceived or experienced intensely enough. But they are individual (as against social) initiations. They initiate us into deeper levels of experience, into a more focused connection with birth and death, perhaps, but they do not bond us into the social body. Nor are they specific enough – they do not necessarily convey the specific content – the specifically whole-male-making or whole-female-making healing message – of sexual initiation. In themselves, these 'general' initiations would not be enough to structure or support coherent holistic men's and women's communities.

The Generation Riddle

The next point I'd like to take up concerns discrepancies around age – the fact that it is mostly middle aged women and men who are coming forward asking for help through what was traditionally a rite of passage of adolescence, and the other fact that today's adolescents also need help. Let's first ask about the essence of initiation. It is a stepping out of the family into the community, into the world. It is a welcoming in among equally sexually potent adults. At the physical, social and psychological levels it is a rite of individuality, selfhood, empowerment and responsibility. And at the archetypal and spiritual levels it is an entrance through the portals of the sacred. It is a crossing of the threshold, the edge, where the worlds meet and overlap. 'Welcome!' say the elders, 'Now we stand together before the beauty, the magic, the mystery and the meaning.' On this level the qualities that are called forth are humility, wisdom, compassion and endless appreciation.

Is this what our middle-aged seekers need? Or do they already stand beyond family, in self, in authenticity? Are they already bonded in powerful, humble, sacred community? Let's not generalise. Different people have arrived at different developmental levels, have varied spiritual awarenesses, and contrasting experiences of community. Nevertheless, in my experience, few have ever lived for very long in aloneness and acceptance-in-community, in the presence of the eternal magic and meaning. In my experience, most of us in middle-age, myself most certainly included, have a lot of initiatory ground still to cover. Not only this, but it is by covering that ground *together* that we find community. Even if I have shared a lot, and grieved a lot, and grown a lot, in private, or in another town – it is only when I am seen unfolding into wholeness (and see my friends doing the same) that initiation can achieve its full meaning – as a social threshold into sacred community. Only by witnessing and being witnessed can we develop deep faith in each other. And the depth of this faith will determine the depth of the community.

But what about the teenagers, who, as it has so often, so correctly, been said are almost totally without deep guidance? I have written elsewhere that, precisely because initiation is a social affair, a welcoming *into* the social body, we need to first build the social body of initiated adults – into which to then initiate the younger men and women. I still feel this is true, but on the other hand, where is the social body into which the middle-aged initiands are being welcomed? It doesn't exist. They are building it out of themselves. Perhaps therefore, at the same time as the middle-aged are self-initiating, to whatever degree they feel capable (and calling for outside assistance wherever they feel they need it), the middle-aged can facilitate initiatory work with teenagers, aware that it lacks a social context (as does their own). Because the middle-aged might not feel ready, but what can they do – leave the teenagers to peer guidance and cultural pressure?

This does not mean that middle-aged men should concoct and impose an initiatory curriculum. But just as they were co-creating their own initiatory journeys with their own peers, they could co-create with the young men. The young men might be invited to learn to listen to the guiding spirit of the co-creative process, and then encouraged to shape their own initiatory journeys together with the facilitators. The older men (holding the context of detachment from family, and attachment to self, purpose and spirit), might offer questions like 'What is man?', and 'What qualities do you feel you need to develop?', and then help the young men evolve their own initiatory journeys and rituals. In this way the young men would be both respected in their individuality, and assisted in going beyond themselves.

For these young men the challenge is the cultivation of an independent, relational self. If I was guiding a group of teenage boys the sense of the initiatory moment (which might span several years) that I would try to hold would be: 'I have been my parents' child until now. Now I need to find myself. Like them, I have now become a sexual being. I am not them. I am me. How can I remain true to my body and my heart? How can I stay close to spirit? I need to practice authenticity. I need to learn boundaries. In this lies my nobility. At the same time, as my sexuality rises and my sense of self strengthens, I feel sublimely excited by life. I enter the community of adults with a huge 'yes'.'

And perhaps, as each local community of initiated women and men (of all ages) begins to expand, and time passes, and experience thickens, it will be in more and more of a position to offer guidance and facilitation, and to welcome newcomers in. And perhaps, within a few generations, it will be only the young women and men who will need to be welcomed in.

Beyond Correctness

All of this is, at best, sketchy. We need to experiment locally – upon ourselves. As a culture, we lack experience in such matters. We need to experiment, and come to different conclusions, and compare learnings… And the question of differences brings us back to many of the remaining 'challenges' listed above. The search for 'the correct' definition of masculinity or femininity, or for 'the correct' body of information to be passed on at the time of initiation, or for 'the correct' anything, for that matter, presumes that such a thing actually exists. And does it? Is there a 'correct' way to transmit initiatory information, for example? Even if there is (which I doubt), in our individualistic, anti-authoritarian culture we are unlikely to ever reach agreement on 'the one right way for everyone' to do anything.

And it's not only bitterness or stubbornness… We're also aware of the insights of cross-cultural studies. Different cultures, in different eras, have held different beliefs, and created different cultural forms to express those beliefs. And if every culture that has ever existed has refined its own ideas and rituals, why can't we, here, locally? Why should we be limited to searching for one clear-cut idea, and one ideal ritual format for our whole culture – why not let every community create its own? Why not go beyond the search for 'the correct' way, and agree to let every community formulate and express the holistic outlook in its own chosen way? Why not encourage our own and each other's communities to evolve differently, according to our different moods and tones and atmospheres. And perhaps, by reclaiming the right to create initiatory (and other) cultural forms in whatever ways we feel appropriate, we will be laying the foundations for a lively, varied, empowered holistic culture.

For communities to co-create their own rites of passage – their own ways of communicating the journey of wholeness through the generations – is a sublime and precarious affair. But what other option do we have? Our individualism is a fact, we do not want to re-establish absolute hierarchy (we are defiantly democratic), we have seen beyond 'correctness' – beyond the ethnocentric dogmatism of 'we are the only way' – and we value tolerance, co-operation and flexibility. Today, co-creativity seems to be the only realistic, practical basis for a holistic culture.

Initially, the co-creative response means that each initiation group must go beyond the search for 'the correct' way to decide, for example, when someone is ready to be initiated – into the frightening and exciting responsibility of finding its own criteria. Groups may or may not look outside the group for advice or expertise – but their own consensus, their own collective voice, has the last say. Should the initiand participate in designing his or her own initiation ceremony? Should initiation be a one-off, a series of annual events, or what? To start with, as I see it, the co-creative community must give every initiation group the opportunity, and the respect, to shape its own fate. Only gradually will each community begin to gather its own experience – and then, as that experience evolves, be in a position to offer guidance to new initiation groups. Guidance which, by definition in co-creative community, will itself be forever evolving.

And if we are to travel together, working together towards conscious, co-creative holistic communities, we will have to call upon our highest ideals and deepest resources. When a group seeks to formulate, for example, its own definition of masculinity or femininity, or its own language and symbols of initiation, it will be forced to stretch and test its co-creative powers: its psychological awareness and skill, its level of empathy and respect, its unity, its trust in itself and its trust in life. And it might do all of this brilliantly, or it might not – it might do it disastrously, at first. But each group's stumbling, picking itself up again, and perhaps sharing its up and downs with other groups, will be the community learning process. The community forum subgroups responsible for womenswork and menswork might organise conferences and gatherings, women's and men's 'community houses', and community literature in order to facilitate this process.

This might make us feel insecure. Where's the authority? Where are the boundaries? But let's be blunt about it, humanity has tried the path of 'only one correct way' – and it is divisive (dividing us into for's and against's, friends and enemies), and it is grounded in arrogance and dishonesty (after all, how can we ever know ours is the only way). And co-creativity is all about involvement and empowerment, intimacy and communication, honesty and unpretentiousness, and art-in-life and co-creation with spirit. I, for one, would like to see my children's children growing up in a community grown from such seeds.

The Personal Challenge

Finally, although I have hinted at it, there is still one challenge I have not responded to directly, namely: 'where is the male or female community-of-the-initiated into which the initiand enters? Including, of course, the initiators, the elders?' In my opinion, at the moment, we just have to acknowledge our poverty. At worst we are a culture in self-destruction, at best we are a culture in-recovery. We are where we are. What can we say? We do not live in holistic community. If we want it, we'll have to build it. It's up to us to become the community-of-the-initiated. Some of us might know one elder here, or one elder there, or sometimes we might want to call in an elder from outside the community, but – if we're talking about a culture of wholeness – its up to us to become that community-of-elders. It's up to us to knit the community together, to cultivate the common language, the language of owning emotions, of speaking from the heart, of honouring other people's perspectives, of deep respect for beauty and the unknown – to become articulate in the language of co-creativity.

And its up to us to nourish real, local social structures that embody that language. Grand men's and women's initiation workshops and weekends, at best, can offer 'general' initiation, in the sense used above. But in my opinion, they can never provide the social context of full initiation. Strangers from different places come together, form a temporary community, and often share a profound experience. But full initiation – initiation which is both mystico-philosophically and socially significant – can only take place within the context of an ongoing, grounded, day-to-day community. If my male initiation is to be meaningful in the community, at least some of my brothers must know me inside out. I must have allowed myself to be seen by them – again and again, over the years. They must have watched me heal. They are my witnesses. They silently testify for me. Their acceptance is my standing in the community.

None of this can really be put into words. But all of this immensely ambitious experimentation in social transformation will ultimately rest on this: have our initiatory journeys been cut-off, intellectual concoctions? Have our brotherhoods and sisterhoods colluded to keep things superficial and safe? Or have we made love with our shadows? Have we cried and sweated and bled? Do we now sit in humility with our equals, and stand in nobility in the great unknown?

How broken open have I been in the company of my brothers? And how re-made in my wholeness? If my initiation is real, and yours, brother, and yours, sister – we will become elders, and we will welcome in the young people, and we will be part of a society that has not yet existed.

Some Afterwords

One question that's been raised about this approach to initiation concerns its *power*... Traditionally initiation has been an extremely powerful event – overseen by deep elders, casting the initiands into new depths of perception. There was a life-death edge. It was a rebirth situation. To say one had been initiated meant everything. Others had also survived that edge.

The question is whether we will we be able to co-create initiatory ritual of similar power. Will we be able to co-create situations that cast each other into the depths of whole perception? Firstly, the concept of the initiation group implies that initiation will be a journey, culminating in ritual – that initiation is thus both gradual and sudden. And the tendency might be to assume that the gradual is somehow less powerful. I would question that. I would say that without the gradual, the sudden can be devastating and damaging – that, in fact, the power of the final ritual totally depends upon the strength of the preparatory journey. Also, the journey itself is a long series of sharings, processes, rituals, projects, experiments and celebrations – powerfully touching different initiation group members at different times. Not only this, but sometimes, along the way, we find we have been powerfully touched without knowing when or how. I would not underestimate the subtle power of the gradual.

But in terms of the final ritual, as to whether we will be able to co-create life-confronting situations or not – I don't know. Different initiation groups in different communities will respond differently. Some might wish to take risks – with drugs, fasting, isolation, physical austerities... Undeniably, the initiatory moment takes place in nakedness in the unknown. As with all creativity, what we make will take shape in the making.

A second much-asked question is 'What's the need for separate gender groups, or gendered initiations? Why not all travel as one?' One response...

Firstly, I feel we do need to travel as one. And the holistic thinking and vision of holistic community in this book is one of togetherness regardless of sex or sexual preference. Together, children, men and women, we are all members of the one community. We all belong to the central, holding community forum. And we develop projects in all four spheres together. Even if we split into gender groups, we always return to the mixed-gender forum. Regardless of gender we share the practical, mystical journey of co-creative community.

But why split by gender at all? My sense is that women have a collective story, that men have a collective story, that each sex needs to make sense of its story for itself, and that the presence of the other sex can disturb and distract. The collective cultural story of woman now speaks of rage, and that of man of shame. A difficult combination. It doesn't help the men to have ten thousand years' worth of rage at patriarchal abuse dumped upon them. And in the end, blaming doesn't help the women empower themselves either. The men need to find their own way out of their place of shame, and the women out of their place of anger.

And each way out is a way into a new sexual wholeness. Something archetypal enters single-sex gatherings – something ancient. Elisabeth has told me, again and again, how women together seem to generate a quality of being that is quintessentially female – not stereotypically 'nurturing', not even neatly 'yin' – just something that leaves her deeply appreciative of woman. And as I have sat around the night fire in the company of men (despite our holding exactly the same set of values as the women) an essence, a presence, that is somehow very, very male has arisen between us.

Nevertheless, if there was great resistance to separate gender work in a community project, and a desire to create a single initiatory path for both sexes – then that is where their co-creativity would lead them. Personally, I feel that separate gender work is one crucial element in avoiding a homogenous, characterless, unisexual monoculture.

2. MEN'S MATERIAL

Introduction

Having introduced the idea of the initiation group in the first part of this chapter, 'Men's Material' goes on to explore the difference between initiation groups and support groups. It could equally have been entitled 'Women's Material'. But like a lot of this book, because it stems from my own experience, it is focused from the perspective of male healing and empowerment.

The Balance experiment has many dimensions, but the aim of the menswork is this: to start men's initiation groups, create a support network for them, and then, as each group completes its initiatory journey, to encourage the growing community of initiated men to both welcome in the adolescents, and to take up the mantle of elderhood. Big ideas. Big ideas, yes, but, on the whole, developing very well. The biggest obstacle has been, at root, a theoretical one: what is the difference between a so-called initiation group, and any other men's support group?

Let me begin with a question: what is the 'material' we men of our times all (or almost all) wear – the material we wove around our boys' bodies – the survival material – when there was only (or almost only) gutless spirituality in the air, and only (or almost only) heartless materialism on the ground? I would say: the corruption of our sexuality, the loss of our wildness and wilderness and love of the night. The loss of each other, the loss of ourselves. Little or no dignity. Little or no peace, or trust, before the mystery. Little or no relation-ship with truth – little or no image of a Great Spirit to grow into. This is the material we wear in common. We almost all feel tight and restless and disjointed and misled...

Please tolerate my generalising. My point is our collectivity – and that if another kind of culture is to emerge, if we are to ever bless and guide the boys, and if we are ever to mature into community-nurturing elders, we need to: (i) recognise this *collective* men's material, without pinning it down, and (ii) find massively acceptable ways of working through it.

The crucial vehicle for this, as I see it – for those of us who are neither boys nor elders, for the central bulk of us – is the initiation group: more specific than our usual sharing/therapy groups, consciously focused on collective men's material, on male cultural conditioning (looking at mothering, men-and-women, fathering, men-and-men, the social stereotypes, new images of masculinity, and so on), the initiation group is on a thematic journey culmi-nating in ceremony and celebration. It is a very deliberate group   consciously initiatory, and consciously engaged in social reconstruction.

And I believe we need to ride these vehicles in the all-leaders-no-leaders sensitivity of co-creativity. This is, of course, something many men will need training in. 'All-leaders-no-leaders' does not mean a bunch of hardened indi-vidualists all pulling in different directions. The understandable flight from authority, in which most of us are cultural participants, can be reflected in peer groups in needless fractures and endless meandering. Co-creativity, on the other hand, is a pact of awareness. It is an agreement to all be led by no one.

One of the most important aspects of initiation is that it defines us within our community, it defines us socially, it is a 'socialising' process. The initiation group initiates us into community in two ways. Firstly, it takes us beyond 'my stuff' into 'our stuff', beyond 'my path' onto 'our path'. And secondly, the very process of co-creativity, of learning to travel together as one, is itself an expe-riential path into community.

Initiation Groups and Support Groups

Men's initiatory material. Co-creative initiation groups. Communities of initiated men. Another kind of culture. These are the concepts we're looking at. But let's go back to the beginning. I want to stress the point that the full agenda of men's initiatory material will not be covered, automatically, simply by meeting regularly in a men's support/sharing group.

To detach from mummy, to heal overdependence (and underdependence) on women and the need to abuse women, for example, is surely a primary port of call on the initiatory itinerary. Now in a men's support group a deep sense of togetherness might develop, an ability to depend on men might develop, a sense of male self-esteem might develop – just by being together, over time, in openness and vulnerability – and all of these feelings and qualities will be helpful in detaching from mummy, but they're not enough. We also need to dive down deep into our babyish idealising and demeaning of women, together, and stay there, and only there, for as long as it takes.

To do a bit of 'sharing' on the subject, or even to spend an evening or two 'workshopping' the subject, is not enough – not if our initiations are to be substantial, not if our communities of initiated men are to have real meaning. If we're working with mother issues, and men-to-women relational issues, then the whole initiation group, at meetings and between meetings, has to be consciously engaged in cultivating a new attitude towards woman – remaining aware of the tendency to lock into programmed, patriarchal attitudes, wary of becoming submissive, castrated, all-good 'new men', wary of getting stuck in guilt and shame when the volume of the 'old masculine' overwhelms us, and aware of the need for patience and tolerance.

In other words, for a men's group to be truly initiatory, it has to participate in a series of prolonged, focused, collective processes. Although many wonderful qualities can develop naturally and spontaneously by sharing together and supporting each other, groups that only share don't stay down in the roots and the muck for long enough – nor fly high together for long enough – for the work to get done, for the transformation to be held and claimed and integrated.

And yet the tendency when we come together in men's groups is to drift into the sharing-supporting mode. It hasn't been enough, in my experience, just to say 'this is an initiation group, not a support group.' The need to be heard, to open up, to break down, is so great (and the support group is the model we're so familiar with), that we quietly, gradually, overlook the difference between general support and an initiatory journey.

I do not, for a moment, underestimate the value of 'working with what's there', or with whatever's 'up' for an individual, or for a group. But, just as working to a pre-set agenda can be an avoidance of the uncomfortable issues itching away just beneath the surface, to work only with 'whatever emerges in the moment' can be an avoidance of the depth that comes from prolonged focused attention on a specific theme. And initiation, as I see it, does need focus. Not all of every man's wounds are male-wounds. Not all of every man's wounds are typical of our culture. But those which are specifically male and observably collective – they are the subject matter of the initiatory focus. Let there be support groups before and after initiation, and in tandem – but let's acknowledge the exceptional and vital category of initiation groups.

Let's return to the example of male-female relations, and let's say that a man has just shared on the subject of seeing women as sex-objects, the madonna/whore syndrome, his inability to unite his love and his passion. Various scenarios can now unfold:

(i) men say: 'Yes, that really resonates for me too', 'Yes, I'm really hearing you', and 'Thank you for being so brave as to share that difficult stuff.' And another group member then begins to share about a problem related to work, or

(ii) someone says: 'Yes, this is powerful subject matter – why don't we dedicate an evening to *all* sharing on this?' And it happens, and it is, undeniably, a powerful session. And then the group gets into something else, or

(iii) the group realises that these are archetypal issues, issues of Oedipus and the Puer and the Shadow Lover, and that they are collectively, epidemically, relevant. The group agrees that if their initiatory journey is to have depth and power and social currency these issues need to be examined extensively, thoroughly, with real guts, tenderly, on and on, until there's a real sense of fresh air awareness around them – the spaciousness for shame and guilt to transmute, and the spaciousness for the heart and belly and balls to fill with new, more fulfilling and more exciting yearnings. Which is, of course, what I would refer to as the initiatory option.

This extended, thematic focus does not preclude working with 'what's coming up' for someone. It's not an absolute either/or. We don't need to become initiation fanatics. A group member's distress (unrelated to the group's theme), may or may not be best supported within the group's formal meeting time. Space can always be made for individual issues, if the group chooses to. But the group would then be consciously leaving the collective path, and later returning to it consciously. It could depart and return to and from support-group-mode and initiation-group-mode as it pleased, but with awareness, because of its conscious self-definition as an initiation group. And sometimes the 'deviation' might end up taking the group where it was trying to go all along. To have a sense of route and destination doesn't mean there can't be unexpected adventures, re-visions and plan-changes along the way. To have a sense of destination is not to predetermine the group process, but to set useful boundaries.

To share with each other, to hear and be heard, to support and be supported – is vital. To organise workshops on various themes is vital. Perhaps some groups need to be support groups before they can be initiation groups. But if we are to build a deep and real men's community around the axis of initiation – a deep, powerful, attractive social alternative – then we need to become clearer about what we mean by initiation. If it is not only a ceremony, but also a journey, then what does that journey entail – through what lands does it need to pass?

But I do not intend to try to list or categorise or even outline the contents of a men's initiation itinerary. There are lots of books about. My concern here is with how to use the books. My aim is to point out that such an itinerary exists. My intention is to link personal recovery and social reconstruction.

A Note on the Soul-Wound

Nevertheless, there is one wound I do want to mention – one land of pain through which, in my opinion, every initiatory journey must pass. Although maybe it's not exactly a land to be visited, more a way of visiting – and I would not mention it if I felt it was being properly attended to. I am referring to the deepest wound, to the collective soul-wound, to the dullness of the spirit to which we are so comfortably accustomed. We have forgotten the tingling in the heart, the spine, the stomach and at the top of the head. We have lost the body-soul resonance which situates the everyday in eternity. This is, so to speak, the wound of wounds. By attending to this wound, I believe, we acquire the qualities we need in order to attend to all of the others. Not the knowledge, but the qualities. By attending to the soul-wound we might not understand exactly how the mother-wound affects us, for example, but we develop the sense of centre, the courage and the forgiveness we need as we unravel her web.

In my experience, there is reluctance and shyness, and even hostility, to the deliberate soothing of the soul-wound. Back we slip into the well known, basically humanistic, sharing mode. Humanistic, and I would even say mechanistic, in the sense that sharing deals mainly in cause and effect within the psychological field – its substance is the analysis of the push and pull of psychological, or emotional, forces.

Once again, therefore, there is subject matter that will not be automatically covered by a men's support group. Group cultivation of silence and stillness – not as a denial or transcending of the pain, but as a strengthening to face it – will not happen automatically. Group-cultivation of openness and connectedness, of appreciation of beauty, of gratitude, of limitlessness – all of this needs to be continually readdressed. This holds and sustains the initiatory travellers. When the soul-wound is being tended, the group can become imbued with an undefinable delicacy, ease, largeness, and sense of presence.

As I see it, the strength to address the whole itinerary of collective wounds comes from the relative healthiness of the soul. So if we consciously nurse the soul-wound, we stand a much better chance of completing the journey. And the community of initiated men that has travelled and arrived with this kind of understanding will be a sacred community – not sacred as against profane, but sacred in the sense of possessed of love of life.

Co-Creativity as a Path into Community

I said at the beginning that in order to establish the community of initiated and initiating men we need to: (i) recognise the collective material of initiation, without pinning it down, and (ii) find massively acceptable ways of working through it. I now want to look at this second point.

Let us suppose that a group of us have agreed that collective initiatory material does exist – and that we're ready to explore it. We stand enthusiastically poised to embark together on a mighty, grand, cutting-edge and intensely intimate journey. Where to begin? Who decides? How will we move from theme to theme? How will we know a theme has been covered? How to decide the theme to come? When to give space for individual issues? How much space? And how to decide when the destination has been reached?

Psychologically superior to the democratic vote, is the principle of consensus. But beyond the often arduous process of consensus is the this-worldly spiritual experience of co-creativity…

> *Sky diving, in patterns,*
> *holding on to ourselves.*
> *Flying that fine, infinite line.*
> *Without letting go,*
> *falling into*
> *the soul of the sky.*

In these lines I try to highlight the subtle, dynamic tension between self and other, and between part and whole, characteristic of co-creativity. To co-create we need to hold, simultaneously, an awareness of ourselves (and others) as individuals and as parts of a group whole. Not only this, but to co-create is to travel the line of infinity. It is to experience the presence of a group whole which is more than the sum of the people who are its parts. In co-creativity, somehow, some sort of mystical energy seems to wrap itself around the group.

We need to see ourselves as if from outside, as participating parts. We need, for example, to be able to see ourselves as expressers of the polarity of forgiveness, in dialogue with other equally valid participating parts who are expressing the opposite polarity of, say, rage… *then* we're co-creating. When we hold this non-oppositional awareness of ourselves as being facets of the whole, reflectors of particular aspects of the situation, then we can experience a presence with a beauty and a direction of its own.

On the other hand, co-creativity can't take place if we negate our individuality. The collective consciousness of co-creativity is a collectivity of present individuals – of people being themselves. Pride is self-inflation, in which we overstate our contribution to the group whole. Shame is a self-negation, in which we minimise our contribution. Both distort the formation of the group whole. And competition is like the right leg kicking the left, and crippling the group.

> *Each of us rooted in our tree of life,*
> *each at our centre of the world –*
> *we spin, we whirl,*
> *into the music we turn –*
> *the music, the music, wo–ow the music!*

The faster we dance,
the slower our feet.
We can see the forest!
We can see the trees!

However, as we know, on some days we're more 'centred' than on others -
and on some days we're not centred at all. Not only this, but individually we
go through phases of months or even years, being more, or less, centred. So
to expect a group to agree on the principle of co-creativity and to then
suddenly, immediately, permanently, experience the unity and sublimity of the
universal mind is, to say the least, optimistic. More realistically, we might
expect our co-creativity to be sometimes smooth, sometimes jagged, sometimes explosive, sometimes ecstatic, sometimes confused. But the struggles and
the smooth times themselves become our deepening experience of community.
The learning of co-creativity is itself the path of meaningful community. And
just as group practice of meditation or sacred dance can sooth the soul-wound,
co-creativity can sooth the soul-wound by offering us the opportunity to be
fully ourselves in the presence of others.

And perhaps we already know more about co-creativity than we realise...

Our two sex-proud bodies
have felt uniquely each other.
The duvet is fallen on the floor forever.
The summer-air dust floating
through the pores in our skin.

I believe co-creativity is 'massively acceptable' because it is suited to the
egalitarian and open postmodern mind. Furthermore it facilitates unity and
direction. Not only this, but it soothes the empty, aching modern soul by
suggesting some sort of guiding presence – something beyond the group's
conscious reach, something with a mind of its own, something that speaks in
hints and moods. Something quite mysterious...

And if we can distinguish between the initiation group and the support
group, and find enough strength and skill to complete our (male and female)
initiatory itineraries in co-creativity, then we will gradually recreate probably
the most important of all the structures of the communal sphere. The rites of
passage of initiation into manhood and womanhood are the centre point of
both gender communities. And strong, alive men's and women's communities
must generate satisfaction, stability, unity and productivity, in all spheres, from
the emotional to the economic.

The Communal Sphere: Partnership

THE MODEL OF THE FOUR SPHERES OF PARTNERSHIP

Introduction

The other pillar of the communal sphere is partnership. Much of what follows might appear dry, theoretical – packed with numbers of spheres and cycles. And initially this might feel disappointing. After all, at best, partnership/marriage is so wet and real, so magnetising and passionate. It is such a naked landscape – so exposed and exposing. So crushing, so freeing. From a chapter on partnership we might want something less intellectual. The intellectuality here, however, is heartfelt – it is not cut off. And my hope in forwarding this social theory is that it might be of support in a most intimate way. It is an abstract analytical framework to support communities of couples as they pierce their pain, and break open, and find their gorgeousness and the ecstasy of simplicity.

Here we are looking at community – at community reconstruction. We are talking about partnership not only in terms of 'coupleswork', of growth-work – even in its most mature, refined, transpersonal forms. We are looking at partnership as one of the foundational structures of stable, trans-generational community. And we are asking how this structure might be imbued with the depth and beauty of the coupleswork so many of us are already engaged in. We are exploring the possibility of gradually constructing communities in which couples can travel alongside other couples and share a holistic vision of intimate relationship, and be supported by intimate, holistic community structures.

Situating Partnership within The Four Sphere Model, and a Few Words about Models

Allow me to state the obvious: that all models and maps are a matter of convenience. They are working models. They are helpful. But they are certainly not absolute, exclusive categories. It might be argued, for example, that everything I have placed within the communal sphere should be situated within the personal sphere. There is, as I have discussed, a sense in which seasonal celebration is very personal – a sense in which all of us pass every year through a private autumn, winter, summer and spring; an intrapsychic annual cycle of introversion and extroversion. And similarly, there is a sense in which rituals such as wedding are also intensely personal, or at most, significant primarily for the wedding couple.

And yet we also travel through the year together – humbled by the elements, humbled by time. And a wedding is also a collective reconnecting with the beauty and power of commitment to a shared journey of love. As Sobonfu Somé says in her book *The Spirit of Intimacy*: 'Every single person in that tribe, in that village, in your family, is going to get married that day. You are the one giving them the opportunity to do that. And so, people in the village will say, 'I'm getting married on such and such day', even though it's somebody else's actual wedding.' (1997, p.42)

The delineating factor is unity. Wedding and partnership belong to the communal sphere because they unite the couple to each other, to their children, and to each other's relatives, ancestors and friends. And seasonal ceremony belongs to the communal sphere because it invites community unity, as does all ceremony – unlike personal ritual or solitary prayer.

Ultimately, all of the spheres are inseparable. But models give us categories with boundaries and let us see what overlaps how and where and why. They make concepts applicable. And that is precisely the aim of the models of the four spheres and of the two communal cycles – to be of help in grounding and practically establishing the very nebulous concept of community.

I mentioned the two time cycles of the communal sphere in the chapter on the four sphere model: 'Within the communal sphere there are two cycles:

i. the collective time cycle (the passage through the year – daily and weekly observances, seasonal ceremony and celebration, etc.)

ii. the individual time cycle (the passage through the phases of an individual life – the rites of passage of birth, initiation, partnership and death, etc.)'

But why situate partnership on the individual time cycle? After all, by definition, it can hardly be a solitary affair. And have I not already said that partnership involves the whole community, either directly through kinship or indirectly through empathy and resonance? Yes, partnership knits the community together. Like all rites of passage it is communal. But within the communal sphere partnership lies on the individual time cycle because its timing is specific to individuals. Whereas seasonal celebrations are not. For all of our lives we all experience the seasons all of the time. But in any given year births, initiations, partnerships and deaths may or may not touch this household on this side of the town, or that household on the other side of town. These events aren't constants. They are sporadic. The rituals and observances of the various rites of passage constantly flicker through the community. Reverence before the seasons turns in a slow, unbroken flow.

The question becomes one of 'how?' We might agree on the importance of nurturing the two cycles of the communal sphere, and specifically, on nurturing the community structure of partnership, and even more specifically, on nurturing growth-work based partnership. But how to proceed? What concepts, skills and social forms do we need?

As I said in the chapter on the community forum, there are spheres within spheres. Wherever we might situate partnership within the four sphere model, or even within the communal sphere, it itself has four spheres. And if subgroups are to step forward at the community forum to take responsibility for the development of coupleswork within the community, it would be wise to consider the four spheres of partnership.

The Spheres of Partnership

1. The Transpersonal Sphere

The second sphere, which in the context of partnership work I call the psychological sphere, is extremely painful. It calls for great honesty and bravery. It means great exposure and confession. It is a noble endeavour. It is humbling. It extremely sincere. It is also absolutely exhausting. And for a couple to be exclusively dedicated to the psychological sphere, ever untangling their inter-knotted patterns, ever unburdening themselves of their 'stuff', however noble their intentions, is a sure way to knock all of the passion and joy out of any relationship.

What is needed is a context for the psychological sphere. The psychological sphere needs to be held within a transpersonal vision. It needs to be held within the understanding of the first sphere, which in the context of partnership work I call the transpersonal sphere. I quote John Welwood on this at the end of my discussion on relationships in Section One. The personalities live in the psychological sphere. Our beings inhabit the transpersonal dimension. And these two beings need nourishing. Our compensations and projections get enmeshed and entangled and need clearing. This keeps the psychological sphere clean. Similarly, our beings also need to be tended. We need to learn to create the sacred spaces they love – in which they can breath. We need to learn about ritual and meditation and creativity. We need to learn to connect with them in order to refresh ourselves with their overview, their vision, their wisdom and their compassion. They are our relationship parents. We need to be more than two wounded children. We need to be able to parent ourselves.

2. The Psychological Sphere

In this chapter we are not talking about the premodern model of partnership (as decreed in both holy and secular books of law), or the modern model (as seen on the romantically-flushed big screen). We are discussing a relationship option that has only recently emerged within our culture. Only a hundred years ago the very idea of couples travelling together on mutually supportive journeys of healing-into-wholeness would have been inconceivable. The necessary psychological vocabulary was only just being stuttered. And it is only since the 1960's that we have had the kind of mass psychological literacy necessary to make growth-work relationships a viable cultural option. However, even today, as we enter the twenty-first century, the number of couples who would say that their relationship is dedicated to self knowledge, or wholeness, or growth is minimal.

Nevertheless, this is the second sphere of partnership we need to develop, the psychological sphere. This is the sphere of learning to listen to oneself and to one's partner, of discovering each other's needs and learning to express them, of getting to know the parts each one acts out within the relationship, and the patterns in which the relationship gets repeatedly stuck. There are many books written about this sphere, and they are vital.

3. The Collective Sphere

All of this is easier said than done. Suddenly, en-masse, we are called upon to formulate our own way of being in relationship. There is little guidance and plenty of distraction. Most of us are ill prepared, and even for the most prepared it's extremely difficult to attend to both the psychological and transpersonal spheres of partnership amidst the everyday pressures of the washing up, and the children's illnesses, and walking the dog, and exams, and teenage rebellions, and so on, and on, and on... Above all, it is difficult because we live in a culture that doesn't encourage us, or make space for us, to tend these spheres within any relationship.

This is why, if we are to re-invent long-term committed partnership within our culture, if we are to redeem it, and re-stabilise our communities – since it is one of its most central structures – then we need to create structures of mutual support. Couples need to support other couples, and to receive support from other couples. We can, of course, receive support from individuals, but the beauty of couples supporting other couples is that we become mirrors for each other – mirrors in which we see our own interlocks and blocks, and through which we can come to see ourselves with compassion. In a couples group there is thus an almost automatic nurturing of both the psychological and transpersonal spheres.

In the context of partnership work I call the third sphere the collective sphere. It is centred around the couples group. And the couples group also demands its skills. Issues that arise in our relationships also arise in the group. We fall into our usual projections and transferences. Subgroups form, individuals get scapegoated. We collude in our avoidances. Again, there are books. And in all spheres training is available. At the same time, we don't need to be experts. We can learn as we go – and we do. My point here is simply to name the spheres I believe we need to develop if we truly want to establish communities with a shared approach to partnership as a journey into wholeness.

Our experience of couples groups has been that they require great commitment, and that not that many couples are yet ready to open themselves to other couples. But then again, as I said above – culturally, these are early days. Meanwhile, free of traditional cultural imposition, within the couples group each couple can formulate its own vision and interpretation of holistic partnership. Unlike a traditional society, in which marriages all look much the same, a co-creative, holistic society cultivates unity in diversity. And already, in one couples group in particular that has been going for several years (the one, in fact, that has been going the longest), I have observed something that I can only describe as a sense of extended family. It is, of course, far too early to draw any grand conclusions, but I suspect that couples groups could have far-reaching social implications.

4. The Structural Sphere

Finally there is the fourth sphere, the practical sphere, which in the context of partnership work I call the structural sphere. It is the area of form, of formalisation – of ceremony and expression and commitment. We all know the statistics: more than half of those who wed divorce, and, of course, that statistic only includes those who wed. More and more couples don't even bother – having little respect for the religious institution, and little use for the secular. Such couples avoid swearing vows of commitment – perhaps wisely, because, generally speaking, those vows are worth very little, as likely to be broken as to be kept (in fact, if the statistic is to be trusted – more likely to be broken).

Couples devoted to growth-work and self-development are no exception. They say: 'We worked through what we needed to work through together, and it was time to move on.' And so they divorce, and off they go to seek out someone who is more compatible with what they see as the next stage of their development. 'J. was good for me while I was working on my inner child, now I'm looking for a man with whom I can explore my inner teenager.' I am being flippant – slightly unfairly, because sometimes one does arrive at a barrier through which only one of the couple is ready to pass, and the other has to be left behind. The problem is that so many commitments are flippant.

The upshot of all of this is that we go to weddings and (i) anyway this is X's fourth, (ii) Y, we know, had a series of affairs while feigning faithfulness to his last wife, and (iii) looking around at everyone else there (accompanied by their step children and their partners' step-children from previous relationships) we realise that everyone there is at least once-separated, or in the process of separating at that very moment (including ourselves), and, therefore, much as we love the wedding couple, and much as we admire the sentiments being expressed, and much as we wish them well – we aren't taking their wedding very seriously.

This makes for very superficial community. Even if individually everyone is dedicated to their own path, and aims at the highest integrity, the community body has little or no cohesion or substance. It has little faith in its couples, and thus it offers little support. If, on the other hand, couples first passed through an exploratory phase, through what we once called 'engagement', but in which, this time, they applied their psychological and transpersonal understanding, and in which they were held and witnessed by the other members of their couples group – then, when they came to their wedding day, and their witnesses testified to their struggles and growth and sincerity and love, we might begin to take their commitment vows more seriously.

Being in a couples group one soon develops a sense of the dynamics and particular flavour of the other relationships. One gradually senses each couple's level of psychological knowledge and skill, and the degree of transpersonal connectedness and holding each couple allows itself. And one watches as everything evolves. If I went to a wedding at which a couple was about to commit for life, and I heard from the members of their couples group that this couple had been to heaven and hell and back during their five year engagement, that this couple had learnt to include every aspect of themselves within the relationship, and that they felt met by each other, and complete with each other – well, I suspect I would be genuinely touched by their ceremony. And I would be more likely to believe in them – and my faith (and the whole community's faith) would support them.

We can only begin to imagine the kind of community depth and cohesion that the development of such a fourth structural sphere would bring. In our private devotion to our coupleswork (spheres one and two), we redeem partnership in a very personal way. By developing the collective sphere of couples groups and the structural sphere, we redeem partnership as a community structure. We redeem community. We re-birth it – with a more inclusive and integrated body than it has ever had.

And in discussing more serious ways of ritualising our commitments, I am not speaking against separation. I have seen couples groups hold couples through crises – when they would have otherwise, rather immaturely, divorced. I have seen couples groups support couples through painful endings, and bless the necessary parting. And I have seen the ceremonial redemption of divorce – divorce which was not whimsical, which was not an avoidance – where the witnesses have spoken, much as they might have done at the couple's wedding, of the integrity of their journeys. Like the wedding I have described, such rituals of parting also strengthen the community body.

In Conclusion

If we want a new quality of community we need to attend to the quality of all four of its spheres. One of these is the unifying communal sphere, and initiation and partnership are perhaps its most essential features. How to attend to partnership? My aim here has been to set out the model of the four spheres of partnership in order to help us focus our efforts.

Although in this chapter I have not spoken directly of the four spheres of initiation, I have discussed the theory of initiation (sphere one), initiation as a journey through gender conditioning (sphere two), initiation groups (sphere three), and the practicalities of reconstructing meaningful initiatory ritual (sphere four). Community forum subgroups wishing to develop initiation and the men's and women's communities might like to reflect on these four spheres of initiation.

Of the millions of couples around us, some have seen the opportunity for growth in committed partnership. And they process their struggles (sphere two). But few of them, even if they are disciplined and dedicated within their personal spiritual paths, set time aside to honour the spiritual path of the relationship (sphere one). And of those few who honour the beauty and pain and greatness of commitment to travelling together into the unlimited unknown, even fewer (unless they are in deep crisis) share their disillusions and shames and recurring scenarios, or even their sexual breakthroughs or their deep, mutual faith, with others outside the relationship (sphere three). And of the few of the few of the few who remain, few, as yet, have stood before their neighbours and called their witnesses forth, and in (sphere four) sacred space been seen in their brokenness and their ordinariness and their unspeakable divinity.

But our civilisation is not as it always was. And it will absolutely certainly not stay forever as it is now. Many people yearn for community. Not just for the practicality of shared amenities, but for a sense of collectivity, and parallel journey – a sense of flock. A sense of flying home together – into the unknown of the here and now. And intentional communities on the outskirts of our culture have their place, but we can't all move home. We need to consider how we can weave community within our local areas – beginning with whoever is prepared to travel, and learning as we go. The models of the four spheres of community, the two time cycles of the communal sphere, and the spheres of partnership and initiation are elementary sketches based on limited experience and a lot of speculation. But we are beginning.

The Balance Project

1. EARLY LEARNINGS AROUND CO-CREATIVITY

[This essay was first published under the title 'Creative Community' in the spring/summer 1996 edition of *Achilles Heel* – the radical men's magazine. I have reworked it for this book, but the basic theme is the same.]

The Balance vision has always been of people pushing beyond the introversion and individualism of their various personal quests, into the unknown territory of community reform, of cultural modelling – into realising the vision of a dynamic, co-creative questing social body. In practice, it is a kind of 'alternative social engineering'.

The project began with a primary focus on the communal sphere, and specifically on developing a network of men's and women's initiation groups, and 'conscious marriage' partnership groups.

It began when Elisabeth and I had the chance of a month without the children. We lived that month naked in a cave in a cove in the south of Spain – where we fought and danced and swam our way into a deeply present ritual space. Then on our return to Devon I wrote this:

> To stand naked
> before the mystery of life –
> naked in the unknown...
> yes!
>
> To stand untamed –
> men, women,
> flesh, blood,
> under the sun, under the moon...
> yes!
>
> To love and hate
> in awareness.
> To grow whole,
> gradually, bitterly, gloriously...
> yes!
>
> To know
> the psychology of our being –
> to know
> oneness and difference –
> to know
> dignity and humility,
> significance and insignificance –
> to not know...
> yes!
>
> To affirm all of this
> and intuit the pivot point,
> the edge,
> of wise action –
> and build houses and homes
> and live together...
> this is balanced community.

My path, like that of many of us, had been long and tortuous. After my hippie years of hitching and smoking and magic and freedom and chaos, for a decade I'd played the part of a shaven, robed Hindu monk – in a fundamentalist sect. By the time I'd finally risked damnation (or, at least, rebirth) and fled into therapy, I'd been something of a ghost. I hadn't been able to integrate into the trivial and vicious cartoon universe of modern culture, but nor had I been able to bear the self-deceit, self-denial and babyish arrogance of a rigid, archaic spiritual culture.

But throughout the healing – the confessing, the sobbing, the raging, the growing up – I'd continued thinking and writing. In re-finding myself I had not become anti-intellectual, and it was in researching spirituality and politics at Lancaster University that my thinking had crystallised. Firstly, I'd come to understand that the social structures of premodern cultures were all intended to facilitate transformation. By transformation I meant unfoldment in open-ness to and awareness of the great mystery of life. And I was not romanticising 'ethnic' cultures, not minimising their dogmatism, oppression, ethnocentricity or fanaticism – I was referring to their intent, as they saw it. In Mircea Eliade's terms, all premodern cultures were 'sacred' cultures.

Secondly, it was clear to me that the social structures of modern culture did not attempt to facilitate transformation. And we were so blandly accustomed to it. Our social vision, our social expectations, were so low. We were so disem-powered. No, even worse: we'd lived under the tyranny of an anti-transformative culture for enough generations to have forgotten. It was the stuff of fairy tales, of wickedness hanging over the land, of spells and of loss of memory. It was a mass hypnosis. Millions upon millions of us were drinking life from an empty glass.

Thirdly and finally, I'd come to believe that today's challenge was to create postmodern social structures to facilitate transformation. And by 'post-modern' I meant structures which acknowledged the individual, which did not impose, had no absolute hierarchies, were open, flexible and travelled into the unknown.

So when we returned from the sparkling skies and seas of our cave life in Spain, my call was about courage, and rawness close to life and death, and about holding each other – but there had been plenty of forethought. I knew the areas I wanted to work in – the social structures I considered, anthropo-logically, to be the basic building blocks of a culture: the men's community, the women's community, partnership, community celebration (focused around the seasons), and practical community organisation (touching on eco-issues, transport, trade, and so on). And I knew these social structures had to be nurtured in a postmodern mood, in a mood of co-creativity.

My approach to weaving together local, transformation-facilitating men's community and women's community was this: initiation was the rite of passage that linked children to adults to elders – that wove the gender commu-nities. And I saw initiation as both the process and the outcome of collective healing journeys. So I planned to convene co-creative initiation groups, and network them through community conferences, festivals and so on. The long-term vision was to establish cores of initiated adults and to watch this lead, eventually, to the reconnecting of the generations... There were many open questions (some of which I addressed in 'Looking Practically At Initiation'), but I had a workable plan for approaching the recreation of these two basic social structures.

I had a similar approach to the couples work: if partnership was to be a shared transformative journey, neither the traditional model nor the romantic model was enough; we needed to empower each other in creating and developing our own models. So, again, I would convene groups, link them through community magazines, conferences, and so on – and another transformation-facilitating social structure could begin to emerge, gain status and become public property.

However, as we all know, it's not what you know, it's how you know it. And when, by word of mouth, the call began to circulate, and men and women began to congregate for the first men's initiation group and the first women's initiation group, I came up against my own inexperience and immaturity. My own, and that of others. Not so much in terms of my ideas for community reconstruction, as in the 'how' of co-creativity.

At Lancaster I'd experimented with co-creative ceremony, I'd written an article on co-creativity (entitled 'Flexible Form' and rewritten for this book), and co-creativity was one of the buzz-words of our marriage. But what I still didn't appreciate was that co-creativity is not the automatic result of the inter-action of assorted individualistic inputs – it has to be a conscious collective orientation. It is a principle, and it has to be agreed upon in advance. It is not something we automatically do. Even among people who are extremely experienced in growth-work (as many of these people were), how many of us are familiar with experiencing ourselves as parts (albeit unique parts) of a creative process taking place on many levels? It is something we need to agree to all focus on, and practise.

In 'Flexible Form' I'd contrasted the fixed form of tradition with the form-lessness of modernity, and I'd proposed flexible form as a way forwards – a way of working co-creatively which preserves the focus and continuity (of form), and allows the unpredictability and sense of responsibility (of formlessness). What I didn't appreciate was just how 'collectivised' the consciousness of a group needs to be in order to co-create – that to co-create we need not only to stay close to our individuality, but to also hold an awareness of ourselves as part of the larger organism of the group. I'd often talked loosely of 'co-creative social structures', but as my experience matured I became more and more aware that groups needed to first understand co-creativity theoretically – and then come to really understand it, by practising it.

My other large learning around co-creativity was with issues of authority and power. At first, I didn't realise the extent to which I was inviting people to participate in a 'directed co-creativity'. I explained, for example, that these initiation groups were not support groups – that they would, of course, be supportive, but that they were not only for sharing, that they were intended to be sacred journeys through the collective issues of male/female conditioning. People were being invited to co-create their own maps, to decide which lands to visit, in what order, how they would travel. Yes – but although I was inviting them to co-create, I was not giving them full creative freedom. They could co-create, but it had to be a journey, a sacred journey, a thematic sacred journey, a thematic sacred journey with a purpose, initiation. There were parameters. There were conditions upon their co-creativity. And I was not aware of just how 'directive' I was being. This was partly inexperience, but also partly immaturity. And I am still working with issues around self-worth, self-assertion, authority and power.

The same happened in the first partnership group. You could co-create your own model of partnership, I explained, but it had to be a model (and this I didn't explain). And I didn't realise the co-creativity I was suggesting to these men's, women's and partnership groups was so directed because, to me, it all seemed so obvious. How could initiatory work be anything but collective journeying? How could partnership work begin anywhere other than with the moulding of new vessels? And my opinions haven't changed; what has changed is that I realise I have them. And progressively, in all of the groups I have established since, and in all of the groups other Balance facilitators have convened, we have acknowledged our standpoint. We have acknowledged that we hold a vision, that we are sharing a vision, and that we are inviting people to participate in it. But we also claim that that vision is not disempowering. On the contrary, our experience is of unity and empowerment.

Today I still believe that the challenge is to establish transformation-facilitating social structures. I still believe that men's communities, women's communities, partnership and seasonal celebration are fundamental among them. And I still believe these social structures need to embody the principle of co-creativity. Co-creativity still seems to me to be the essential mood of progressive postmodernity. It implies relationship, listening, give and take, trial and error, exploration, responsibility. It is an opportunity to transcend our isolation, and almost paradoxically, to empowerment by being part of something larger. It still seems to me to be the ideal mode for the postmodern mind. But I am now less naive in the degree of competence in the art of co-creativity I expect. And I now take responsibility for the degree of control I exercise when helping facilitate postmodern transformative community.

2. THE KINDRED SPIRIT ARTICLE

[The following essay was first published in the summer 1998 edition of *Kindred Spirit* magazine. I am including it, with grateful thanks to *Kindred Spirit*, because it includes several quite substantial personal testimonies.]

INITIATED IN 1994 BY MARK JOSEPHS-SERRA, THE BALANCE PROJECT HAS BECOME A UNIQUE, ONGOING EXPLORATION OF WAYS TO BUILD HOLISTIC COMMUNITY.

IN VARIOUS GROUPS AND AT VARIOUS TIMES OVER THE LAST THREE YEARS, SEVERAL HUNDRED PEOPLE IN THE SOUTH DEVON AREA HAVE BEEN DRAWN TO PARTICIPATE.

DREW LEITH REPORTS ON THE JOURNEY SO FAR.

In modern times, our sense of community, in even the most general sense, has been of something being worn down, threatened on many different fronts. Rapid change can be seen in almost every realm of human activity and are practically impossible to ignore, yet the more change we witness, the easier it is to perceive it as de-stabilising, if not actively destructive, even anti-life. As individual humans we feel somehow separate from the process of change and are forced to face our own powerlessness in the face of it. Fundamental questions arise such as: am I part of the problem or part of the solution? Where is my power?

Meanwhile, the disintegration of the extended family and the declining significance of marriage as a social framework are matters of historical record. The ongoing collapse of the nuclear family has been more recent; as for the present, whatever form a life-partnership takes, its subjection to increasing pressure from both internal and external forces is generally seen as inevitable Yet a human being in good health (on all levels) is inherently loving, creative, intelligent and co-operative. Balance's vision is to find ways to restore ourselves to good health at all levels of our being, and concurrently to find and to live within workable, holistic structures. It doesn't ask anyone to move home but aims to bond the community that already exists.

The form of Balance at the start was in the setting up of groups – men's, women's and partnership – and seasonal ceremonies and celebrations. Each group was to meet regularly for an initial facilitated period, then be left to follow their own path. Mark makes the following observation about these groups: 'After the facilitated period the groups usually go into 'support group' mode. What happens in this phase is very necessary. It may be private self-development rather than community development, but it is vital nevertheless. You share your struggles, your patterns, give and receive support… But no community structure is yet in place that would enable this acquired wisdom to be passed through the generations. If, however, an initiatory structure were to be set in place, that is something that would give community coherence. Then the work would become collective development as well as self-development'.

This combining of individual and collective growth work is really the cutting edge of what Balance is doing in experimenting with the vision and the practicalities of establishing holistic community. The vision itself is much greater than Balance, which is a specific small part of it. At the core is the belief that we need to be pioneering a new kind of culture, not just a new kind of individual.

Mark elaborates this point: 'Our culture is shifting and can go in one of several directions – to being increasingly materialistic/self-destructive; to fundamentalism; to matriarchal/green spirituality in reaction to what has gone before; or to holism. Many people are working in many different ways to facilitate the shift along the path of holism, Balance being one of the ways. The world is at a crossroads, the possibility of going along the holistic path is not really greater yet than the possibility of going along the self-destructive one. I'm not a 'new-ager' in the sense that I think it's written in the stars. Potentially yes, but there are other potentials too. I feel we are all, every one of us, makers of history, by the way we act, think and feel now, at both subtle and gross levels.'

In terms of men's work, the focus of Balance is on men finding ways in which they can be powerful in their creativity and honour their inner lives. In premodern cultures, the men's community was a crucial communal structure, comprised essentially of three tiers: young men and boys, initiated men and elders. Whilst clearly care must be taken to maintain an objective perspective when looking back in time, there is much we can learn from this structure. Balance has been building a network of initiation groups with the aim of re-creating the male community and its place within the wider social structure.

Chris Salisbury was in the first of these groups. He works for Devon Wildlife Trust and, as someone committed to the vision of holistic community, has a valuable overview of Balance's evolution to date. He is currently in two groups that were initiated by Balance and is also an organiser of the annual three-day camp, Manifest, for men and boys, fathers and sons, now in its third year. I asked him what being a part of that first group had meant to him.

'The basic process was simply to witness each other. I had a strong sense of being met, and to have such a group meeting in my own neighbourhood was really great. Some strong and lasting friendships began in that group. It gave birth to a real sense of community and has certainly enriched the lives of those involved. Even though the original vision of setting in place holistic social structures hasn't really been achieved yet (because in the beginning it was a somewhat haphazard, experimental affair, with many different agendas being followed), the great thing for me has been having a place where I was able to build close and intimate relationships with other men and their families with my family. This is something not easy to achieve in the mainstream culture; you could even say it is actively obstructed. I really enjoy meeting people in the street with whom I am connected at a deep level, who are not just casual acquaintances.'

I wanted to know how possible Chris thought it was to reach the level of actually living a committed community existence.

'It is possible but if takes a lot of commitment, a lot of clarity and a lot of coherence. Naturally enough, none of these were sufficiently there in the beginning. However, I do feel that everyone involved is very grateful for all the things that have sprung up from the founding vision of Balance. Imperfect it may have been, but it did give rise to a lot of things that are now happening – there are many ongoing groups and new ones forming. It is community in a kind of infancy and it is moving along the path towards the vision. It seems to me that was a kind of naiveté in not recognising that actually there is such a lack of commitment generally. I feel it's safe to assume that most people would welcome the kind of community that Mark is articulating, yet what was most difficult was getting the necessary quality of commitment from people. Bringing together a fragmented community into a coherent togetherness is a very tall order, and yet it has endured and is meeting a deeply felt need. The vision has always been evolving. It's not the same as it was. We've all moved on with it and I feel very grateful for its presence in the wider community and for the fact that I've been able to contribute and help shape it.'

Balance has been concerned with issues of authority and hierarchy, encouraging sensitivity to oneself as both an individual and as a part of the body of the group, issues that are perhaps of particular relevance to the women's community. Clio Wondrausch, one of the initial participants of the first Balance women's group, takes up this point when describing her experience of that group:

'Our defining issue, right from the start, was women's empowerment and it still is that. This is a really good clear focus, which means for one thing that we avoid traps such as thinking we're supporting each other when in fact we're just maintaining our victim roles. The vision of community is very important to me, as is knowing that there are other groups under the umbrella of Balance. We are becoming more aware of community, and the group work constantly shows that we are not alone with our issues.

'Being in the group does give me a sense of connection to those times when there were close-knit communities, councils and clans, a feeling of being interconnected not just during the meeting times but energetically too. There is a strong feeling of sisterhood, a bond of love that feels to me like our greatest strength.

'This group is central to my journey. When you are committed to a group, things that have no other place of safety start to come through and be discovered. A big part of this shadow-revealing work is learning how to trust that the other women in the group will still love me. That work is there for us all – seeing how the sharing and the loving make a dynamic relationship. We are committed to really looking at where we are and often find ourselves saying 'this isn't enough' and then taking a long, hard look at how to do whatever the work is that needs to be done. It can be quite difficult relying as we do on our own resources, on our inspiration, without the guidance of elders.

'My hope is that what we are doing will lead us to a place where we are able to help other people make their own journeys, perhaps when we're really wrinkled, really grey women! It would be good to be doing some intentional building of community structures, one obvious place to start being creating a ritual to mark the beginning of menstruation. In exploring and sharing our personal journeys, we are making bonds and this is a kind of community building in itself. More and more it is becoming clear to all the women that this present society doesn't work. Quite a high level of self responsibility is required to be able to take on the challenge of making a difference and it needs this work of bringing out the shadow – not just one-to-one with a therapist – the process is immeasurably more powerful in the company of one's closest companions. To know that we can reveal the most frightening and filthy stuff from within and for that to be all right is so empowering, for both the person sharing and for those holding the loving space. It takes people with true commitment to themselves and to each other to stand together and go forward together in this way; there needs to be a continual re-acknowledgment of our differences and of our oneness. There's a whole world out there and for community to truly work it has to have the capacity to include everyone.'

Katie Ashton, from this same women's group, wrote about the impact on her of the week in Turkey that the group spent together:

'Our experience in Turkey was a magical gift. The tranquillity and beauty, the perfection of our space at Huzur Vadisi awed and enriched us. We made time each day to meet in sacred circle, often sitting in the meadow of the yurts that burst colourfully and softly with spring. Our connection to each other, to the earth and to spirit was deep and enriching, opening us. We were held safe, allowing edges to be pushed, loving challenges to be made, and secrets to be revealed. We walked most days deeper and higher into the forests and ocean views, we walked in beauty. We ate delicious meals prepared by the local family involved in the centre who took us in with open hearts and cried with us when we left. Dark nights full of stars inspired music, dancing and laughter, fires and rituals and our voices soared, weaving into the whispers which gently eased our minds into stillness.'

In his book *Journey of the Heart*, John Welwood describes how two people's love has room to grow only in proportion to their ability to allow their love to lead them to greater connectedness with the whole of life. Balance's experiments with partnership groups are a pioneering attempt to facilitate this by bringing holistic partnership – relationship based on allowing transformation – into the open. These have proved to be wonderfully nourishing, not just for those in the group, but for a wider community, where a sense of extended family has developed, particularly among those who share holistic attitudes.

Alison and Toby Fairlove, as well as being in respective women's and men's groups, are also in a partnership group together. Alison describes the special nature of the partnership group:

'The partnership group feels much more vulnerable than the Women's group – there's nowhere to hide. As trust and intimacy have grown in the group, so we've become more able to open doors which have not been opened outside the couple before. And having other people open their doors opens up our own relationship. Sharing so intimately with others is constantly making the relationship larger, giving the feeling of being accepted and expanded. And it really sharpens the sense of where our individual responsibilities are within the process. The children have also been part of the journey. We've learned as a group to honour their needs rather than exclude them.'

Toby takes up this point:

'In a way our participation as a family has been a gift to others, especially those without children. For me this group is about being witnessed, held, challenged and being able to challenge others. It's also really good fun. And sometimes it's really painful. There's also a lot of love there, which frees up a lot of energy. Somehow it's also, very subtly, an inspiration for me and Alison to maintain the vision and to nurture the sacred garden of our relationship. It's an opportunity to compost the waste, burn the deadwood, plant new seeds and to take cuttings from other people's sacred gardens and to borrow some of their tools. The feeling is that it's so much more nourishing to work communally'.

3. EARLY LEARNINGS AROUND
DEVELOPING THE COMMUNAL SPHERE

Many of us have a sense of a personal journey, a private path of meaning. And many of us are also concerned with the political and economic matters that dominate our culture. Between these very private and very public spheres is what I refer to as the communal sphere. Marriage/partnership, for example, has always been an important communal institution. The collapse of the traditional communal structure of marriage has been well documented. The modern follow-up, the romantic model, has proven unsustainable. And there are now many couples within the holistic movement who see their relationship as a psycho-spiritual path, as a shared journey of unfoldment. But such holistic partnership has not yet entered the communal sphere, it is still a private affair.

Balance's experiments with partnership groups have been an attempt to go a step beyond this privacy – by bringing clusters of local couples together for intimate, long-term support. The intention has been to bring the long, painful and sublime journey of holistic partnership out into the open, and to re-create the possibility of commitment-vows with community credibility – thus re-establishing the pivotal communal structure of partnership. Not only has this proven extremely nurturing for the partnerships concerned and for the community as a whole, but, unexpectedly, a sense of extended family has sometimes developed – which, in terms of re-constructing the communal sphere, is very important because for most of human history the extended family *was* the family. Put differently, instead of talking of the lost advantages of the 'extended' family (as if the nuclear unit were the norm), we might be beginning to confront the huge disadvantages of living in the 'shrunken' family.

Another example is Balance's menswork – the re-making of men in ways that honour their emotions and inner life, and that are powerful in their creativity. The men's community was a critical communal structure in premodern cultures. But if we limit menswork to the private end of the social spectrum, and value it principally as individual growth work, then the male community as a communal structure will never emerge. Thus Balance has been trying to build a network of initiation groups – so that, as the community of initiated men grows, it can begin to welcome in the adolescents, and another fundamental communal structure can mature.

I believe the lack of attention given to this communal sphere, the sphere of collective-developmental structures, explains our inability, so far, to develop coherent, consciously-holistic community. This sphere, the sphere previously the responsibility of the religious traditions, has collapsed – leaving a hole at the core of community. We are left either overly-private or overly-public. We might, on the one hand, have very deep personal inner lives, and, on the other, be familiar with the ins and outs of the international political arena, but for most of us, most of our neighbours are total strangers. If we want deep community, as we so often say we do, then this third sphere of people-structures and collective-journeying is perhaps the missing link.

But how to go about developing the third sphere? Balance began by saying something similar to all of the above, and attracting people to the various groups. It was a direct attempt to develop the communal sphere, in isolation from the other spheres... Many people are looking for more personally, socially and ecological aware cultural alternatives. But one of the many naivetés with which Balance began was the assumption that 'alternative people' all share a holistic approach. In fact, many are stuck in a premodern ascensionism, many are caught in a reactive anti-transcendent 'gaianism', and many are lost bewildered somewhere between the shelves and the till in the supermarket of enlightenments. In other words, I have learnt that we cannot develop the third communal sphere, without simultaneously addressing the first sphere – the sphere of ultimate beliefs. Potentially, holistic community is a postmodern cultural option that unites the collectivity and sense of the sacred of premodernity with the equality, openness and affirmation of the individual of modernity. But, once again, if we are to develop stable, trans-generational holistic communities, agreement on such matters cannot be assumed.

Not only this, but the personal holistic path (sphere two) involves the body, the intelligence, feeling and spirituality. It is not humanistic and psychological (neglecting the spiritual), and it is not inhumanly spiritual (neglecting our humanity). The holistic path is as shadowy as it is light, as physical as it is otherworldly, as personal as it is transpersonal. It is not about denial, but neither is it 'anything goes'. It is about integration, synthesis and wholeness. It is about relatedness, difference, embracing polarities, and paradox. And all of this has to be understood and agreed upon if we are going to develop communal structures together. Both our ultimate beliefs (sphere one) and the way we construe our personal journeys (sphere two) will impact upon the way we work together.

This brings us into the whole area of authority and hierarchy, and possible dogmatism and disempowerment. After all – who says what's what? Who's to say what holism's *really* about? And who's to say how holistic community is to be structured? Balance has been working with concepts such as co-creativity, flexible form and the four spheres but, as I explained in 'Early Learnings Around Co-Creativity', however egalitarian, democratic or sensitive these structures – they are structures. They exist. They have been put in place by one or more individuals, and these individuals need to be named. They hold authority. In a new project others might hold authority by virtue of age, educational background, wealth, and so on, but whoever has brought Balance into a local area carries an authority on all that Balance represents – and this needs to be owned, and spoken aloud. What is clearly spoken can't become shadow.

But we need to go further... Whether it is myself, or someone else, who is facilitating the development of holistic community in a new area, our authority needs to be gradually shared. In other words, we cannot just impose our outlook, even 'owningly'. We cannot come in and pompously declare that the holistic experience is one of erotic awareness – and expect everyone to follow. We need to allow people the space to compare their outlook with ours – and to decide for themselves whether it is an imposition, an articulation of what they already believe, or a new, insightful and exciting path.

For some people what we are offering will be a useful, uniting expression of what they already know. In fact, it will only be possible to hand over our authority to people in the local community who have touched their own knowing of sex-heart-spirit openness. To them we will be providing the community with a common vocabulary. These people were already authorities – not by virtue of position, but by virtue of realisation. Similarly, it will only be when the community has experienced the beauty and efficacy of co-creativity and flexible form that it will become an authority on its own methodology.

Particularly in the first few years, I didn't stand in my own authority. Perhaps understandably, because, after all, I wasn't an authority – I was just heading up the experimenting and exploring. But I found it difficult to stand even there. I found it difficult to hold the various groups in a united sense of exploring community development together. When I facilitated groups I'd speak about the larger community vision that holds Balance's work, but I didn't insist on it. People were often coming mainly for the specific group, and I wouldn't want to be pushy. Men were participating in a men's group, for example, for their own self-development. They didn't necessarily share an interest in community development.

But although people were often coming mainly for deep companionship and support, few if any were opposed to community development. In fact, I am sure that if they'd been welcomed into the groups via a different structure, then whatever interest they'd had in community development would have been maximised, rather than minimised. For example: when there were already a few men's groups and a few women's groups, and a new men's group was forming, the new men could have been invited to a first evening at which all of the involved men and women were present. Not only would they have heard of the personal experiences of the participating men and women, but they would have automatically felt a sense of growing community.

That would have been an improvement. It would have made it clearer that something more than just a self-development programme was evolving. But what? Perhaps a network re-creating the community structure of initiation, or a network of support groups? But community is more than the structure of initiation, and more than emotional support. There are also the understandings of the first two spheres, there are many other communal structures, and there is the whole realm of the practical sphere. Why not also welcome newcomers into all of that too? I came to see the necessity for some sort of basic community meeting-ground or community forum around which all of the groups and activities, agreements and projects in all four spheres could revolve.

One way in which I did try to bring the groups together was for seasonal celebrations, at the equinoxes and solstices. Seasonal ceremonies and celebrations offer the opportunity for a community to bond deeply in ritual-space. And we have had some wonderful celebrations – from candlelit midwinter processions and spiral maze-walks, to spring enactments of the return of Persephone from the underworld. But participation has almost always been low.

Not only has it been low, but often group members have not come, and people who were not in any of the groups have come. And they were very welcome. But I now feel that if I'd held a stronger focus on community development (as against just self-development, or even shared journeys of self-development), then members of the individual groups would have felt more of a sense of belonging. The weakness of that focus, plus our opening up the equinox and solstice ceremonies to absolutely anyone, meant that we lost the opportunity for the members of the various groups to share sacred space and bond in deep community. We've often co-created strong and beautiful gatherings, but if more people had come, and the majority had been group members and their families and friends, then our celebrations would have been a much more powerful nurturing of holistic community.

The other area that has suffered from Balance's neophyte lack of clarity and confidence is the fourth sphere, the practical sphere. The obvious was not stated: that unless we wish to perpetuate the traditional division of church and state, or the secular privatisation of higher and deeper values, then our psycho-spiritual communities need to also be committed to mutual support at the level of shopping, washing clothes, transport and trade. Concerns which inevitably lead to holistic political activism. But because there was no unified focus, and because this core fact of holism was not being clearly stated (due to a lack of attention to sphere one), Balance was largely ungrounded and apolitical. Of course, people connected at the practical level in thousands of small ways – exchanging skills, and offering each other domestic and professional support. And those people who were more involved in think-global-act-local community politics would sometimes motivate others to get involved. But the practical sphere of how we manage our physical survival needs was not seen as an absolutely vital level of community, nor, due to the lack of a community forum, was that attitude facilitated.

Just as assumptions about outlook and path (spheres one and two), need to be addressed from the beginning of any project, this fourth practical sphere also needs to be included from the beginning – alongside our work with the communal sphere. In fact, the overarching lesson I have learnt while trying to cultivate the communal sphere is to not be afraid of authority, to own it and to share it out, and to use it to encourage a unified, focused four-sphere approach.

The Blood and Roots of Community

COMMITTING TO COMMUNITY

As in a fairy tale, in which two travellers set out from furthest that-way and furthest the-other-way, and meet at the mid-point (the centre of the world) – holism is a sacred-erotic place of meeting.

There the flesh rises to meet spirit,
and spirit rises within the flesh.

From my personal story, and from the story of my work within Balance, it is clear that I am walking from furthest the-other-way – I am arriving from the land of spirit. Half way to the centre (a quarter of the way across the world), in a rather colourful town, I meet therapy, and groupwork, and the mytho-poetic movement. Then as I get closer and closer I begin to hear about alternative economics and community politics. And when I arrive madness and sanity finally meet inside me. Expansiveness and definition become one. Beauty finally makes perfect sense.

Others are walking from furthest that-way. They are coming from the land of facts. And they too have a half-way city of honesty and vulnerability and revisioning of the self. And as we cannot but do: each one pausing to eat and drink there relates what they learn to what they already know. By the time they leave they use green banks, campaign against ethnocide, and support socially responsible trade. And when, at last, they arrive at the mid-point of the world their sanity is set ablaze by their own madness. They no longer need a reason to be right. And they see all they ever had was faith.

The poem and prose with which I want to end this book tell of the direc-tion of my journey. The poem tells of my embodiment – of my spirit materialising. And the prose that follows tells of someone who is moving from the first sphere towards the fourth. I appreciate that others will be arriving from the other direction – from the fourth to the first.

But this last piece is not only about meeting at the mid-point. I actually have faith that some of us, if not many of us, will meet there. Whether that means anything so grand as a holistic postmodern culture, I do not know. But I do believe we will meet, and cultivate co-creativity, and nourish the four spheres, and nurture deep community. But this last chapter adds a last word…

It returns to something I mentioned at the very beginning of this book… In the preface I wrote: 'we might even say that this book is about the next step in 'the consciousness movement' that has been evolving, large-scale, since the 1960s… This book is not about applying an individualistic 'holistic attitude' to a certain subject matter – be it gardening or economics. It is about the next step for the holistic attitude itself. It is about a broadening out. Because how can we develop community while at the most profound, gut-soul level our life-attitude (however holistic) remains secretly, supremely individualistic? And for the most part, it does. For the most part, our growth-work is purely personal. The family is shrinking away. And even our politics is the work of groups of individuals tied only in ideological unity. There is rarely a sense of travelling together – of commitment to each other, to each other's families, and to the local land we live upon together. Why not? Because this would call, and does call, for a new sense of collectivity. Not a new theory of collectivity, but a new experience of collectivity.'

Because even if we agree on the philosophy of holism, and on the socio-political vision of a decentralised society, even if we are walking the same sacred-erotic path, even if we have flown in flock in co-creativity, and have no doubt at all about the four spheres – what will bind us to those around us (as against all others), and to where we are (as against all elsewheres)?

Whatever direction we have come from, whether we need to ground or to lighten up, community will not cohere without commitment. And commitment itself needs time to cohere within us. It threatens our identity and our free will. It shakes up questions of purpose and destiny. When we commit to an involvement, we know that in that involvement we are going to be using up our life-minutes... But if we do not name what we do not have, we will never have it.

There are perhaps three essential commitments we need to consider:
• commitment to each other
• commitment to our land
• commitment to spirit

(When I say commitment to each other I do not mean to our partners or to our closest friends, I mean to the people of our community – whether we know them well, or like them or not. And when I say our land, I mean 'where we are' – the ecosphere, the biosphere to which we belong – whether urban or rural.)

Of course, they can be separated: we can be committed to each other, but not to the land. To spirit, but not each other... But in terms of holistic community there is only one commitment. Within it there is commitment to each other, to the land and to spirit. There is commitment to each other in and through our shared spiritual journey, and in and through our shared embeddedness in the land.

Clearly, even though we might agree on all of the ideas and models and methods in this book, and feel enthused to develop holistic community together, it is unlikely that, as yet, we will feel a deep sense of commitment... And although I could imagine 'community commitment enhancement programmes', I wonder if any programme could ever reach the inner substance of commitment. What, after all, moves us to commit?

(i)
I have been with spirit,
in spirit,
somewhere away from this world
for a long time.
I enter body,
I enter the flesh of the world...

(ii)
I breathe.
I enter body.
I go down.
I down.
I ground.
I breathe.
I enter ancestral blood,
ancestral semen.
I am flesh
handed down,
handing itself down.
I am reborn of burial grounds
of people who prepared the world
for me.
I am the past becoming.
I am the flesh of my people.

(iii)
I feel you
deep in your breathing
next to me...
As flowers give seeds
give flowers give seeds,
we are the tip of the flow,
we are the forward-dying moment –
endless flowerfields,
endless seedfields,
endless flowerfields
are we.

(iv)
I breathe. I remember
my body.
I re-enter.
I enter beloved embeddedness.

I relax down. I enter the ground.
Every cell of me fed
on food fattened
on sunheat and rainwater and soil.

Where do I choose to end?
The air circulating around me
swirls within me.
I tire with the night,
I rise with the sun.
I am a walking plant.
(I love to lie in the grass.)

(v)
My brain is packed
with ideas
my memory layered
with stories
my mind arrayed
with images
of the outside.
Deep felt concepts,
like embeddedness,
now in the human collective,
float through me.

Holism,
flames about me.
My embeddedness
in the flesh of the world
and my embeddedness
in spirit
intertwine and interpenetrate
and merge and burst.

And this joy
is not of me,
and it is mine.

And this joy
is not of me,
and it is mine.

I am a man. I live with a woman, a teenager, a child, a dog, a cat, two fish, a garden and a house full of things. I have deep, sacred values. As have all my friends. Who also live in various permutations of with-partner, without-partner, with-pets, without-pets, in their own houses full of their own things. Things, almost to the last safety pin, manufactured in not very deep or sacred places, by not very deep or sacred processes. And together, of an evening, we often talk about community. Particularly, of course, about deep, sacred community.

And I especially talk a lot about community. I teach about community. I write about community. I sleep-think about community. I imagine and envision community, and schematise and formulate action plans to develop community. But how much have I actually got? And why?

Community, I have always felt, is about travelling together, in commitment to each other – into the unnameable unknown. It is not about travelling alone. It is not about our personal journeys, vital as they may be. Each of us having a personal journey doesn't in itself, automatically, bond us in community. Community, for me, has always been, above all, a communally held sense of travelling as one. As ourselves, but as one.

I'm in a men's group. That's weekly. It was convened around the theme of sexual healing. We've travelled together for a year. There's a dozen of us. Right now we're creating a re-commitment ritual, to stay together for another year. A re-commitment to our theme. But how committed are we to each other? What'll happen if one or two men leave? What will happen to our commitment to them? And what is the relationship between commitment and community?

I'm also in a couples group, with three other couples. That's fortnightly. That's a deep place too, like the men's group. To have opened our relationship to other couples, to have let them see inside, and to have seen inside theirs, has bonded us. No doubt about it. We're close. And after each meeting we all go home to our houses with-children, or without-children, full of our own things. Nor would I have it any other way. I want my space. Why then, with all of this closeness, do I still feel a lack?

I think about my parents. I live in Devon, they live in London. And about my sister, who lives in Brazil. And about my brother, who lives in France. Maybe we're an extreme example. But that makes us an excellent one. Because my point is that despite being so dispersed, we're still connected. Family: connection. Friends to whom I have shown my soul: where are they now? Family, whose values are so different: still in contact. Friends, whose values are identical: we've lost touch. Why? What is this bond of blood, that still seems to grip us? And how much longer can it hold? With every generation, it seems, the bond is stretched thinner, the blood is watered down.

I think about blood and tribe, and I think about the soil. I think about blood and ancestors and bones. I think about women bleeding into the earth. I think about death, and flesh returning to the land. I think about walking over hills and knowing whose blood and bones have fed them. Once we were bonded by sex, love, food, work, fear. We lived in need – of our fields, of our animals, of the each other. We stuck together, like any species. We birthed and ate and died together, like the mice and crows and ants. We were embedded in our surroundings, like the badgers and oaks and grasses and rocks. Now we think we're not. But breasts still dribble milk. Babies still suckle. Children still grow. We still see in sunlight, and breath in our sleep, and eat and urinate and defecate. We think we're out of nature, above nature, detached somehow. But we're not. It's foolish to even talk of 'returning to nature'. We've forgotten what we are. We've forgotten that we too grow on the land. And…

> no land,
> no roots.
> No roots,
> no family trees.
> No family trees,
> no forest of community.

The roots of community feed on our blood. We need to re-commit to where we are, to the land we're living upon, to where we are together – whether the land is grassed or paved, whether the air is pure or fumed, whether we can hear silence and birdsong or traffic and machinery. We need to become blood brothers and blood sisters, before spirit – in and through the land we're upon. Then, when we've committed to staying put, and we're looking after our locality on behalf of our children's children – then we will really, really start to care about our local water and waste. Then we will really begin to protect it. We will protect the right of local people to care for local land. We will protect our right to love it. And we will feed it with our blood and bones. And by coming together, and staying together, for our land, for our locality, for local autonomy, for local democracy, for deep, sacred democracy – we will become a committed, deep, sacred community.

I think about love. And family. And friends. And the thinning of the blood. And the deep, sacred values in my men's group and couples' group. And my longing and discontent. And I think about political alienation and apathy, and disenchantment and disempowerment. And I remember a thousand conversations about community. But it feels like we're still preparing, in our self-development and self-help groups – preparing our souls for when we're ready to spill our blood. It feels as if our growth-work groups and spirit-work groups are a subtle readying for the time of embodiment, for the holistic opportunity – when we'll slowly come back to earth, when we'll embed, and commit to wherever we are, and blend our bloods for generations, until community is reborn.

I want to be here to stay. I want you to be here to stay. I want to commit. And I want you to commit. To each other. To here. And to the journey. To the heart. To the body. To spirit. I've had enough of spirituality for spirituality's sake. And I've had enough of lifeless, shallow, impersonal centralised democracy. I'm ready to stand in spirit, and unite my blood with yours, and let it fall upon the land, and grow the generations.

And yet, and yet, and yet… it feels like an enormous sacrifice of my independence and freedom. It feels like another marriage. And…

> *do I choose these friends,*
> *above all others,*
> *as my husbands-and-wives-in-community?*
> *Is this the land of my heart?*
> *Am I ready to lawfully wed*
> *this land,*
> *until in death from it I do part?*

Or maybe it's enough, for now, at least, if I can commit myself to the land I'm upon, while I'm upon it…

Meanwhile, here I sit. The man of my house. The woman of the house has gone out in our car-thing. On top of the cupboard there are stacks of deep, sacred books and magazines. The teenager's at college. The child's at school. I've been offered a job. It would mean moving out of the area. The cat and dog are asleep here next to me. The fish are upstairs in their glass box. In every direction I'm surrounded by more things. More things, and, in my imagination, as my mind travels out in all directions, more people, like me, alone in houses, and offices and fields and streets, aching, like me, for deep connectedness, deep community. And some of them, like me, I am sure, also readying to commit.

Select Bibliography

Books

The McDonaldization Of Society, George Ritzer (Sage, London, '92)

Modernity and the Holocaust, Z. Bauman (Cambridge, '89)

The Sane Society, Erich Fromm (Routledge and Kegan Paul, London, '56)

Where The Wasteland Ends, Theodore Roszak (Faber & Faber, London, '74)

Of Water and The Spirit, Malidoma Somé (Penguin, London, '95)

Small is Beautiful, Fritz Schumacher (Vintage, London, '93)

A Brief History Of Everything, Ken Wilber (Shambhala, Boston,'96)

We've Had 100 Years Of Therapy, Hillman &Ventura (HarperCollins, San Francisco, '93)

The Sibling Society, Robert Bly (Hamish Hamilton, London, '96)

Sitting In the Fire, Arnold Mindell (Lao Tse Press, Portland, '95)

The Different Drum, Scott Peck (Arrow, London, '87)

Psychosynthesis, Roberto Assagioli (Thorsons, London, '93)

Women Who Run With The Wolves, Clarissa Pinkola Estés (Rider, London, '94)

Knights Without Armour, Aaron Kipnis (Putnams, NY, '91)

Journey Of The Heart, John Welwood (HarperCollins, London, '90)

The Spirit Of Intimacy, Sobonfú Somé (Berkeley Hills Books, Berkeley,'97)

Magazines

Positive News

Kindred Spirit

Caduceus

Resurgence

Sacred Hoop

Green Events

New Internationalist

The Ecologist

Permaculture

Achilles Heel

Contacting Balance

LOCAL-FOCUS WORKSHOPS

Local-Focus Weekend Workshops have an eye towards practical application, to groups of local people developing holistic community together – to people taking the ideas and the feelings beyond the workshop setting.
It's not that we expect people to agree to this before coming on a weekend, but these workshops are for people who are hoping that the weekend will live up to its promise, and inspire people (including themselves) to engage in developing holistic community locally.

INTRODUCTORY WORKSHOPS

You might prefer to come along to an Introductory Weekend Workshop. These weekends aren't locally focused, but offer the opportunity to experience the ideas in this book. You might feel they're the best place to start.

WORKSHOPS FOR GROUPS

We also offer workshops for existing groups, intentional communities, organisations, etc.. These workshops are adjusted to different situations and needs.

PERSONAL DEVELOPMENT WORKSHOPS

These workshops are called The Sacred and The Sensual and use meditation, body and voice exercises, sharing from the heart, and ritual in order to help people situate their own journeys within the context of the holistic path ~ and to perhaps take another step.

ALSO

If you have any other needs, questions or suggestions – please do contact us.

YOU CAN CONTACT US

By post at: Balance, PO Box 57, Totnes, Devon TQ9 5ZL, UK.
By e-mail at: balance@lineone.net

AND YOU CAN KEEP IN TOUCH

Through 'Holistic Community', our biannual newsletter. Subscription by donation – minimum £5/year UK, £8 Europe, £10 elsewhere

YOU CAN ALSO VISIT OUR WEBSITE

http://website.lineone.net/~balance

Response Form

☐ I would like to participate in a Local-Focus Weekend Workshop in
_____ (name of area)

☐ I would like to participate in a Local-Focus Weekend Workshop in
_____ (name of local area),
and might like to help set one up. I would like to know more. (It would help us if you
could tell us about yourself, and how you see your local area, on a separate sheet.)

☐ I would like to participate in an Introductory Weekend Workshop

☐ I would like to participate in The Sacred and the Sensual Weekend Workshop

☐ Our group/organisation, _____ (name of
group), might be interested in a Group Workshop. We would like to discuss this further.

☐ I would like to keep in touch for a year via *Holistic Community*, the biannual
Balance newsletter, and enclose a donation of _____ (minimum £5/year UK, £8
Europe, £10 elsewhere). Cheques should be made payable to 'Balance'. From outside
the UK: pay by a sterling draft on a British bank, or a Eurocheque with your card
number on the back. Sorry, no credit card facilities available.

Name

Address

Telephone

E-mail

Please return this form to: Balance, PO Box 57, Totnes TQ9 5ZL, UK.